Heroes of the RNLI

Heroes of the RNLI

The Storm Warriors

Martyn Beardsley

PEN & SWORD HISTORY

First published in Great Britain in 2020 by
Pen & Sword History
An imprint of
Pen & Sword Books Ltd
Yorkshire – Philadelphia

ISBN 978 1 52672 576 9

Typeset by Mac Style
Printed and bound in the UK by TJ Books Ltd,
Padstow, Cornwall.

FSC
www.fsc.org
MIX
Paper from
responsible sources
FSC® C013056

Pen & Sword Books Limited incorporates the imprints of Atlas,
Archaeology, Aviation, Discovery, Family History, Fiction,
History, Maritime, Military, Military Classics, Politics, Select,
Transport, True Crime, Air World, Frontline Publishing, Leo
Cooper, Remember When, Seaforth Publishing, The Praetorian
Press, Wharncliffe Local History, Wharncliffe Transport,
Wharncliffe True Crime and White Owl.

For a complete list of Pen & Sword titles please contact

PEN & SWORD BOOKS LIMITED
47 Church Street, Barnsley, South Yorkshire, S70 2AS, England
E-mail: enquiries@pen-and-sword.co.uk
Website: www.pen-and-sword.co.uk

Or

PEN AND SWORD BOOKS
1950 Lawrence Rd, Havertown, PA 19083, USA
E-mail: Uspen-and-sword@casematepublishers.com
Website: www.penandswordbooks.com

Contents

Acknowledgements

I am shamefully bad at keeping records of those whose help I have benefitted from during the lengthy process of putting a book together, so I apologise in advance to anyone whose name I have missed from the following list. I would like to thank my editor, Ting Baker, and all at Pen & Sword for their help and encouragement; Patrick Boyle, descendant of the two men of that name involved in the *Stolwijk* story; Nicholas Leach of the Lifeboats Enthusiasts Facebook page who helped with finding pictures; John Harper and the Grace Darling Society for advice and an interesting discussion regarding where Grace lived and died in Bamburgh; Lesley Crow, Sheila Harrison and all at the Newbiggin Maritime Centre; and especially Jeanette Hensby, for her invaluable help with the research and general moral support.

All images from Wikimedia Commons, unless otherwise stated.

Introduction

The Royal National Lifeboat Institution has to be one of the most undervalued and taken for granted organisations in the country. If there is an emergency around the coasts of Britain and Ireland, we know that those familiar bright orange, hi-tech boats will soon be racing to the scene. I suspect many people assume that such a large, professional and well-equipped organisation must be government-funded, but, of course, this isn't so – as those of us old enough to remember the Blue Peter appeals will appreciate! The body was founded nearly 200 years ago (as the Royal National Institution for the Preservation of Life from Shipwrecks) with money from public subscriptions, and has continued to be reliant on donations ever since. Even I had to keep reminding myself after writing about another dangerous, gruelling exploit that these men were *volunteers who took time out from their real jobs and risked their lives for others in the worst possible conditions for no payment.*

What became the RNLI was originally run on a fairly informal basis, without specialised boats or equipment – in fact, as we shall see when we look at the Grace Darling story, there were times when volunteers preferred to take out their own sturdy vessels rather than risk putting to sea in the boat they had been provided with.

The idea of bestowing medals for gallantry stems back right to the beginnings of RNLI: initially gold and silver, with the bronze being instituted much later. It has to be said that when it comes to awarding gold medals, there has always been a bias towards coxswains and 'rank' in general (many early recipients were naval officers employed by the coastguard). In one way this makes sense – awarding golds to every person involved in a rescue could increase the numbers issued by as much as tenfold and 'devalue' its prestige, at least in a numerical sense. As it is, under the system that has always obtained, RNLI gold medals are quite rare; it is often said to be the lifeboat version of the Victoria

Cross – but harder to win, on the basis that fewer have been awarded. But still, there are cases, such as the engineer of the *City of Bradford II* during the *Gurth* rescue, who as we shall see stayed at his post while almost up to his neck in icy seawater, working the lifeboat's controls with numb fingers by feel alone, where the awarding of a silver rather than gold doesn't seem quite fair. But in general the system worked well, and I have come across no complaints or grumblings. The coxswain represented the crew, and from that perspective the gold was for them all – and more than one coxswain said as much.

I freely admit to a certain bias in my selection of stories for this book, since during the course of my research my imagination was especially captured by the rescue missions in the earlier days, when a few men in open rowing boats went out to save lives in the teeth of a gale and worse, weather bad enough to overpower large ocean-going vessels.

I always planned to divide the book into sections allocated to subjects such as wartime rescues, winners of more than one gold and so on. One of the categories I had in mind was going to be called something like 'Family Affairs', where members of the same family were involved in a rescue and/or were following in a family lifeboat tradition. However, it soon became clear that lifeboat crews, especially in the early days, so often came from such tightknit communities that such a criterion would apply to almost every chapter, so that idea was never really going to work!

As it is, there will be some overlap or seeming incongruity with the dividing up of the stories between sections; for example, there is a section on wartime rescues, but Henry Blogg, who did partake in such, is in a different category. I have simply chosen to allocate each story to whichever section seemed most appropriate while at the same time trying to maintain as much balance between sections as possible. And Blogg is an example of another feature of this book – which is that while the rescues themselves are interesting and sometimes awe-inspiring, the rescuers themselves are often just as fascinating. I was keen to make this a book about the people behind the rescues just as much as their exploits, and have gone to great lengths to dig out biographical information wherever possible to help bring the names to life.

Part I

Genesis

Chapter 1

The Man Who Started it All

Sir William Hillary

It was a stormy start to March 1824, with sleet and snow adding to the fierce winds. On Wednesday 3 March a London sloop, the *Margate*, put into Yarmouth Roads having had its master and ship's boy lost overboard. Another London vessel was driven ashore on Haisborough Sands, Norfolk, one of many such incidents around the coast. The following late afternoon, a large group of eminent men issued forth from the London Tavern on Bishopsgate in the city's financial district, turning their collars against the wind as they made for their carriages. The tavern was an elegant, neo-classical building, big and tall for its time, featuring a banqueting-cum-ballroom on the upper of its three floors, and a large meeting room on the floor below. On this particular afternoon it had been the venue for a gathering that would have significant and long-lasting consequences, and the emerging gentlemen were in buoyant mood despite the weather, for this was the inaugural meeting of the National Institution for the Preservation of Life from Shipwreck. It had been chaired by no less a figure than the Archbishop of Canterbury, and had as its patron the king himself, soon leading to the prefix 'Royal' before its name. His Majesty wasn't present on this day, but in attendance were numerous MPs, leading City figures, naval men and others – including the anti-slavery campaigner William Wilberforce, and one Captain George Manby, whose name will crop up elsewhere in this book.[1]

There was a slight note of discord at the meeting when thanks were offered to Sir William Hillary as 'the father of the institution'.

---

1. Although the Association was to be financed by donation, the government did play its part by donating fifty-eight of Manby's mortar devices.

One member ventured that Manby had proposed such an idea 'long ago' and asserted the captain's own claim to be called the institution's 'father'. But the fact is that it was Hillary whose efforts in drumming up interest among those with the necessary clout had led to a preliminary meeting the previous month, which in turn paved the way for this official launch. Hillary himself, perhaps surprisingly, doesn't seem to have been present, but this day saw the realisation of his dream of establishing a national life-saving organisation with bases and equipment strategically situated around the coasts of Britain and Ireland, manned by volunteers and funded by public donation.

In the same year, the awarding of gold medals ('medallions') for outstanding acts of bravery came into being, and Hillary himself was awarded an honorary one as founder of the Institution. But within six years of that windy day in London, this man, who had made Douglas on the Isle of Man his permanent home, was in possession of three further golds for actual rescues, something that would be achieved by only one other man. There is a natural temptation to imagine that the organisation of which Hillary was the architect, its founding father, would be, shall we say, *generous* when it came to deciding whether he was deserving of its highest honour. But I believe the stories that follow will show (and these are not the only such rescues in which he featured during his life) that he was every bit as deserving of the awards as the majority of the others who earned them.

The *Förtroendet*

There had been storms lasting several days in the early part of December 1827, and one ship caught up in them was the *Förtroendet*, a Swedish barque with an English captain, Andrew Ackerman. She had been making her way from Marseilles with a valuable cargo of madder (a plant that can be used in dyes) intended for Glasgow. When she reached the British coast she called in at Derbyhaven, some miles to the south of Douglas on the Isle of Man, to pick up a local pilot and a few more hands to supplement her crew of twelve for the completion of her trip. But upon attempting to head north on the last leg of the voyage, the intensity of the gales led Ackerman to divert to Douglas Harbour. When even this proved impossible, he dropped anchor just outside, in the southern part of the bay, but this didn't prevent the barque from being carried towards the nearby rocks of St Mary's Isle. When the inevitable collision occurred, it destroyed the *Förtroendet*'s rudder, leaving her helpless.

All of this hadn't gone unnoticed from the harbour in Douglas, and it wasn't long before a combined rescue operation was underway. Hillary, approaching 60 years of age, soon had the lifeboat out, in which as well as his volunteer crew he was accompanied by his colleague Lieutenant Robinson, along with a Lieutenant Greatrex. Luckily, there was also a Revenue cutter, the *Swallow*, anchored in the bay. She lowered her boat to join Hillary's men, and a couple of other local boats put out from the shore.

The initial plan was to tow the Swedish ship to safety, but this was scuppered when she struck the rocks again, holing her below the waterline. It was now left to Hillary's lifeboat to take the crew of the *Förtroendet* off before the rocks and waves could inflict even more serious damage. Hillary had his boat anchor a little way off and then cautiously veer down on the barque. This went without a hitch; all of the crew and even some of their belongings were taken into the lifeboat. But she was now somewhat overloaded, especially in view of the worsening weather, and Lieutenant Strugnell, commanding the *Swallow*'s boat, now came alongside to relieve her of some of her burden.

All were safely got to shore, and housed by the Isle of Man Shipwreck Association – another brainchild of Sir William Hillary. Over the course of the next couple of days the continuing storms gradually battered the ship into a complete wreck. It was a good example of a well-co-ordinated rescue mission, but as the *Cumberland Pacquet* pointed out, Hillary and his men were, 'as usual, the first to aid the wreck and save the crew'. Hillary had earned the gold medal of the institution he had been responsible for creating.

The *Eclipse*

After a stormy night on 13 January 1830, continuing into the next day, daylight revealed a large sloop on the rocks near Castle Mona, which had been the coastal home in Douglas Bay of the recently deceased 4th Duke of Atholl. She was the *Eclipse*, a Glasgow vessel, and had been on her way to Liverpool. With distress signals flying and water flooding the ship from the waves breaking over her, four of her crewmen had managed to get to shore in one of the ship's boats. But with the force of the wind not abating and the tide coming in, it wasn't a method that could be risked by the *Eclipse*'s master and two crewmen left on board.

There was a new lifeboat in Douglas Harbour, intended for Ramsay, but she had yet to be launched and the work of preparing her for sea hadn't been finished: in particular, the watertight compartments that helped to prevent her from capsizing hadn't been fitted. Nevertheless, Hillary was determined that this was the time for her maiden voyage. With the help of bystanders, he and his loyal coxswain, Isaac Vondy, headed for the wreck with a larger than usual crew of twelve, which allowed for each oar to be double-manned and gave them a better chance of fighting through the towering waves. This they did, and the lifeboat was able to get alongside the *Eclipse* and take the remaining men off. There was almost a last-minute disaster when a sudden surge of big waves came one after the other and threatened to turn the boat over, the sea filling the parts of the boat where the watertight compartments should have been. It was later estimated that she took in nearly half a ton of water, and Ackerman, the experienced master of the *Eclipse*, knew full well that the lifeboat was close to sinking. But those crew who could be spared from rowing baled furiously with their hats, and the crisis passed. The almost completely waterlogged lifeboat was run onto the beach, where there was no shortage of helping hands to help all aboard to the safety of dry land.

Local opinion was that even despite the lack of watertight compartments, no other craft could have withstood what the lifeboat had been through, and great praise was heaped upon not just Hillary (who was to receive a second gold) and Lieutenant Robinson, but the boat's builder, a local man.

The *St George*

In November 1830, the Royal Mail steam packet *St George* anchored in Douglas Bay to deliver its usual batch of post to the island. During the night a storm blew up, gradually increasing in intensity till the packet's anchor cable parted and she was blown towards two notorious sets of rocks: St Mary's Isle as mentioned above (also known as Conister Rock), and Pollock. The *St George*'s master, Lieutenant Tudor, soon had the men at their stations and the ship's engines fired up, but in trying to reverse out of danger while battling with the power of the waves, the ship collided with the St Mary's rocks 'from which', as the local press reported, 'few vessels that once strike ever escape'. As well as ordering the firing of distress rockets to alert those on shore, Tudor had the foremast cut down for the building of a raft so that his crew could at least reach the safety of the island, hopefully to be rescued when daylight came.

Hillary's Fort Anne home overlooked the bay, and when he saw what was unfolding, he dashed down to the pier. There he met a group including Lieutenant Robinson, William Corlett, agent for the company that owned the steam packet, and coxswain Isaac Vondy. They quickly gathered together a crew of fourteen men, and put out in the lifeboat. There first attempt was on the weather side of the *St George*. They lowered their anchor and tried to approach stern-first by letting out the cable. But the conditions proved too rough. Hillary and one or two others now proposed taking the lifeboat in on the leeward side, which would be the normal side to approach from – were it not for the fact that it in this case it meant they would be precariously positioned between the wreck and the rocks – something that Lieutenant Robinson strongly advised against. He was overruled, but his worst fears came perilously close to being realised.

When they manoeuvred into position, the lifeboat was thrown about so much that she sustained as much damage as if she had been involved in a battle at sea: most of her oars were lost, her upper works were damaged, including some of the watertight bulkheads; and her rudder was smashed. Worse than that though, in the midst of the fight against the elements, Hillary (who couldn't swim), Corlett, and two crewmen were swept into the frothing sea. The boatmen managed to haul the last three back aboard fairly swiftly; Hillary only survived by grabbing a rope dangling from the boat's side and clinging on grimly until the crew could turn their attentions to him and manhandle him back into the boat in a battered and bruised state. He must have been in excruciating pain throughout, since it was later discovered that he had broken six ribs. They were now faced with the difficulty not only of saving the crew of the *St George*, but of how they could extricate themselves from the tight spot they had got themselves into. Their options were severely limited by rigging and debris from the cut-down foremast obstructing their way, St Mary's Rock itself, and another solitary rock emerging from the sea a little way off from it.

Luckily, the lifeboat was equipped with an axe. With a rising tide and waves washing over the boat and threatening to swamp it, the implement was used to hack away the rigging, clearing an escape route. The twenty-two men of the *St George* clambered from the rock into the lifeboat, bringing with them buckets from their ship for baling. The remaining intact oars were manned, and all on board made their bid for freedom.

It was a tough fight. The boat was thrown against the rocks twice and filled with water, but she remained afloat, and then there was a lucky break when they were washed into the calmer lee of St Mary's Isle, where they were able to gather themselves and strike out for home. About a quarter of a mile from shore they were met by two boats that had come out to their aid. By this means some of the men were transferred from the crowded and badly damaged lifeboat, which itself was taken under tow for the remainder of the return journey. Everyone was returned to the beach without the loss of a single life.

Lieutenant Tudor of the packet soon afterwards wrote to Hillary telling him that he and his men had seriously considered hailing them to keep them away, considering it was too dangerous for them to attempt a rescue: 'There did not appear to us, amongst the heavy breakers then rolling upon Conister, the slightest chance of escape for you, and which, from the crippled state of the lifeboat, when she afterwards left the wreck, was so nearly proving the case.' Tudor hoped that Hillary would 'long live to preside over an establishment your philanthropy gave birth to and in which your humanity has always placed you amongst the foremost and most active of its members'. Hillary and Robinson both received gold medals for this action, while Corlett and Vondy earned silvers.

William Hillary was born in Liverpool in 1770 to a merchant father who owned a sugar plantation and property in the West Indies, but grew up in a humble Wensleydale cottage with his Quaker parents. When he was 30 he fell in love with and wanted to marry the very eligible Frances Elizabeth Ffytche, whose father, Lewis, was a wealthy landowner. It was a match that Lewis, sceptical of Hillary's true motivations, opposed; Hillary biographer Robert Kelly (*For Those In Peril*, 1979) refers pointedly to his subject's 'expensive tastes'. The couple eloped and married anyway, but although Frances would become very wealthy on her father's death, for now she had very little money of her own and Lewis Ffytche's refusal to help caused them to struggle financially. Tensions eased somewhat when Lewis' daughter made him a grandfather; the financial reins were loosened, and Frances was allowed to move into the family's Danbury estate in Essex.

They were still, though, far from wealthy. When war with France resumed in 1803 after a brief hiatus, William took the extraordinary step of raising a veritable private army, complete with infantry, cavalry and artillery. It was ready to fight the French should they invade, but it was only achieved by borrowing very heavily. Even selling property from his own family estate and dipping into an inheritance from the death of his brother in Jamaica was still not enough to keep pace with his outgoings.

The king had been impressed by William Hillary's dedication to the cause (rewarding him with baronetcy) but his wife, seeing their financial future looking bleaker by the week, wasn't. The couple finally split after a little over seven years of marriage, with Frances retaining and remaining in what had been their marital home in Essex, and Hillary – now Sir William – selling the plantation (which he had never visited) in order to finance the renting of Fort Anne at the southern end of Douglas Bay on the Isle of Man. He later bought the place, which was never actually a fort but a mansion that had been built at around the time he married Frances. It was a magnificent building and gave a sweeping view out over the sea – a panorama that played a part in inspiring the founding of Britain's lifeboat service.

The lower cost of living on Man no doubt contributed to Hillary's choice of destination, but he did take an active interest in local life, and mingled with the men of the fishing fleet down in the harbour. Someone else he mingled with was Amelia (Emma) Tobin, at 26, twelve years his junior. Her parents had died, and she was living with her brother Caesar, a major in the local militia. As with Lewis Ffytche in the case of his daughter, Caesar wasn't keen on his sister's growing attachment to this incomer – not least, of course, because of the inconvenient fact that Hillary was still married.

To avoid the scandal of a divorce, Hillary took advantage of a loophole in the law. Although divorce in England was only possible by Act of Parliament, in Scotland mutual consent alone was sufficient. There would still be some doubt as to whether a 'divorce' obtained in Scotland by an English couple would be legally recognised in the latter country, and the situation was even more complicated than that. Even if the marriage were not recognised, bigamy was not actually illegal on the Isle of Man. The final hurdle, though, was still whether Hillary could then remarry – because although the *law* on Man didn't recognise bigamy, the *Church* certainly did. Thus, the final step in this tortuous business was to go back and marry in Scotland – where, since the divorce was acknowledged, marriage could hardly be denied. And so it was that in the summer of 1813 Amelia Tobin became Mrs Hillary at a private ceremony in the little village of Whitehorn, on the coast of what is now Dumfries and Galloway, and conveniently directly north of Man by fishing boat.

Hillary may not have been the best manager of personal finances, but he wasn't the chancer that his first wife's father feared. For one thing, he seemed to have genuinely loved Frances Ffytche, even though it went pear-shaped within a few years; and, anyway, the idea of him as some sort of cad doesn't really fit with other aspects of his life, behaviour, and the way those who knew him described him. For example, the huge amount he spent on his private militia was born out of a desire to do what he thought was right and necessary for his country, rather than an act of personal vanity. In *The Lifeboat Baronet*, Janet Gleeson quotes an acquaintance as saying Hillary was 'a man of military bearing, of more than medium height...' with 'kindly sympathy shown in every lineament of his face'. And bear in mind that if Hillary hadn't been capable of 'thinking big', perhaps even over-optimistically, then many more years would have passed and many more lives may have been lost before a national lifeboat service came into being. Manby *suggested* a lifeboat service; Hillary made one happen.

And it seems to have been the move to the Isle of Man prompted by his relationship complications that led to his lifesaving inspiration. Shipwrecks off the island were as common as elsewhere around Britain and Ireland, but it is the loss of two ships in particular, during 1822, that is often cited as prompting Hillary to call for an organised lifeboat service.

In October of that year, the navy cutter *Vigilant* foundered on the infamous rocks of St Mary's that have featured above, and Hillary personally led the mission to save her crew. Two months later, six crewmen of the navy brig *Racehorse* that hit a reef on the south of the island were drowned, along with three local fishermen attempting to rescue them. This latter tragedy, in particular, is often cited as the one that finally inspired Hillary to campaign for a lifeboat institution. But as Janet Gleeson points out in *The Lifeboat Baronet*, he lived miles from where the incident took place, didn't take part in the rescue, and probably wasn't even present. In fact, in his own words Hillary refers not to these famous incidents or any others, but to a more generalised inclination towards 'maritime affairs', in which he had long had an interest. It's inconceivable that he didn't very quickly learn of the wreck of *Racehorse* and subsequent loss of life though, and within months he began actively trying to drum up support (at his own expense) from among the great and the good for what became the National Institution for the Preservation of Life from

Shipwreck. As we have seen, the 'Royal' prefix was added thanks to the patronage of George IV, and, finally, in 1854, the name was somewhat streamlined to become the one we are familiar with today: the Royal National Lifeboat Institution.

Part II

The Navy Men

Chapter 2

Devastation in Lyme

Charles Cowper Bennet

The Royal Navy reigned supreme during the protracted wars with Napoleonic France and her allies, and the courage and professionalism of its officers played a big part in that story. But the war had been a big financial burden on the government, and when the fighting was finally over there was an urgent need to make drastic cuts to a navy that was now far larger than was necessary for peacetime. The inevitable wholesale mothballing and even scrapping of ships meant that large numbers of officers found themselves without employment and on half-pay, but there was one avenue open to at least some: the coastal services whose prime duty was the intercepting of smugglers etc. Even long before the war, the Revenue cutters had been active and commanded by naval officers. While the Revenue cruisers could roam far and wide, the Preventive Waterguard, often referred to as the Preventive Service, was established in the early nineteenth century to patrol the coasts closer inshore as well as on land ('Riding Officers').

An attempt to unify these services as the Coast Blockade came in 1816, which became the coastguard service a few years later. Most chief officers of the coastguard were lieutenants from the Royal Navy. But although the primary role remained the catching of smugglers, going to the aid of vessels in distress was also part of the remit – and remains so to this day.

On the night of Monday 22 November 1824, a gale hit the southwest coast of England, and steadily increased in intensity over the next twenty-four hours, causing havoc both at sea and on land. Many a ship was caught out, in some cases losing their whole crew.

There was a particularly high tide on the 23rd, and such was the force of the storm that even the venerable old Cobb at Lyme Regis, where several vessels were sheltering, was in danger of giving way, and sea water was washing up into the streets of Lyme itself. At least one shop was destroyed entirely, and dozens more were damaged. The house of the famous fossil hunter Mary Anning was, like many others, flooded, and she had to hurriedly move her precious collection upstairs.

The famous promenade was destroyed, the Cobb House was battered to destruction by the waves, and all of the domestic dwellings in the same row were flooded out, sending their inhabitants, unable to walk along the Cobb wall because of the mountainous waves breaking over it, scurrying to flee in little boats. The Revenue cruiser the *Fox* sank opposite the Assembly Rooms (which overlooked the sea, and which Jane Austen had visited twenty years earlier) with two crewmen drowning. Then, at 7 am, the old frontage of the Cobb began to collapse, and the sea came crashing in. Now that the defences had been breached, it was no longer the safe haven of normal times. All vessels anchored there were driven from their moorings, and among them a schooner and two sloop were swept right over the quay walls.

Watching from the Custom House in Lyme Regis were Charles Cowper Bennet, in command of the coastguard there, and two of his men: William Porter and John Freeman. They witnessed a London merchant vessel, the *Unity*, being carried out of the harbour and swept helplessly eastwards along the coast. They would almost certainly have trained their telescopes on her, and been able to pick out the terrified crew scrambling up into the shrouds and lashing themselves there for some degree of safety – no doubt praying that the mast itself would not go by the board.

Bennet and his two colleagues dashed along the coast following the *Unity*'s progress, until she ran aground near Charmouth. A boy among the ship's crew either didn't lash himself securely or perhaps at all, and through exhaustion he lost his grip and plummeted into the sea. Carrying ropes they had brought with them, the coastguard men made their way down to the shore, rescued the boy from the frothing seas, and as soon as the tide had ebbed they were able to clamber on board the beached ship and help the three remaining crewmen, one virtually unconscious, off and to the warmth of a Charmouth inn.

Bennet was presented with his gold medal early the following year, and the local press reported that John Freeman, who was given a silver along with William Porter, had, 'in his lifetime, rescued many of his fellow creatures from a watery grave'. Unlike many ships during that storm, even the *Unity* herself survived. When conditions improved she was refloated, then refitted at Lyme's shipyard and relaunched the following year.

Charles Cowper Bennet was born in Donhead St Andrew, near Shaftsbury in Wiltshire, but spent most of his life in Lyme and became a leading local figure, serving for a time as a magistrate. He is invariably referred to as 'Captain' Bennet (and sometimes 'Benett' or 'Bennett' – I'm following the spelling in the Navy List and census returns) at the time of the 1824 drama, and it seems almost certain that he must have used that title himself since that's how he is described in the censuses of 1841 and 1851, and census returns were filled in by occupants themselves. However, his naval records categorically show that he was promoted from lieutenant to commander in 1814, and didn't make the jump to captain until July 1851 (after the census of that year was have been taken).

When Charles died in 1877, his (second) wife Agnes paid for a stained glass window for Uplyme church in memory of her husband. They were both buried in the churchyard there.

Chapter 3

Necessity is the Mother of Invention

Joseph Clarke

The second ever recipient of the gold medal for gallantry, six months after Charles Fremantle (see Part IV, Chapter 18), was Lieutenant Joseph Clarke, RN, of the navy's Coastal Blockade Service. In November 1824, the brig *Juno*, en route from Jersey to Glasgow, was caught in a storm off Beachy Head where Clarke was based, and began drifting towards the shore at Birling Gap.

Not having any conventional life-saving equipment, Clarke struck on the idea of getting the men under his command to remove the lashings from their hammocks and splice them into one long line. He then led them out into the tempestuous surf, and after a fierce battle with the elements, Clarke got his makeshift rope to the crew, by which they were able to haul themselves to safety.

Realising that the *Juno* was still intact, he and two of his men boarded her and took down her topgallant and topmasts, then lowered two anchors to prevent her from being washed towards the cliffs. This act saved both ship and cargo, and on behalf of himself and his crew her captain, Francis Lefevre, offered thanks, saying that he had 'no doubt that every man on board must have perished, had it not been for the resolute exertions of Lieutenant Clarke and his men'. His relief can be better understood when considering that the cargo was uninsured and being transported at Lefevre's own expense and risk.

Joseph Clarke was 34 at the time of his gold medal-winning exploits. He had joined the navy at the age of 17, following in the footsteps of five of his brothers – all of whom had been killed during the Napoleonic wars. Joseph himself had seen action on numerous occasions in a variety of warships, and was wounded at least once.

He joined the Coastal Blockade Service in 1819, and undertook a number of life-saving missions, which brought him several other rewards, including a gold medal from the King of the Netherlands for saving a Dutch crew of six.

Chapter 4

Holy Terror

George Joy

In January 1825, the sloop *Robert and Janet* was in a collision with another vessel, necessitating a return to her home port of Stornoway for repairs. It proved to be an omen of worse things to come.

By May of that year she was at sea again, calling at Liverpool, and in October she found herself carrying a load of slate to Leith, having previously picked up several passengers from Longhope, Stromness: a governess, Miss Thompson, three young girls (the eldest being 14) and a boy under her care, and an 'old man'.

On the morning of Friday, 22 October, concerned onlookers at Berwick spotted a sloop in trouble off the coast about eleven miles north of Lindisfarne (then known by its alternative name of Holy Island). The ship was wallowing, 'sails torn to pieces, rigging all disordered'; the sea was running so high that she couldn't work into the harbour, and no boat could put out to help. After several hours in this desperate battle with the elements, the unknown ship, 'from the north', at last got out to sea and it appeared that she would be able to clear Holy Island, to the relief of the watchers from the shore. But their optimism was misplaced. The mystery sloop was the *Robert and Janet*, and rather than clearing Holy Island, it would prove to be her final, fatal destination.

By the afternoon of the 23rd, attempting to take refuge in Holy Island harbour in a heavy gale, the *Robert and Janet* ran onto rocks within sight of the island. She was badly damaged by the impact, and the savage waves immediately began to smash the ship to pieces; tragically,

McKenzie the master, two of his crew, and all of the passengers were drowned during or soon after the ship foundered. (The body of one of the girls was later washed up on Shoreston Sands, near Seahouses.)

An observer wrote to the local newspaper that when he arrived at the spot on the coast of Holy Island closest to the ship, to his dismay he found at least 200 men looking on without trying to do anything to save the survivors, who could be seen clinging to the rigging of the disintegrating sloop. He tried to launch a six-oared galley, but the seas were too heavy for him to stand any chance. But help was at hand.

'I at last, with tears in my eyes, implored them to assist in bringing a cable over land', he recounted, so that it could somehow be taken out to the *Robert and Janet*. Luckily, the revenue cutter *Mermaid* was in port, and 'four intrepid fellows' from her crew joined him in the boat led by her chief mate, George Joy. For some time they feared they wouldn't be able to fight their way to the ship, the waves and current driving them back time and again. But with a tenacity and indomitable spirit typical of navy seamen of the day, they stuck at it and managed to get close enough to extricate two crewmen and the ship's boy. But after all this time exposed to the intense cold and waves the survivors were in a bad way, and even before Joy and his *Mermaid* shipmates could get the victims back to land, one of the men had died.

The 'intrepidity and skill' of Joy and the men of *Mermaid*, without whom there would probably have been no survivors from the *John and Janet*, was rightly applauded.

There is some issue over both the name of the sloop that was wrecked in this case, and even the date of the incident, with some accounts giving it as the 22nd and even 30 October, rather than the 23rd. The tragedy certainly couldn't have happened on the 30th because stories began to appear in the press on the 25th. Then, there is the surprising amount of confusion about something as basic as what the sloop was actually called. In the reports of the day there are mentions of the *John and Jessey*, *John and Jessy*, *John and Janet*, and *Robert and Jannett*. But the most widely used name, and the one *eventually* appearing in the authoritative *Lloyds List* (despite having originally being given as the *Robert and Jennett*) is the one I have gone with: the *Robert and Janet*. This is almost certainly the correct version, because the movements of this Stornoway sloop can be traced back several years in shipping movements as reported in the press.

George Joy was an experienced seaman, having served in a variety of warships before joining the *Mermaid* revenue cutter as second mate in 1821.

Chapter 5

In the Line of Duty

Howard Lewis Parry

One of the shortest and most tragic careers of any of the RNLI gold medal winners featured in this book is that of Lieutenant Howard Parry. He was born in Frindsbury, Kent, in 1792, the son of a navy man, and by the time he was 11 he had been entered into the navy himself as a ship's boy, a not uncommon age at that time. Of course, Britain was at war with France during that period, and, after serving in several other ships, he was transferred to the *Tonnant* in 1805, and while still only 13 years old Howard found himself involved in perhaps the most famous sea battle of all time: Trafalgar.

The *Tonnant* was heavily engaged. Although Nelson's tactics on the day led to a British victory, they meant that many of the British ships would come under fire before they could bring their own guns to bear. The *Tonnant* had sails and rigging shot away as she approached, then found herself sandwiched between one French and one Spanish ship, and while engaging became the focus of a much bigger Spanish three-decker, which fired on her as she sailed past, destroying masts, rigging and sails. Parry and the rest of the *Tonnant* crew fought on, and had almost overcome one of the Spanish ships she was alongside when yet another vessel of that nation arrived on the scene and began pouring broadsides into Parry's ship. Luckily, one of the leading British warships, the *Bellerophon*,[1] put herself between the two and dealt with the newcomer.

The *Tonnant* was now engaging the French ship *Algésiras* from such close range that the gunners had no room to run their cannon out through the portholes after reloading, and had to fire them from

---

1. Into whose hands Napoleon would later surrender himself.

within the ship. Eventually, a party from the *Tonnant* boarded the *Algésiras* and took possession of her. By the end of the battle, Parry's ship had incurred twenty-six deaths and fifty casualties among her officers and men.

Even after Trafalgar, Howard Parry led an eventful life. In 1810 he was on board HMS *Dolphin* carrying 275 French passengers to England when a virulent form of typhus fever swept through the ship, killing eighty-nine people and laying many others low, including the bulk of the crew. Parry himself contracted the disease, but managed to keep working. A report afterwards praising his efforts stated:

> It would be impossible to describe the scene which this ship presented during her home voyage, and the duties which devolved upon Mr Parry were such as to create wonder how they could have been performed. The whole service of attending the dying and the dead devolved upon him (assisted only by the gunner's mate) and this in addition to his other duties as an officer of the ship... [He] suffered many weeks in Haslar himself from fever... The captain said it was entirely owing to his efforts that he had been able to bring the ship in.

Then in 1811 he was on board the frigate *Grasshopper* as part of a convoy escorting a number of merchantmen. They encountered a fierce gale, which sank four of the warships, resulting in great loss of life. Parry begged to be allowed to try to save some of the crew of one ship, the *Hero*, but although he set out to do what he could, the conditions defeated him; he couldn't reach her 'and had distress of seeing most of the crew perish'. To avoid meeting the same fate, the *Grasshopper* was obliged to run ashore on the coast of Holland, which had sided with Napoleon, and Parry and his comrades were taken prisoner. It was Christmas Eve. They were forced to march to France, a seven-week slog of up to twenty-five miles a day. Once in their French prison, they had to endure a diet of black bread and water. Parry sold most of his possessions, including his shirt – presumably to raise money for food – but kept his Book of Common Prayer.

After the Napoleonic wars had ended, as we have already seen, the Royal Navy drastically reduced its number of ships and men, and like many other officers, Parry sought employment in the coastguard service. His task mostly involved chasing smugglers, but, with the lifeboat service in its infancy, also included rescues at sea. Parry's most noted – and final – such mission took place in November, 1831.

By now his naval rank was that of lieutenant, and he was Inspecting Commander of the coastguard station in Rye, Sussex. Sometime during the night, a large French fishing lugger, *L'Aimee* of St Valery, ran aground in Rye Bay, in the mouth of the harbour. Parry decided that he was going to go to her aid in his own galley, but this entailed hauling it half a mile overland so that it could be launched within sight of the distressed vessel. This was accomplished, and with four of his men he set off into the teeth of a buffeting storm for *L'Aimee*. There were too many sailors to take off in one go, so this rescue entailed four dangerous and damaging trips, during which twenty-one of the crew were brought ashore. There were still ten men aboard the lugger, however, but Parry's galley had taken such a battering from the heavy seas and repeated contact with *L'Aimee* that she was barely seaworthy and he could not risk getting so close again. He had taken this into account, however, and on his previous trip he had got the men left on board to thrown him down a line, which was paid out from the lugger as he took that boatload ashore, and had it secured on land. By this means, the last ten crewmen were able to haul themselves to safety. Parry received his gold medal a few months later, but the gods hadn't finished with him yet.

By the time of his gold medal-winning incident, Lieutenant Parry was 40 years old, married with four children, and had saved numerous lives in the twelve months or so he had been with the coastguard. But the main task of that service, that of preventing goods being brought in from France and other places without paying the appropriate taxes, still had to be performed. In the public eye there is a certain roguish charm about smugglers and smuggling, and in one sense it is understandable. Duties on things like foreign wines and spirits were so ridiculously high that they would be beyond the means of most ordinary folk without an illicit trade. For that reason, it was barely seen as a crime in the eyes of many and it wasn't unusual for local worthies, including clergymen, to be involved.

But unlike the popular, romantic view of smuggling, clashes with the authorities could be brutal and bloody. There may well have been a few Customs men who were prepared to turn a blind eye, especially locals who would have known all those involved, but the naval officers joining the service after the war were a different breed. They were used to strict discipline, things being done the right way, and not backing down even in the face of overwhelming odds – as they often were in Customs role unless a nearby militia or company of dragoons could be called out, which itself took time.

At approaching midnight on 1 February 1832, less than three months after the *l'Aimee* rescue and a month after he had been awarded his gold medal, Lieutenant Howard Parry had received a tip-off that smuggled goods were to be landed this night and was patrolling on the beach at Camber with two of his men. Others were on a different part of the beach, and out of the darkness he saw and heard a distant alarm pistol being fired by one of his officers.

'Come on, my boys!' he cried, and they ran in the direction of the alarm. When they got to the shoreline he saw a boat and a number of tubs[2] nearby. At that moment, knowing the game was up, a large body of men who had been lying flat on the beach, hidden in the shadows, rose up like ghosts before him. There were maybe a hundred, but some estimates suggest far more – large-scale organised smuggling could involve ~~small armies~~ groups of men acting in different roles: someone to signal to a ship when the coast was clear (a 'spotsman'), lookouts, carriers, armed guards ('batmen', so called after the cudgels they carried, but a small number might have firearms) and others.

Undaunted by the odds against him, Parry presented his pistol, barking, 'If you advance, I will fire.'

The response was flashes in the darkness and the crack of pistol shots. Parry returned fire, but had been hit almost immediately, and

---

2. A type of wooden cask.

collapsed, blood from five wounds turning the sand around him red. When he had come to his senses, a smuggler loomed out of the darkness towards him brandishing a long heavy stick,[3] ready to strike. Parry struggled through the pain to raise himself into a sitting position, while reaching for a second pistol inside his coat. He discharged it at his attacker, who disappeared into the midnight gloom. Whether he was hit or not, Parry couldn't tell. It later emerged that one of the smuggling party was shot dead that night (and another wounded), but there was a fair amount of shooting going on in the darkness, and it was impossible to tell who had hit whom.

The smugglers' cargo had been mostly brandy from Boulogne, and the smuggling gang, according to common practice, consisted of two groups: the 'company', i.e. the actual smugglers, who were unarmed, and the armed 'protecting party'. Edward White, in a separate group of four or five of Parry's men, saw at least a dozen armed smugglers, some with muskets, and was shot in both thighs during the battle. Another coastguard man, Henry Best, was surrounded and beaten with sticks and musket butts and left for dead.

Parry and the other wounded men were carried to a nearby cottage, and from there to their own homes where two local doctors attended them. Among Parry's injuries were two musket balls embedded in his shoulder, along with a large nail, which had seemingly been used as an improvised round. He also had one finger almost shot off. Three of his men were severely wounded and one, probably Edward White, required a leg amputation. But the coastguard men also left their mark. In addition to one shot dead during the battle, six are said to have died of their wounds subsequently, including one bayoneted in the abdomen, and numerous others were left with life-threatening wounds. The gang got away with most of the brandy, but the coastguard managed to retain twenty-six tubs.

Lieutenant Parry was rightly praised for his bravery, as were those with him, and, within weeks, he was promoted to the rank of master and commander as a reward for his actions on that night. But it can have brought him little cheer, for his body was shattered and his active

---

3. Parry believed it to be a cut-down hop pole, about 7 feet long.

career was as good as over. Unable to work, he was placed on half-pay. He received a further promotion to the rank of post-captain, as well as being awarded a pension for his wounds, but he never served aboard ship or worked for the coastguard again. He spent his last years in Gloucestershire, living in the parsonage house of Newland with his first son, who by that time was the curate of St Peter's church there. He died on New Year's Day 1869, aged 77.

Chapter 6

I Shall Board Her at Daybreak

John Row Morris

The seas off Dundrum Bay, near Newcastle, County Down, where the tides from the north of Ireland meet those from the south, had a reputation for shipwrecks. The SS *Great Britain* was to run aground on sandbanks here in 1846. That was more down to navigational error, but when the *Richard Pope* met the same fate twenty years earlier, it was as the result of what a witness described as a 'terrible hurricane' and a huge surge of water that carried her on to the sandbank at low tide, leaving her on her beam-ends.

The barque was carrying a general cargo of dry goods from Liverpool to Sierra Leone, when calamity struck at 4 pm on 6 March 1826. There are some discrepancies in the reporting of events that follow. Some say that 'at least two boats' put out to try to save the *Richard Pope*'s crew but were beaten back. However, an eye-witness in a letter to the press described a group of young men, said to have been local fishermen, displaying 'intrepid courage' reaching the barque through mountainous waves and taking off one crewman. Fearing they would have to save themselves, a group of eight (some reports say only five) crewmen lowered the vessel's own boat about half an hour later, and headed for shore. Sadly, their boat was overwhelmed by the waves and they ended up in the sea. A different group of young men struggled for three-quarters of an hour to save them, but our witness said they only managed to get one back alive.

By then it was getting dark and further attempts were impossible. A letter appeared in local newspapers, unsigned, but probably from the eventual gold medal recipient Lieutenant John Row Morris, inspecting commander of the Newcastle coastguard, talking of fears for the *Richard Pope*'s captain and remainder of the crew still left on board – almost certainly lashed to the rigging and exposed to the elements, as was the usual and almost unavoidable course of action in such situations. 'I have two boats manned,' said the writer, 'and shall board her at day-break.'

As soon as it got light on Tuesday the 7th, Morris and six of his men headed out for the stranded barque, and there was possibly another boat from the shore also involved. (One account says that Morris had also made an attempt the previous day but hadn't been able to get close enough.) This time the rescue went well, and the captain and remaining crew were extricated from their refuge in the rigging. Those still alive were brought back without incident, but sadly one had died in the night from exposure. The coast was 'strewn with pieces of wreck and cargo'.

There is more confusion as to the numbers lost and saved, but at least seven, and as many as ten men were rescued.

John Row Morris was born in Rotherhithe into a naval family. His father was master of a naval vessel, and his brother became a rear-admiral. John himself served in the navy from the age of 15. In 1794 he was on board the *Alfred* at the historic Glorious First Of June battle, and was also involved in the Battle of Basque Roads in 1809, by which time he had been promoted to lieutenant. He had reached the rank of commander when he joined the coastguard service in County Down in 1820. He died in Bryansford, County Down, in 1850 at the age of 78.

Chapter 7

Manby's Mortar in Action

Charles Holcomb Bowen

On the afternoon of New Years' Day 1827, the smack *Rose* of Wick, a regular trader in the waters off the east coast of Scotland, sailed from Wick with a general cargo of herrings, grain and other goods, bound for Leith. Her master was James McBeath, and he also had on board nine passengers: five men, three women and a young child who was blind.

As the ship progressed on its southerly journey, the wind, which had been blowing from east-north-east, veered towards the north-west and strengthened considerably. Sailing conditions were challenging, but things took a turn for the worse when a leak was discovered below at around 10 pm McBeath ordered men to the pumps, but despite their best efforts it eventually became clear that there was more water coming in than being pumped out, 'to the great alarm of the passengers'.

Aware of the growing urgency of his situation, the master decided that the only way of saving everyone on board was to run his ship ashore. At 2 am the light at Kinnaird's Head was sighted, which meant he should be able to round the head and take the *Rose* into Fraserburgh Bay, rather than make for Peterhead, which had been his initial idea. He had all sail possible made given the conditions, but it was a losing battle. It would be impossible to get into Fraserburgh harbour, and there was by now a foot of water in the cabin. McBeath's passengers pleaded with him to run the ship on shore wherever he could without delay, and he concurred, fearing that if he waited any longer they were all doomed. The smack ran onto rocks about half a mile south of Fraserburgh town; no one was injured by the impact, but the waves were now crashing over the little ship, and there was a bitter sleet and snow shower to add to the mix for the terrified passengers. McBeath had a distress light hoisted, in the hope that it would be spotted by someone on the coast. It was.

The coastguard always had someone on lookout in such conditions, and at around 3 am the plight of the *Rose* was discovered. Word was passed to the commander of the station Lieutenant Charles Bowen, and all available men of the Fraserburgh coastguard station were called out.

They hastened along the coast to the spot closest to the ship. The heavy snow made it hard to pick her out but they eventually located her and saw that she was in a perilous situation, in danger of being dashed to pieces or washed off the rocks in a sinking state. In these horrendous conditions they couldn't put a boat out, but Bowen and his men had brought with them Captain Manby's mortar device for firing a line out to grounded ships. Their first attempt failed to reach the *Rose*; the second shot was accurate, but when the line landed across the ship it presumably snagged on something because it broke. But it was a case of third time lucky. The shot carrying the line was thrown across the deck near the mainmast, and the smack's crew were able to attach a hawser to it, which was hauled to the shore.[1] By this means a cot was sent across to the ship, in which all nine of the shivering, exhausted passengers were pulled ashore. The local chief magistrate, Lewis Chalmers, and his wife took the bedraggled bunch into their own house where they were could recover from their ordeal in warmth and comfort for the night. But the night's work wasn't over Lieutenant Bowen and his men.

The coastguards were being aided by onlookers who had gathered at the scene, along with the masters of other vessels already anchored in the harbour, and while the *Rose*'s rescued passengers were enjoying the Chalmers' hospitality, this group remained at the scene for several hours more, at times waist-deep in the icy water, not only bringing off the ship's crew, but also salvaging most of the cargo she had been carrying.

---

1. The ball fired by a Manby mortar is often described at this period as a 'hooked shot'.

The coastguard's local inspecting commander was so impressed with Bowen's professionalism and modesty that he wrote to the Comptroller General of Scotland's coastguard recommending him for some sort of award, and allowed his letter to be made public in the newspapers.

Lieutenant Charles Holcombe Bowen was born in approximately 1772, probably in Meline, Pembrokeshire (where at least two of his siblings were born). He doesn't seem to have come from a seafaring family, but he and his four brothers all joined the navy, with Charles being the only to survive the wars with France. He was promoted to lieutenant the year after Trafalgar; at some point he joined the coastguard service in Scotland, and that country became his permanent home. He was initially at a west coast station, before moving to Fraserburgh, just north of Peterhead on the east coast. We know he lived at a house on Broad Street, Fraserburgh, thanks to an 1829 advertisement in the *Aberdeen Press & Journal* announcing that, Bowen having vacated it, it was now being used as retail premises by the Misses Greig, who had arrived from London with a fine selection of the 'present fashions', including bonnets, dresses and stays. Bowen almost certainly moved to Rathven, about forty miles west of Fraserburgh, because that's where he was living when he died in 1833, aged around 61.

Chapter 8

The Rescuer Rescued

James Lindsay

The day after the New Year of 1827 had been ushered in, the Inverness sloop *Lively*, with a crew of three and one female passenger, was driven onto the coast near Fort George, a few miles from Inverness, in heavy weather. The sloop's own boat, in which those on board might have escaped, was swept away in the incident – but bad luck turned to good when, upon being thrown ashore by the tide, it was commandeered by the chief officer of the local coastguard station: Lieutenant James Lindsay, RN. He, along with two of his men – William Cork and Alexander Gray – took the boat back out into the crashing waves and managed to work it alongside the *Lively*. Before they could get anyone off the sloop, however, the surging waves swamped Lindsay's boat, forcing them to scramble onto the vessel whose crew and passenger they had come to save. Now, they were victims themselves.

Everyone on board was exposed to the cutting winds, and the waves repeatedly cascading down onto the ship, and Lieutenant Lindsay had to keep a tight grip on the woman to prevent her from being carried away to her death.

Thankfully, there were more coastguard men watching from the shore, and they were able to come to the rescue in their own boat, returning Lindsay and his two men, along with the four from the *Lively*, to the safety of land after a three hour ordeal. The value of the coastguards' rapid action was demonstrated when the sloop was dashed to pieces within thirty minutes of the rescue.

James Lindsay had been a lieutenant in the Royal Navy since 1815, and is probably the officer of that name who served on HMS *Britannia* at Trafalgar. He died in 1845.

Chapter 9

An Officer and a Scholar

Christopher Jobson

Saturday 17 February 1827 started out cold but clear and bright on the east coast of Scotland. During the afternoon, however, the brisk north-westerly wind veered to the east, becoming gale force and carrying with it a snowstorm which caused havoc among the shipping in the area. Some vessels took refuge in harbours, but others didn't make it. A sloop bound for Dundee lost her mast and ended up on the rocks; luckily, her crew used the mast as a floatation aid and made it safely to shore. As the wind approached hurricane force, other vessels were overcome and ended up ashore.

One of these was the *Clyde* packet, which had set out from Aberdeen and was making for Glasgow when it was driven onto rocks to the west of Arbroath. The local lifeboat put out and fought to reach her, but was forced back by the breakers and the danger from rocks. The only other option was to fire a line from the Manby mortar, and the coastguard hurried through the snow to get their equipment in position.

Under the guidance of Lieutenant Christopher Jobson, a line was successfully fired over the smack and secured by crew, which allowed the lifeboat crew to haul themselves towards her. The boatmen helped two women and their two children aboard, followed by two crewmen – but then disaster struck. A wave threw the boat against the hull of the packet, swamping her and toppling everyone into the sea. Worse still, a rope had caught around the ankle of one of the women, almost ripping her foot off.

Seeing the drama unfold, Jobson and others from the shore waded out into the icy water to do what they could. Considering the task they faced, the outcome was as good as could be realistically hoped for. One of the children was lost, but everyone else was dragged to safety. The woman who became snagged in the rope, however, subsequently lost her foot such was the extent of the injury; to make matters far worse, she was the mother of the drowned child.

Lieutenant Jobson had been ably assisted by both his coastguard men and various seamen and townsfolk who had gathered near the wrecked packet – one of whom was his own wife. It was Elizabeth Jobson herself who tried in vain to resuscitate the drowned child and tended to the other. Her husband was awarded the gold medal for his courage, and within a month he was in action again.

In the early hours of 7 March, in very similar conditions to those prevailing in the *Clyde* packet event, the sloop *Alice*, carrying unslaked line from Sunderland to Perth, came to grief about 300 yards off the coast near Elliot, south of Arbroath. The lifeboat was launched to try to take off the crew of three, but once again despite the best efforts of the crew they couldn't get close, and soon their own boat was swamped.

Lieutenant Jobson and his men arrived with their Manby equipment, but the first attempts ended up with lines being snagged among the rocks. By now, things were getting desperate for those on board the *Alice*; not only was she being dashed to pieces by wave and rock, but a fire had broken out below in the cargo of lime. Jobson joined the lifeboat crew in making one more effort, this time fighting its way to the sloop and taking off the master. Sadly, the other crewman and a boy were lost.

Lieutenant Christopher Jobson was from England but settled in Scotland after joining the coastguard in 1815. He was approximately 42 at the time when he won his two gold medals. He and his family were living in Stromness when he died at the age of 56 in 1841. An obituary in the local paper described him as 'an excellent commander, an indulgent officer, and accomplished and elegant scholar, and a kind and affectionate parent'.

Chapter 10

Mentioned in Dispatches

Roberts Bates Matthews

R obert Matthews knew only too well what it was like to be shipwrecked.

As a young midshipman he was on board the heavy frigate *Apollo*, part of an escort protecting a large convoy of merchant ships from Cork in April 1804. What no one on board realised was that an iron tank they had on board was affecting the officers' compass readings. Believing they were well clear of land, the warship grounded off the coast of Portugal. Worse still, because of the gale-force conditions and poor visibility, over twenty ships of the convoy had been following close behind the *Apollo* and also struck bottom. Very many died, some from the actual grounding, and others subsequently from exposure. More than sixty of the *Apollo*'s crew lost their lives, including the captain, and seven ship's boys. Matthews was one of the 'lucky' ones left clinging to the wreckage in freezing conditions until help arrived.

On the night of 10/11 October 1827, by which time Matthews was a naval lieutenant and inspecting commander of the Lowestoft coastguard station, fierce winds caused several ships to put into ports along the east coast of England with storm damage and lost anchors, and at least five were driven ashore and wrecked.

One of these was the *Lord Duncan*, carrying coal from South Shields. She struck the Newcombe Sands, and there were great fears for the safety of the master and his six crew. The possibility of getting a boat out to them had to be discounted, but, thankfully, Lieutenant Morris and some fellow coastguard men were soon on hand with their Manby mortar. They succeeded in firing a line over the ship, which was secured by the crew, enabling them all to be hauled off one-by-one.

Robert Bates Matthews had health problems for most of his life, making his work and achievements with the coastguard even more admirable. When, as a teenage midshipman he had been wrecked on the *Apollo*, his entry in the *Naval Biographical Dictionary* reports that he and his colleagues were left for three days, only partially clothed and with no food. 'So great was the shock to his constitution that he never recovered from its effects.' The following year, while serving on a naval schooner protecting an American ship that had gone onto rocks, he received a hand injury serious enough for him to be awarded and naval pension, even though he was able to continue to serve.

The very next year he was given charge of a recaptured British merchant ship that came under attack from four Spanish privateers. He was mentioned in dispatches for the way he extricated his ship and brought her safely home. He was promoted to lieutenant in 1810, but his health problems meant that he was unable to join the 110-gun *Hibernia*, though he did later serve on other ships before a posting to the Barry's Head signal station, County Cork.

He joined the coastguard at Lowestoft in 1820, finally retiring, again though ill-health, in 1831. Whether the problem was still with his hand is uncertain, but it is reported that he underwent two surgical procedures. Born in Canterbury, Kent, he died in London in 1858, aged 73.

Chapter 11

Tragic Coble Rescue

John Brunton

In May 1824, two Royal Navy ships, the *Hecla* and the *Fury*, sailed north in search of the North-West Passage in an expedition under the command of the renowned explorer William Parry. They were pushing the frontiers of exploration – in fact, attempting what we only know today to be the impossible in a wooden sailing vessel, and they ran into trouble. The *Fury* was damaged and ultimately abandoned, and the *Hecla* was forced to return to Britain fifteen months later. This was fortunate for both one particular individual, and a large number of future distressed mariners: because on board was a young midshipman, John Brunton, who would go on to be decorated for his bravery in that field.

The Arbroath schooner *Triton* was carrying a cargo of rye from the port of Liebau (now known as Liepāja) in Latvia, to Newcastle. She almost made it, but not quite. In the early hours of 1 December 1828, about forty miles from port, the 100-ton vessel was carried towards the coast near Newton-by-the Sea; she struck the rocks at about 3 am in the pitch darkness, without anyone on shore or in the seas around her realising what had happened.

Those on board, namely Thomas Ford, the master, four sailors, three ship's boys, and one passenger, scrambled up the rigging into the masts as the waves battered the broken hull beneath them.

When daylight revealed the *Triton*'s plight, Lieutenant Brunton at the coastguard station was notified, and he quickly assembled a team to transport the Manby equipment down to the shore. Unfortunately, the ship was too far off for the mortar to get a line to her, and onlookers could only helplessly watch the harrowing sight of distant figures plunging one by one into the waters and disappearing beneath the waves, as their energy failed them.

But some remained, and now Brunton approached a group of fisherman on shore and offered to lead a rescue party out to the wreck in one of their coble boats[1] if enough would volunteer to come with them. Despite the dangerous conditions for such a small boat, four of them stepped forward without hesitation, and soon they and Brunton were pushing off into the wild surf. Twice, the waves drove them back towards the shore, but they persevered, and finally reached the Triton. By now, only three men remained clinging to the ship's rigging, and only one of those had sufficient strength left to help his rescuers to lower him down into their boat. The gale was worsening, and the chances of them being able to get the coble back to shore intact were rapidly decreasing. It would be impossible to get the dead weight of the two remaining sailors down from their position high up the mast, and, tragically, Brunton and his men were forced to get the coble clear, leaving them behind.

Even then disaster nearly struck, so perilous was the state of the sea by this time. Very soon after pulling away from the schooner, the fishing boat was swamped by a great wave, tipping everyone on board into the sea. Luckily, they all recovered the boat, and because on their outward journey they had paid out a line that was secured and manned on shore, their boat was hauled back in.

At some point during the drama, one of the fishermen who had volunteered to accompany Brunton, called Robert Rutter, had his hand smashed so badly that he lost a finger. He was unable to work in order to support his family for some time to come, so the £20 reward given to all those who took part would, in 1828 when it would quite possibly have represented a year's wages or more, have gone a long way keeping his family in food and other basic necessities.

Lieutenant John Brunton went on to be awarded a silver medal when he joined a lifeboat crew in rescuing the crew of a Whitby merchant

---

1. Cobles were traditional open boats with a flat bottom and a high bow, largely confined to the north-east coast.

vessel that came to grief on Boulmer Rocks, a few miles south of the Newton coastguard station. He left the coastguard in 1846 and took on the role of governor of Northumberland Gaol.

Unlike almost all of the navy men featuring in this book, Brunton didn't come from a naval or seafaring family. In fact, his background could hardly be of greater contrast, because he came from a Norfolk theatrical family: his father (also John) was an actor, comedian and eventually theatre manager; both John senior, his father and his daughter had appeared on the stage at the Covent Garden Theatre in London, and all had quite big reputations in their day.

Father and son may have trodden divergent career paths, but in a rather sad way they came together in death, since they died within two days of each other in 1848: John senior in London, his son in Morpeth, at the age of just 53.

Chapter 12

Never Give Up

Jimmy Haylett

On the evening of Wednesday 15 November 1901, Charles Sneller, a Caister lifeboatmen of over forty years, was walking home with coxswain Aaron Haylett from the lifeboat station. They had been checking on the *Beauchamp*, one of their two lifeboats, concerned that the tide was so high that it had been washing round the skeets upon which she stood and threatened to lift her off. Satisfied that the tide had turned and the water was now receding, they decided to go home. But along the way they noticed the lights of a vessel not too far out to sea, and assessing her position and the stormy weather, Aaron said to his colleague, 'If the wind comes out a bit, we shall have to be after that fellow.'

Inside the station, a keen lookout with telescopes was being kept. The weather had been fine at the start of the day, but the sea had grown steadily rougher and the barometer had dropped so dramatically that many boats of the fishing fleet had elected not to go out. Towards midnight the storm had truly broken, with a lashing rain and boiling sea. This was not an isolated meteorological event, but part of what became known as the Great Storm, which hit the whole of the east coast of Britain and claimed 46 ships and 200 lives.

But not all local boats had stayed in port. The vessel Aaron Haylett and Charles Sneller had noticed was the *Buttercup*, with Captain James Smith and two hands, a Lowestoft smack on her way back from the fishing grounds. Eventually fearing that his boat was being driven towards the treacherous Barber Sands, Aaron's prediction came true when Captain Smith decided to send up distress flares. They seemed to light up the whole sky on that dark winter's night; when the coastguard station saw them they sent up their own rockets, and the Caister lifeboat station signalman, Harry Knights, acknowledged then tolled them alarm bell, its ominous alert echoing around the dark, rain-swept streets of Caister.

The bell woke Jimmy Haylett, a man looked upon as the father of the Caister lifeboatmen. He was 78 years old and had been retired from the lifeboat service for several years, but it was a case of once a lifeboatman always a lifeboatman, and when he heard the familiar tolling at around 11 pm he instinctively ran down to see what he could do, arriving at the same time as the men mustering for the launch.

There were two lifeboats at Caister by this time: the larger *Covent Garden*, and the *Beauchamp*, named after Lady Beauchamp who had presented the boat to the station. The latter craft was chosen for this mission because she was smaller and didn't draw as much water, making her better suited to a rescue closer inshore and near sandbanks. The *Beauchamp* was not a self-righting lifeboat, as had become common, and this was to prove a somewhat contentious issue in the days to come.

The coxswain of the *Beauchamp* was Jimmy Haylett's son Aaron, who cried 'Heave off, or those poor fellows will be drowned!' The crew scrambled into the boat and she was ready to go half hour after the alarm had first been raised. But at the first attempt the raging surf overcame them. She had to be hauled back onto the skeets using a capstan, ready for another try. It was nearly three exhausting hours before they could get her away. During this time there was a regular switching of crewmen because some, often working up to their waist in water, got so saturated with icy water that they were sent home to change clothes and new men were brought in to replace them; this happened two or three times in some cases. Little did they know it, but this constant chopping and changing would prove to have been a deadly form of musical chairs. When the *Beauchamp* did finally put to sea, things went from bad to worse.

Coxswain Aaron Haylett ordered the hoisting of her two sails once they were clear of the beach. As they were heading off into the darkness, Aaron called out to Sneller, 'Charlie, look out and keep a light on the beach.' Sneller duly fetched a 'duck light' from the station, but such was the gale that it kept blowing out and he would have to rush back inside several times to re-light it in the coming minutes.

Jimmy Haylett stood outside the store house looking on, and at approximately 3 am he saw the red light from the *Beauchamp* disappear from view, swallowed by the night. Approximately half an hour later, his grandson Fred, who had been home to change out of his wet clothes, came hurrying to him. He was worried.

'Are there any people on the beach? Because I heard someone shout.'

Then Jimmy himself heard it: shrieks coming from the sea, which 'pierced even the howling gale and the roaring of the billows'. It was too dark to make anything out, but the old man ran northward along the seafront in the direction of the 'piteous cries'. Fred grabbed the duck light, which had been left on beach to guide lifeboat back in, but he ran so hard that it again blew out, and he had to go once more go back to the station to re-light it.

In the meantime, about fifty yards north of where the boat had been launched, Jimmy came upon a sickening, heart-rending scene. There at the water's edge was the lifeboat, partially submerged. Worse still, she was upside down, her hull glistening in the darkness from the waters that continued to crash over her. She was being rocked, lifted and dropped by the merciless seas, and almost as soon as he arrived on the scene Jimmy saw a man's upper body appear from underneath it after one such shifting of the boat. The crewman was trying to drag himself clear but was being held in by a rope that had become wrapped round his feet, so Jimmy plunged into the surf, pulling out his knife as he ran. He quickly cut the rope, grabbed the struggling man by the collar and pulled him free. So distressed was old Jimmy by the terrible scene before him that he couldn't even take in who he had rescued, even though he knew the whole crew perfectly well, and had to ask '*Who are you?*'

In fact, it was his son-in-law Charles Knights, and Jimmy helped him stagger ashore. Thankfully, he was no longer alone because other men were arriving to assist. A large number soon converged on the beach once word got round; the lifeboat men who hadn't been on the crew but who had been away to change into dry clothes raced down to the spot, with most getting soaked again as they waded up to their necks in water trying to help. Jimmy ventured back in and rescued Jack Hubbard, then once more to the aid of his own grandson, Walter, whom he helped to haul to safety. Attempts were made to lift up the boat to see if more could be saved, but the sea continued to toss the *Beauchamp* (almost the length of a double-decker bus) about so violently that they had to keep running clear to save themselves. It reached the point where the distraught onlookers at the water's edge could only stand and watch the crashing waves toy with the boat.

It was half an hour before the first corpse was washed clear of the upturned boat, this being William Wilson, 56. He was married but had no children. Next came Jimmy's grandson by marriage, Harry Knights, just 19 and on his first 'shout'. He was the son of the rescued Charles Knights. Harry was followed by John Smith, known as 'Shepherd', and the only non-Caister man in the crew. He left nine children fatherless. Jimmy had just managed to grasp him before his body floated away, but then he had to endure the sight of his son, James Henry Haylett, being given up by the upturned wreck. He was 56 and a father of ten. The final man to emerge in this way was William Brown, another father of ten. By now it was around nine in the morning, and the storm was abating.

Dr Case had been on the scene and even attempted to resuscitate a couple of the apparently dead men, William Wilson and 'the lad' Knights, but quickly realised that such efforts were futile. Even the survivors were in a bad way. Apart from the effects of exposure and the violent buffeting they had endured, they had taken plenty of water into their lungs. Dr Case did what he could at the scene, but the state of medical knowledge of the day meant that he could do little more than administer 'restoratives' – probably brandy and/or smelling salts, after which the men were quickly taken to their homes, where the doctor continued to minister to them.

The news spread through the whole village and beyond, and as dawn broke crowds of people flocked to beach either to see if they could help or in a desperate search for family members. Distraught women, protected from the driving rain and wind only by shawls over their heads, were 'running hither and thither making anxious enquiries after husbands, brothers or friends'.

Towards midday, the conditions were such that it was possible to attach lines to the *Beauchamp*, and through the strenuous efforts of around 250 men, she was finally righted – and in doing so gave up her remaining victims. In what must have been a horrific sight for all looking on, but especially father Jimmy, Aaron Haylett the coxswain fell out when the boat was turned. The other two were George King and Charles Brown. King was yet another father of ten and the sole financial support to his widowed mother. His father, Joseph, was one of those who died in 1885 when the yawl *Zephyr* was wrecked going to the aid of a grounded schooner. Charles Brown also left behind several children. Both were entangled in rigging and 'much knocked about'. This meant that all the crew were accounted for except one: Charles George. (A rumour circulated in Caister at the time that he had leapt clear before the boat capsized, but it was never substantiated.)

Villagers congregated throughout the day at the corner of Tan Lane, which led to the lifeboat shed, and in afternoon the church bell tolled and the blinds of the houses were drawn. For those whose loved ones had been members of the crew, their sad journey ended at the little white-painted lifeboat station, where the eight recovered bodies were now lying on floor, covered with a sail.

The inquest opened very soon after the tragedy. The alarm had been raised late on Wednesday night, with the rescue operation continuing into Thursday morning; the inquest began on the Friday, but this was too soon for the survivors, who were so badly affected by injury, shock and exposure that they could not be there to tell what had happened. The main concern was over Jimmy Hubbard, who had taken a lot of water into his lungs and was having breathing difficulties. Because of this, the coroner announced his intention to deal with the formalities and glean what information he could during this session, then adjourn in the hope that the surviving crewmen might be well enough to make the second session. It was held at the Lord Nelson Tavern, but first the jury had had to perform the onerous task of viewing the bodies, which were still laid out at the lifeboat station. It was, ironically, a sunny day with a calm sea. The jurors walked past the *Beauchamp* herself, now righted, with her broken spars and tangled rigging stowed onboard, and the damage to her structure clear to see. Inside the shed, the sail covering the victims of the terrible night was pulled back. Their arms had been placed across their breasts in the then customary manner, and 'their heads and faces bore painful traces of their awful experience'.

Although none of the survivors was in a position to take their place at the inquest, white-haired old Jimmy Haylett did attend, and the coroner was happy to take his testimony even though much of it was second-hand, gleaned from the sick-bed of his son-in-law Charles Harry Knights. It was at this first session of the inquest that Jimmy Haylett was reported as uttering a phrase that has become part of lifeboat folklore.

There had been some discussion about what had caused the lifeboat to end up where it did, and Jimmy, after having discussed it with Knights, was unequivocal. After the difficult launch, in trying to reach the vessel in distress the *Beauchamp* had initially been sailing well and had completed two tacks, but she failed to respond to the third tack: she had 'missed stays'. By the time they had made another failed attempt to go about, they found themselves too close to the shore to do anything other than turn the boat's head for the beach. She didn't drift ashore, Jimmy emphasised, but was deliberately run ashore. He explained:

> There was no other remedy. In weather like that it is uncertain whether a boat will stay or not. If not, she must come back to the beach ... Poor souls – they couldn't do anything else.

It was at around this time, during the discussion about 'missing stays', that the coroner asked Jimmy to clarify that the crew had not given up the rescue.

This shouldn't be seen as a challenge – his questioning was polite and sympathetic throughout, but it was his job to ask the kind of questions that, for the record, would be expected to be asked of witnesses. The reason this is significant is that old Jimmy Haylett's reply has become part of lifeboat legend – and, in fact, has been adopted as an RNLI motto and forms the title of more than one work about the lifeboat service. The problem is that the famous version of Haylett's reply is almost certainly not completely accurate. When the coroner asked him to confirm that the rescue hadn't been abandoned, he was (and still is) widely quoted as saying 'Caister men never turn back'. But this was most likely due to a reporter paraphrasing what was said, and perhaps interpreting his own shorthand notes some hours after the event. Newspapers back then plagiarised each other routinely – in fact, it seems to have been accepted practice. A report appearing in a local newspaper would be replicated verbatim, often without attribution, in numerous others around the country within a day or two, and again in the national press if it was a big enough story. In this way, the 'Never turn back' reply caught the imagination of the public and spread quickly – so quickly, in fact, that by the time of the second sitting of the inquest, a moving little vignette took place when the coroner read out a letter from a member of the public in London. He had been inspired to write to say how proud he was to hear those 'nobles words' uttered by Jimmy Haylett: 'Caister Lifeboatmen never turned back'. They were, he said, words worthy of Nelson himself. He even sent a half-sovereign to be passed on to Jimmy, who was visibly touched. (And interestingly, neither he nor the coroner queried the 'Never turn back' phrase.)

The most accurate account of the exchange came in the *Yarmouth Independent* of 23 November, which, to me, is the least sensational and most reliable account. It began with the coroner pretty much inviting Jimmy to contradict him for the record: 'The crew had not given up?' Jimmy's reply was 'No, sir. They would never give up – it's against our rules' to which a juror quickly added: 'They are not that sort of blood.'

But the 'wrong' version immediately captured the imagination of the British public, leading to ever more melodramatic renderings in different publications, such as '*Caister men never turn back when there are lives to rescue*'. In one account, a rather mangled version of the juror's supplementary remark is even put into Jimmy's mouth for added effect: 'No,' proudly replied the old Tar. 'Caister men never turn back. It is not in their blood'. A poem called 'The Caister Men Never Turn Back' was published just a month after the disaster.

I'm sure that both Jimmy and the coroner felt the catchier version that was popularised to be perfectly valid in that it captured both the meaning and the spirit of what he had actually said. In fact, Jimmy himself used a variation of it not long afterwards at a public meeting held to inaugurate a fund for the families of the men who had drowned. One of the speakers was the rector of Caister, who announced to applause that he was particularly pleased to see 'that grand old man of the sea' present, James Haylett, who said at the inquest 'The Caister men never turn back' (further applause). The rector quite correctly prophesied that 'these words were destined to become memorable'. After more speeches from dignitaries and discussion regarding the raising and apportioning of monies, there were calls from various parts of the room for Jimmy Haylett to say a few words. He rose to his feet to thunderous applause. After a few introductory words, he reflected on the night of the disaster. Nobody could know, he said, what it felt like for him to be alone in the rain and the dark, the first man to come upon the sickening sight of the upturned boat. He added (to more applause), 'I have never turned back. I always go for what I start for. I hope I shall always stick to my post as long as I live. I am 78, and if spared twenty or thirty more years (laughter) I shall go out again and do what I can.'

Technically speaking, of course, the Caister men did 'come back'. But it was unavoidable and for sound nautical reasons, and there is no doubt that they would have tried again and again had the freak wave not tipped them over.

At the subsequent inquest session, five days after the first, a fuller picture of what had befallen began to emerge.

Only two members of the crew were well enough – just – to attend. Walter Edwin Haylett was accompanied to the Nelson by grandfather Jimmy. The descriptions of his appearance at the court are poignant. He appeared 'very ill, and was greatly distressed, bending his head upon his hands, and sobbing for some time before he was able to speak'. Walter was given a seat near the fire and allowed to wear his cap in court. He wore an overcoat with the collar turned up, and a black 'wrapper' around his throat. The other was Charles Knights, 'who showed signs of illness'. He related that he had nearly been thrown clear when the boat went over, but was caught up in the lifeline running round the sides. The boat ended up virtually on top of him, badly injuring one of his legs and leaving him with his bottom half inside and his upper body outside. He was trapped like this for about five minutes with the waves continually washing over him, trying to shout for help. His were probably the cries that had alerted and Fred and Jimmy Haylett to the unfolding drama. He was fighting to free himself when old Jimmy arrived and pulled him free.

Walter Haylett, who had served nine months in the Royal Navy and had been in the Naval Reserve for ten years, described his own 'remarkable escape'. He had been completely entombed by the upturned boat. There were holes in the bottom (of which more later) and when he peered through one of these out into the gloom he saw a shadowy figure on the beach (almost certainly old Jimmy). Not wanting to wait – or perhaps aware that it would be almost impossible to right the boat, he waited for the next occasion when the waves lifted her up, then made a dive for freedom. He didn't make it all the way out, however, and like Knights his leg was also crushed and he was pulled clear by grandfather Jimmy Haylett.

When asked to describe how the capsize came about, Walter explained that the *Beauchamp* was handling well given the atrocious conditions. They were able to tack to port and starboard, but then she fell into a hollow and was hit on her bow by what he described as a 'hob gob' sea, 'putting her head off'. It was so dark that Walter, standing aft, could not see the men in the forward part of the craft. They attempted to tack once more and managed to get the sails full again for a few seconds, but she refused to come about and by now hadn't sufficient leeway to get clear, so it was decided to turn her towards the beach. At first, she was propelled in that direction on the crest of a wave, but then a much bigger wave hit her starboard quarter just as she touched the beach, levering her over.

When the bodies had been viewed, it was noted that none were wearing cork life jackets, and this would be one of two issues relating to safety and policies that would be raised more than once during the course of the inquest – both of which had to be inquired into but were, in my opinion, ultimately red herrings. In addition to the absence of life jackets, the other main matter, as we shall see below, was the fact that the *Beauchamp* was not a self-righting lifeboat.

It became clear that the crew of the Caister lifeboat were ambivalent at best on the subject of wearing life jackets. Jimmy Haylett reported that none of the crew were wearing the cork jackets on the night of the disaster, and declared that 'There would not be a living soul if they had' because such accoutrements would prevented them from getting out from under the boat. Charles Knights said emphatically that, 'If we had, [worn life jackets] none of us would have been saved.' It was, Jimmy said, 'God's mercy' that they were not wearing them. When asked why they were not worn routinely, other than on this specific occasion, he said that with them on the crewmen were more likely to be knocked out of the boat when a heavy sea struck. The other point he made was that they hampered movement at crucial times. 'Often when we have the lifebelts on we chuck them off when we near the wreck, in order to give our arms more liberty. I very seldom use one myself.' Fred Haylett backed his grandfather up on this point. Walter Haylett was slightly more equivocal. While admitting that he didn't 'believe' in life jackets because they proved a hindrance when launching, he did tend to wear his once the lifeboat was under way, but even then the only reason he was able to offer up was that they 'prove very warm' – perhaps not quite what the inventor or lifeboat authorities had at the forefront of their minds for the devices.

All of this was, in many ways, a matter of more relevance for future lifeboat operations. It could, no doubt, be argued that the circumstances of the *Beauchamp* capsize were unusual and that in most rescues life jackets were more likely to save rather than jeopardise life; it was more by luck than judgement that not wearing the cork jackets proved beneficial on this occasion. The main point, as far as the circumstances of the capsize of the lifeboat went, was that it happened virtually on the beach, in water shallow enough to stand up in; it was a situation where anyone who had the liberty to do so could have reached shore without the need for a buoyancy aid.

The second of the more technical matters that were pursued during the course of the inquest (and at the Board of Trade enquiry) was the revelation – no doubt surprising to many even at the time who weren't part of the coastal community – that the *Beauchamp* wasn't a self-righting lifeboat. This was not a recent innovation. Such a design had been in use for decades by this time, yet a sizeable minority of boats still were not of this type. Of the 286 lifeboats around the coast of Britain at the start of the twentieth century, fifty were non-self-righting. This wasn't down to cost or availability; such vessels were actively shunned by the men of Caister and other stations on that coast. The *Beauchamp* was built to a specifically Norfolk/Suffolk design, one that the boatmen themselves were consulted on. This type had a hollow 'wale' with 'air cases' running around the side to aid buoyancy; the Caister Beach Company, to which the lifeboatmen all belonged, liked this design because, as Jimmy said, 'When a sea caught her it held her up ... The self-righting class would not do at Caister.' He, for one, would not even go in one, 'for I like to keep them right side up if I can'. Walter Haylett put it even more plainly at the inquest, managing at the same time to raise a rare wry laugh about self-righting boats on this otherwise sombre occasion: 'They have to turn over before they can right again, and by that time you are not much good ...' This might seem like a stubborn, even Luddite prejudice, but remember that these were all still open boats, so Walter's point seems a fair one. The Caister men weren't fools but vastly experienced men, both as regards lifeboat work and in their seafaring 'day jobs', and, in fact, at that time they had saved more lives than those of any other station. Again, with the lifeboat virtually beached, the whole issue of whether or not she was of the self-righting type becomes academic – no boat can self-right when it's as good as on dry land.

We have already heard that Walter Haylett described looking out through a hole in the bottom of the *Beauchamp* – a hole not caused by damage but that was one of several in the bottom of the boat there by design, to allow any water the boat shipped to escape. The way this worked was that the craft had a well running down its centre; the holes were inside this channel and were fitted with plugs. The practice was to pull the plugs out as soon as the boat was launched, allowing the water to fill the well and find its level with the water outside.

When Dr Case had been called to give evidence, he said he was of the opinion that all of the victims must have died quickly, and that William Brown may have been killed outright by a blow to the head. The last three men to be removed from beneath the *Beauchamp* looked as if they had tried to get out but had become entangled in ropes (which sounds like a horrific end and doesn't quite fit with his, no doubt, well-meant assessment of 'near instantaneous' death).

There was a kind of postscript to the inquest later that month when Jack Hubbard, who had not been well enough to appear to give his own account, was visited by a journalist. In those more genteel days the reporter merely called to enquire after Jack's health, and so was somewhat surprised to be invited into what he described as a pleasant but humble cottage near the lifeboat station, to talk to the still bed-bound man. As they climbed the stairs, Hubbard's wife confided that the 'horrors of the accident were never out of his mind'. The man himself was, not surprisingly, still looking exhausted and suffering 'greatly from the severe shock and battering he received' but otherwise appeared to be a 'young hale fellow'. He told a story very similar to those of his comrades – the boat wouldn't come round so they were running for the shore, but just as she got to the beach she turned broadside to the sea when a 'tremendous curling wave caught her and she was over in a moment'. Jack was hit on chest by the rest for the oars, which was how he got his most tangible injury. Perhaps stunned, he didn't try to escape from beneath the upturned boat, and, in fact, didn't expect to emerge alive. 'How it was I got clear, I cannot tell …'

Something else that had emerged at the inquest came from the captain of the vessel whose distress signal had set the whole chain of events into motion. James Smith reported that his lugger *Buttercup* had eventually been washed off Barber Sands, and had been able to drop anchor in deep water, riding out the gale till morning. But, of course, the crew of the *Beauchamp* weren't to know that, and, anyway, by the time the fishing lugger had got clear it was already too late for them.

The funeral of those lost in the *Beauchamp* disaster was paid for by RNLI, and the story had struck such a chord with the nation that offers and donations were pouring in, including the promise by the Beauchamp family of a replacement boat for Caister. The renowned Dr Barnardo had written to offer places in his home for any orphans in need – but the local papers remarked, rather sniffily despite acknowledging the generosity of the gesture, that it was thought unlikely that the offer would need to be taken up. Caister lifeboatmen never turned back – and its people looked after their own. The funeral took place on Sunday 17 November, and thousands converged on the church. 'Yarmouth seemed to empty itself … The long straight road that divides the wind-swept marshes was crowded from one end to the other …' The road the cortege would take was so packed as to leave a passage just wide enough for procession. It was a bright but chilly day with a touch of frost in the air when the eight hearses bearing their flower-strewn coffins weaved through the streets to the parish church, drawn by lifeboatmen, rocket brigadesmen and Trinity lighthousemen. The families of the bereaved walked behind, then took their places in the church to the heart-rending sound 'weeping women and sobbing children' taking their seats. 'That grand old veteran James Haylett supported himself with composure.' After the service, the procession moved on to the cemetery, where the coffins were lowered into a single large grave, which had been designed so that the fellow lifeboatmen could all lie together – with enough space left for Charles George should his body ever be found.

One day in January 1902, Dr Case, who had attended the living and dead on the night of 13 November but who was also the secretary of the Caister Beachmen Company, informed Jimmy that he had instructions to take him to Sandringham. It was all rather mysterious, but even though the doctor declined to tell him what the purpose of the visit was, Jimmy went anyway. If he hadn't already guessed at the purpose, a clue presented itself in the form of a royal brougham waiting for them at the railway station to whisk them away to York Cottage on the estate of Sandringham House. There, he was greeted by the Duke of York, the future George V, who asked him about his life-saving exploits and then explained that he was to be escorted elsewhere in order to receive the RNLI gold medal from King Edward VII himself. He was duly escorted to Sandringham House, where he received a warm welcome from the king. Edward had clearly been well briefed, or had perhaps followed the story in the press, because as well as enquiring after the family members Jimmy had lost in the two disasters, he also probed him on the subject of self-righting lifeboats. The medal was then presented, and before the two men parted, His Majesty said he hoped he would live many more years to savour it and perhaps even save some more lives if that were possible. 'I told the king', Jimmy later said, 'that I hoped I might live to be a hundred, and that when he died he would go to heaven.'

The father of the Caister lifeboatmen didn't make the century, unfortunately, dying just over five years after the *Beauchamp* disaster at the age of 82. (Edward VII outlived him by only three years.) At the time of his death, after a short illness in February 1907, another of his grandsons, John, was carrying on the family tradition by serving as the latest coxswain on the station. Jimmy's coffin was carried from the church to the cemetery by lifeboatmen, where he was buried near to his sons. The service was no sooner over than the lifeboat station alarm bell rang out, and the men who had born his coffin aloft ran off to meet the call. The uncanny coincidence was, in a way, a fitting end to the proceedings, and one that, if Jimmy were somehow looking down on it, must have made him smile.

Part III

Soldiers, Sailors, Priests and Civvies

Chapter 13

Agent of Preservation

William Broad

We scarcely recollect ever seeing such a heavy sea come into the harbour
Dorset County Chronicle

When the brig the *Larch* arrived off the coast of Cornwall in early January 1828, the last thing her crew needed was a battle with a tremendous gale when she was so close to her destination of Poole. The men were cold and weary, and most were already suffering from frostbite after a 'dreadful passage' of twenty-one days from Newfoundland bearing fish, oil and lumber, as well as carrying three passengers – a Mr Pearce and his two daughters. But they were buffeted throughout the night of the 6th and into the next day, the storm showing no signs of abating.

Collingwood, her master, decided to run into Falmouth harbour. He would normally have been able to call upon the assistance of a pilot to guide him to a safe anchorage, but the storm had kept them from going out. Collingwood carefully picked his way in, but strayed too close to the Trefusis side of the harbour (a reference to the Trefusis Estate, on the opposite side to Falmouth docks). He dropped anchor, but the *Larch* dragged towards the rocks, and at about 3 pm he hoisted a distress signal from her mainmast. She hit the rocks about around four in the afternoon. The distress signal was responded to not by the coastguard, but a civilian. William Broad, the Lloyds agent for Falmouth, boarded a six-oar gig and he was followed out by one of the local pilots in another boat.

Despite the terrible sea conditions, they were able to pull their way to the brig and board her, but their combined efforts could do nothing to prevent the inexorable movement towards the jagged rocks along the shoreline, which she eventually hit in the darkness with the rescuers on board.

Fortunately, help was at hand on shore. Captain Sutton, of the steam packet *Stanmer*, came up with the idea of carrying tar barrels to the headland and setting fire both to them and the surrounding gorse in order to give the rescue party some light to work by. As the gale-force winds continued, the *Larch*'s masts were cut through and cleared away, and a boat was able to carry a line to the shore. Next, an improvised breeches buoy was rigged up using a cask big enough to hold one person, by which means the crew, along with passenger Pearce and his daughters, made the precarious and, no doubt, terrifying journey to the shore and safety.

It was feared that the ship would be destroyed completely, but, in fact, she was saved and refurbished. In June of that year, she was offered for sale at a local hotel by none other than Broad himself in his capacity as shipping agent:

> now lying in Falmouth Harbour, together with all her masts, yards, standing rigging etc – very deserving of the very first attention ... lately hauled up for the purpose of being immediately fitted out for sea; and on inspection will be found a first-class faithful vessel. Her hull is exceedingly handsome, with a figure head; a fast sailer ...

It's interesting to note that her encounter with the rocks just a few months earlier was not mentioned!

William Broad was no ordinary, desk-bound agent 'having a go'. He was a vastly experienced and well-regarded master of merchant vessels himself, who had once been captured by French privateers. His release only came about when his ship was intercepted and retaken by a Royal Navy ship. He and his family were, and would long be, well known in the town as merchants and agents.

William was born in 1772, and, not long after his brush with the privateers, founded Broad & Co. shipping agents and merchants. At the time of the *Larch* event, his office was on Church Street; he later had his own business and domestic premises erected on Arwenack Street close to the Custom House (by which time the business name was Broad & Sons) which still exists. The *Larch* hadn't been his first rescue.

In November 1816 the brig *Mary and Dorothy*, a troop transport ship anchored in the harbour for a period of quarantine after returning from the West Indies, parted from her anchor cable and was driven close to the shore. William Broad was one of those involved in taking a replacement anchor and cable out to her, thus saving the day.

William was at his home on Arwenack Street when he died in 1853, aged 80. His sons took over the reins of the business, which continued well into the twentieth century. His obituary, fittingly bearing in mind his gold medal exploits, said, 'He was remarkable for extreme kindness of heart, and for great physical energy, which prompted him on all occasions to acts of daring humanity.'

Chapter 14

Heroism and Tragedy

John Jellard

The Short Straw

Patrick O'Brien, a 15-year-old sailor on board the barque the *Francis Spaight*, knelt on the deck while a bandage was tied over his eyes. Mulville, the seaman standing behind him, held up one of four sticks he had in his hand, and told O'Brien to call out the name of one of the four ship's boys, including O'Brien himself. This would continue till the shortest stick was selected, and the named person would be the one put to death to be eaten by the rest of the starving, desperate crew.

'Little Johnny Sheehan,' replied the youngster.

O'Brien had reprieved his shipmate: it was one of the longer sticks, and duly tossed aside.

Mulville picked out one of the three remaining sticks and held it aloft. 'On whom is this lot to fall?'

Patrick decided to take a gamble. 'Upon myself.'

The gamble hadn't paid off – he had chosen the shortest stick.

The *Francis Spaight* (sometimes erroneously referred to as 'Speight' and 'Sparght') was a 345-ton transport ship named after its owner, a Limerick merchant. Lately, she had been engaged in taking Irish emigrants to America, returning with a cargo of timber. She was on such a return journey on 3 December 1836 when, thanks to what a surviving crewman described as the 'carelessness of the helmsman', she 'broached to'.[1] The ship wasn't sinking; she had been rolled onto

---

1. To suddenly turn broadside on to an approaching heavy or steep sea. This can be caused by carrying too much sail or, as seems to be the case here, poor helmsmanship.

her side, during which three crewmen were lost, as were all of their provisions. The captain had ordered the cutting away of the masts, which had allowed the ship to right herself, but obviously she was now just hulk at the mercy of wind and tide.

And now, just over two nightmarish weeks later, Timothy Gorman, the *Francis Spaight*'s captain, told his young crewman that he must prepare to die, and decreed that the method would be to bleed him to death – either believing that drifting into unconsciousness through blood loss was the most humane method, or because he and his crew, who had been without food and water for nearly sixteen days, were too weak to perform any more violent a method. Apart from three bottles of wine, there had only been a little collected rainwater to keep them going till now. O'Brien made no protests. The only argument came from John Gorman, the ship's cook (and possibly the captain's brother) whom the captain had assigned to make the fatal cut. But under threat from other crewmen that he would become the victim himself if he refused, he caved in.

Patrick O'Brien removed his jacket and held out his right arm, since it was the veins in this limb that were to be cut open. His only request was that if any of the crew were to make it home, they should let his mother know what fate had befallen him.

Gorman grasped O'Brien's wrist and drew the small clasp-knife twice across the skin, but his feeble efforts didn't even draw blood. The youth put him out of his misery by taking the knife from him to do the job himself. For some reason, perhaps because he knew that O'Brien was right-handed, he suggested he cut his left arm instead, which he did, cutting himself in the crook of his elbow 'as a surgeon would'. But through a combination of extreme cold, starvation and stress, his blood vessels had contracted and he, too, failed to cause blood to flow.

The captain now suggested the quicker and more certain means of bringing about the boy's end: cutting his throat. For the first time, O'Brien's resolve and composure deserted him. He pleaded to be allowed to sleep for a while and try to get warm – then, he felt sure, they would be able to bleed him from the arm. When the captain, backed by several of the crew, insisted on carrying out his latest idea, the angry O'Brien threatened to come back and haunt whoever did the deed. It was no good, he was overpowered; the cook was once again ordered to make the cut, once again refused, and once again bowed to the threats from captain and crew.

By now, someone had rummaged around the poop deck of the helpless and dismasted but still floating *Francis Spaight* and found a knife with a bigger blade. A big bowl was held against O'Brien's neck to catch the precious blood, and after further ineffective protests, Gorman, the cook, made the fatal cut. Not all of the men could stomach drinking their former comrade's blood, nor eat the flesh, once the unfortunate O'Brien had been butchered for consumption – but most, driven by hunger, eventually did. Even with that, some of the crew were now becoming almost delirious – in particular the cook himself. Perhaps pushed over the edge by the terrible act he had been force to perform, he seemed to lose his mind completely that night, jabbering and raving nonsense, becoming aggressive and throwing his clothes around. Or so the story goes, as told by an anonymous member of the crew. The cook's 'madness' provided a convenient excuse for the crew to target him as their next meal, and when morning came he was dispatched in the same way that O'Brien had been.

By the end of the same day, two more crewmen – Michael Brehane and another of the boys, George Burns – lost their minds and became so wild that the others had to tie them up. Burns was bled to death like his late colleagues, while Brehane spared the remaining crewmen the grizzly task by conveniently dying a 'natural' death. They were both cut up and consumed as before.

If the crew of the *Francis Spaight* could have just lasted this long (and it's by no means certain they could have) then neither the deaths nor the cannibalism would have been necessary. Because the next morning, lookouts spied a distant sail – and it was heading their way.

The Rise and Fall of John Jellard

In October 1835 a brig called the *Freedom* of Teignmouth, Devon, carrying among others the master, John Cousins, and a seaman called

John Towell, was wrecked off Labrador. Fortunately, none of the crew drowned, and from Labrador they embarked on the schooner *Hero*, bound for St John's, where they might get a passage back to England. But the unfortunate men from the *Freedom* soon found themselves in trouble again before they had got very far, when the *Hero* ran into such a fierce gale that her crew, exhausted from battling against the elements 'went below, leaving the vessel to the mercy of the winds and waves'. Fortunately, Cousins and Towell were made of sterner stuff and took charge, eventually guiding the ship into St John's. Here, they did find a ship to take them home: she was the *Angerona*, whose master was John Jellard.

About five days into their voyage, a dismasted ship was made out in the distance, which seemed to have crewmen still on board, and Jellard ordered the *Angerona* to alter course to investigate. What they saw as they approached the *Francis Spaight* shocked even the hardiest among them: human body parts were neatly arranged around the poop deck like a display in the window of a butcher's shop.

But there were still the living to be saved, and despite a gale blowing, Captain Jellard stripped down to his shirt and asked for volunteers to accompany him and brave the heavy seas in the ship's boat in a rescue attempt. Three men offered their services, one being the indefatigable John Towell, despite him being only a passenger on this voyage. Jellard was able to go because his other passengers included experienced seamen such as Cousins, formerly master of the *Freedom*, and one Captain Kemp of Dartmouth, both of whom were able to continue to manoeuvre the *Angerona* so that her returning boat could safely come alongside on both occasions. There can be no doubt that without the selfless actions of all these men, those left adrift on the *Francis Spaight* would have suffered miserable, lingering deaths.

With four men needed at the oars in these atrocious conditions, the *Angerona*'s boat wasn't big enough to take all of the eleven men they found on the *Francis Spaight*; an initial batch of six cold, feeble and drenched crew were transferred to the *Angerona* first. Shipping a lot of water in the rough seas, the boat came close to capsizing, yet Jellard and his fellow volunteers immediately pitted themselves against the elements once again. To the sound of the rousing cheers of their shipmates, they returned with the remaining five seamen. While the *Francis Spaight*'s exhausted survivors were tended to below, the *Angerona* resumed her course for England, arriving safely on 6 January 1836.

When news of what had happened on board the *Francis Spaight* appeared in the press, it came to the attention of the author Jack London and provided the inspiration for his story 'The Custom of the Sea'.

While John Jellard fully deserved his gold medal it seems a shame that others weren't also handed out, particularly one for Towell, who 'only' received the silver medal.

John Jellard was born in Shaldon, Devon, but appears to have set up home in St John's, Newfoundland, and married there the year before the *Angerona* rescue. His RNLI gold medal is even rarer than most, being one of the very few exceptions to the normal rule that the award was really intended for rescues occurring around the coast of the UK. The citation read that despite the rescue being outside the organisation's normal parameters,

> in consideration of the meritorious conduct and exertions of Captain Jellard and the three other persons who assisted him … they have voted the gold medallion of the Institution to be presented to Captain Jellard, and the silver to Mr William Hill, to John Towell and to Samuel Hicks.

He returned to his home village in later years, but hadn't lost his spirit of adventure because in 1856 he commenced a round-the-world voyage in the barquentine *Avery*, which he had successfully completed by the following year. Jellard wrote a book about his voyage, and a plaque to mark his achievement was displayed at the shipyard in Shaldon where the *Avery* had been built. But his story has a sad ending.

Despite the fame the circumnavigation had earned him, the voyage had been plagued by problems. The *Avery* was beset by storms that caused expensive damage and losses of provisions, and to make matters worse there were doubts as to whether the insurance taken out by the vessel's owners had expired before the losses occurred. Whether or not this proved to be the case, we do know that Jellard was in financial difficulties when he departed the Port of London in the *Avery* bound for Canterbury, New Zealand, in February 1860. By this time he appears to have been suffering from depression. He took to drink, and, worse still, laudanum, a freely available and fairly widely resorted to mixture of opium and alcohol used to treat pain, sleeplessness and so on. Not surprisingly, it was highly addictive. With the *Avery* anchored at Lyttelton Harbour near Christchurch, New Zealand, Jellard's crew were aware that he was ill, but at first didn't think it serious. By the time their concerns led to them sending for medical attention a few days later, it was too late. On 28 May 1860, John Jellard, 50, master mariner, was found on board the celebrated *Avery*, dead from a laudanum overdose.

Chapter 15

Soldier, Sailor …

John Torrens

When the morning of Thursday 28 October 1880 dawned in Dublin Bay, the North Bull coastguards observed an alarm flare streaking into the grey skies from the direction of the nearby lighthouse. Scanning the sea for the cause of the alert, they spotted a brigantine that had foundered in stormy seas near the mouth of the harbour. She was the *Robert Brown*, carrying coal from Neath, South Wales, to her home port of Warrenpoint, County Down. An enormous wave had destroyed her wheel-head and caused other damage, leaving her unable to steer. She was not the only casualty of the previous night, when a great storm had swept through the whole of Ireland and Britain leaving a trail of damage on land as well as at sea. In one incident alone, at least twenty-two sailors had drowned when their ship went down off Tynemouth.

Training their telescopes on the scene, the coastguards picked out two sailors clinging to the rigging of the *Robert Brown*, and immediately went into action. The sea conditions were such that they didn't think a rescue boat from their northern part of the bay could make it to the ship, so they sent a man to the Ringsend coastguard station, south-west of them, to summon help. But the heavy weather hadn't just affected shipping – there was serious flooding inland, with some roads near the coast virtually impassable, and this severely hampered the messenger's journey.

At around the same time, Lieutenant John Torrens of the Scots Greys at Pigeon House Fort near Ringsend, had been supervising target practice on the rifle range when he had also become aware of what was happening out at sea, and turned his own telescope on the desperate men on board the brigantine. He collected a group of his men and hastened to the North Bull coastguard station to request that they launch the Poolbeg lifeboat. Unfortunately, her crew were away, having been ordered to carry out practice drills on board the guardship *Belleisle* anchored in Kingstown Harbour several miles to the south. In desperation, Torrens, a keen yachtsman, declared that *he* would launch the lifeboat, and put together a crew of soldiers, some local fishermen and a man called Nicholson of the government steamship *Stanley*; including Torrens, there were twelve men in all. The coastguard officers weren't keen on this plan, and would only agree to it upon receiving a guarantee that Torrens and the military at Pigeon House Fort would accept responsibility for the safety of the lifeboat. Torrens didn't hesitate to give his assurance, and headed his motley crew down to the Half Moon Battery to launch the rescue craft.

The sea was running high and it was no easy task to get her under way, but a launch finally was achieved at about 11.30 am and the makeshift crew rowed through the crashing waves out to *Robert Brown*. The two men they finally managed, with great difficulty, to haul into the lifeboat were the only ones left of an original crew of five. Two had been swept overboard when the ship had got into trouble, and in trying to save one of the youngest members of the crew, a 16-year-old, the master had also lost his life. Torrens and his men rowed the shivering and exhausted survivors to shore, from where they were taken to Pigeonhole Fort's hospital, where Dr Cox, the medical officer (who had helped to launch the boat), was on hand to tend to the survivors of the sinking vessel.

Torrens and Cox, in particular, were highly praised for their gallant efforts. The *Robert Brown*, however, was beyond saving and could only be left to the mercy of the waves and her inevitable destruction.

On Thursday January 6 1881, the same day that Charlie Fish was in the middle of battling with the elements to save the crew of the *Indian Chief* off Ramsgate (as we shall see later in the book), Torrens attended an award ceremony at the RNLI's then headquarters in the Adelphi in London. There he received his gold medal; two of the volunteers he had roped into the venture were presented with the silver, and the whole crew of brave but untrained non-lifeboatmen, received 'double the ordinary reward' for their efforts.

John Arthur Wellesley O'Neill Torrens had been born into a wealthy Ulster family in 1856. He was educated at Harrow, and joined the 2nd Royal Scots Greys when he was around 20 years of age, serving with them for twenty-nine years. He was a lieutenant at the time of the *Robert Brown* rescue, but reached the rank of major before retiring. He then embarked upon a new career in the railways, joining the board of the London, Midland and Scottish Railway Company in 1909. This was no nominal appointment. He was actively involved, becoming chairman a few years later and 'many outstanding developments ... in the company's system' took place under his tenure. He was also involved with other, smaller railways companies in Ireland – on top of which he was made chairman of the Coleraine Harbour Board and was well respected for his work for that organisation too. He even found the time to serve as High Sheriff of Londonderry.

Torrens never married, and after leaving the army he lived with his mother at Cleggan Lodge, the family home near Ballymena, County Antrim, until his death at the age of 80 in 1936. He was buried on the estate, the first to be interred in a private burial ground on a mountainside overlooking the picturesque Valley of the Braid. One sign of his esteem within the railway fraternity is that the mourners included numerous men of that profession, from engineers and station masters to directors.

Chapter 16

The Priest and the Rocket Men

Father John O'Shea

There can have been very few sea rescues organised and led by priests, and surely none that led to the awarding of an RNLI gold medal – none, that is, until Father John O'Shea took the initiative in gathering together a large body of men about him on the beach at Ardmore on the south coast of Ireland, and launching a boat in almost impossible conditions in a desperate attempt to save the crew of the *Teaser* in 1911.

Born in 1871, John Michael O'Shea belonged to a prominent Waterford family, so was pretty much on home territory at the time of the *Teaser* incident. He trained for the priesthood at the Cistercian Mount Melleray Abbey, not far from his home town of Lismore, and by the time our story is set he was the curate of Ardmore in the same county.

O'Shea was part of a large crowd of people who had ventured down to the seashore on Saturday morning, 18 March 1911, when news quickly spread that a schooner had foundered on Black Rock in Ardmore Bay during a gale said to be the worst to hit that part of the coast for many years. She had been en route from Swansea to Killorglin, Dingle Bay, but was driven ashore. Three crewmen could be seen in her rigging – her two masts and her shrouds remained intact – having clambered up to avoid the powerful waves that swept again and again over their broken ship. They were Captain Thomas Hughes; a man called Fox, the mate; and Ordinary Seaman Walsh. When attempts to telephone the nearest lifeboat station failed, probably due to lines having blown down, Ardmore's coastguards rushed to the beach carrying their rocket equipment and managed to fire lines out to the *Teaser*. But the crewmen had already been holding on in that exposed position for some time, and were simply too cold and exhausted to be able to secure the ropes. (At least one of the ropes must have caught hold, however, perhaps after passing over the far side of the ship, for it was to be put to good use in the coming hours.) Seeing their effort fail, and with no lifeboat on hand, Richard Barry and Alexander Neal, two of the coastguards, attempted to wade out to the schooner. It was a gallant but doomed attempt; the water was icy-cold, and huge seas knocked them off their feet every time they tried to make progress. They had to be dragged back to land before becoming casualties themselves.

It was now that the priest went into action. A boat was the only way the *Teaser* could be reached, and he recalled that there was a fisherman's boat about a mile inland. It didn't seem feasible to drag it so far – to anyone but Father O'Shea. He took charge, bellowing above the howling winds for volunteers to help him to fetch it, and in no time he was at the head of a small army of around a hundred people pushing, pulling and generally manhandling the boat over fields and hummocks, along 'boreens' or narrow country lanes, until they had dragged it down onto the beach. Lifebelts had been procured. The rather short, stout 40-year-old priest fastened one on.

'Come, boys!' he cried. 'Who will help me to man the lifeboat?'

Once again, there was no shortage of men to come forward. He was joined by the two coastguards, Barry and Neal, who had recovered sufficiently from their earlier attempt, and had the valuable experience of a boatman named John O'Brien. There were two farmers: Patrick Power and Cornelius O'Brien, who may or may not have had any boating experience but who were surely strong in the arm, local policeman Constable Lawton, and, finally, William Harris, who owned a hotel on Ardmore's Main Street. This was the motley crew that manned the craft that was pushed by the crowd into the frothing waves and spray.

As they pulled closer to the *Teaser* through a blinding snowstorm (one account says that, in addition to rowing, they used one of the snagged rocket lines to help pull themselves towards her), they could see the three crewmen lashed themselves to the rigging; one up in the shrouds, and two on deck. It had saved them from being swept away, but nothing could have protected them from the cold and the pummelling of the waves. O'Shea and some of his crew managed to board the schooner, which was lying on her side at an angle of about 45 degrees and with several of her sails still set and flapping uselessly in the gale. Power and the two O'Briens stayed in the boat and fought to hold her steady, as she could have been being thrown against the schooner at any moment.

John O'Shea first pulled himself up the shrouds to free the man there, but he was in a state of total collapse and a dead weight, and it was impossible to untie him. It seemed clear that he had not long for this world, and O'Shea administered the last rites to him there and then. The acute angle of the wet deck caused one of the rescuers to lose his footing and tumble into the sea, but the coastguards Barry and Neal plunged in after him, and with the help of O'Shea he was hauled out.[1]

Not long after the rescue of their comrade, the effects caught up with Neal; he collapsed from exhaustion on the deck of the *Teaser* and had to be revived before they could continue. The two remaining shipwrecked crewmen were lifted into the rescue boat, but were hardly in any better state than their colleague up the mast – who sadly had now died. O'Shea deemed it necessary to utter the words of the last sacrament to the worst affected one, but he, too, expired before they could reach the shore. The third man was taken from the boat when it landed, but died soon afterwards.

And by now rescuers themselves were reaching the limits of their endurance. In particular, O'Shea had to be helped to a nearby house to recover, and Barry was driven to the coastguard station.[2]

---

1. Some accounts say that the rescuers dropped one of the three crewmen into the sea during the rescue, but O'Shea himself, speaking to a reporter, explicitly states that it was 'one of our own party'.
2. One version of the story says O'Shea gave the last rites to Barry the coastguard. O'Shea himself doesn't mention this, and, while it may be true, some writers have possibly confused the incident with those involving the *Teaser* crewmen who the priest did minister to.

Father O'Shea was presented with an array of awards in addition to his RNLI gold medal, including, eventually, the George Cross. (He was initially presented with the Empire Gallantry Medal by George V in a ceremony at Buckingham Palace, but that award was superseded by the George Cross in 1940 and his original medal was duly 'upgraded'.) The other men who had taken part in the attempted rescue were also given awards, including the Board of Trade's Sea Gallantry Medal.

Astonishingly, for a man who had nothing to do with lifeboats or the sea, the *Teaser* affair wasn't the last of Father O'Shea's rescue attempts, albeit not a gold medal-winning one and he played a much more minor role in his next incident. Just a year after the *Teaser* was wrecked, the *Marechal de Nouailles*, carrying a cargo of coke, coal and limestone from Glasgow, ran aground at the southern end of Ardmore Bay, this time several hundred yards west of Mine Head in heavy weather. There was a crew of twenty-two on board in urgent need of help, one of whom had already been swept into the sea, and the captain ordering the firing of distress signals. The lifeboat based at Helvick put out but wasn't able to get alongside the ship, so the Ardmore coastguard rocket team went into action, including our old friends Barry and Neal – with Father O'Shea also joining them. The state of the roads was such that wagon normally used to transport the rocket apparatus couldn't be used, so the men had to carry the equipment some fourteen miles to their destination, arriving in the early hours of the morning.

Once they had assembled the rocket equipment, they managed to fire over the *Marital de Nouailles*. One way in which the rocket apparatus was used to rescue crew was to fire a relatively light line that, once secured, was used to pull across a stouter rope which, by the use of a sort of pulley system, could transport individuals in a 'breeches buoy': a canvass carrier designed like a pair of 'breeches', with two holes into which the victim inserted their legs and were reeled safely to shore. But the crew didn't seem to know what they were supposed to do at their end, leaving the frustrated coastguards on the shore unable to help. However, the crewman who had been lost overboard was now found clinging to rocks at the foot of the cliffs, and, although he spoke no English, one of the coastguards was able to use gestures to explain how the system worked, and the sailor relayed the instructions to the ship using a megaphone.

Once the equipment was all set up, the crew were drawn from ship to shore along the line one-by-one; Father O'Shea was on hand to give the last rites to four of the crewmen who had been seriously injured by falling spars, though thankfully all survived their ordeal.

Father John O'Shea later left his post as curate in Ardmore to become the parish priest of Ballyporeen in County Tipperary. This was over thirty miles inland, thus bringing an end to his coastal rescuing days. He remained Ballyporeen's priest till his death in 1942, at the age of 71. His gallantry medals were bequeathed, according to his request, to the abbey at Mount Melleray where he had undergone his training in the Church.

Chapter 17

Tragic Hero

Dan Rees

It happened at some point between late evening on Sunday 1 September 1918, and the early hours of the following day. Forty-seven-year-old Dan Rees, respected magistrates' officer, hero of the Lavernock Point rescue of 1907, sat alone in his bedroom, took out his old Colt .45, held it to his head, and squeezed the trigger.

Daniel Esmonde Rees had been an athletically inclined man, interested in boxing and other sporting activities – including boating and sailing. As a solicitor and clerk to the Cardiff Magistrates' Court, this latter interest served him well when he sat on numerous inquiries into shipwrecks off the coast locally.

He was born in Cardiff in 1871, to a father who was also called Daniel Rees and who also, as his son was to, served with distinction as Clerk to the Magistrates. As a youth he went to sea 'for which he had a passionate fondness', though in what capacity isn't certain, before settling down on land and qualifying as a solicitor. He was a hardy man and noted for never wearing an overcoat no matter how cold the weather, and only donning a mackintosh in the very heaviest of downpours. He carried himself in an erect way, but was by no means stiff and dour in character, being known for his genial manner. He married in 1897, but the relationship didn't work out and he was single by the time of his death.

At about 11 am on 16 June 1907, a professional colleague of Rees', solicitor Harold Lloyd, was out near the coast south of Penarth, in what was then the county of Glamorgan, Wales. Gazing out to sea, he noticed a yacht off Lavernock Point apparently in difficulties in what was later described as a moderate gale. He looked on in horror as the vessel capsized, leaving her three occupants floundering in the sea before managing to cling on to their upturned craft. Lloyd's first thought was Dan Rees, who lived not too far away in Sully House, the family home in the village of Sully, and who had rescued people from these waters in the past. It took Dan only three minutes to get down to the shore and launch his own skiff, and he was soon rowing through the heavy sea in the direction of the yacht's distressed. His brother Ivor and nephew Morgan had come down to the shore with him, but had to remain on shore so that there would be enough room in the little boat for the yachtsmen.

Dan laboured for four miles through the waves and managed to reach the vessel. He helped two of them men in as his skiff, only 6 feet long, bobbed wildly about; but she was already crowded and lying low in the water. Taking the last man on board in these seas would have almost certainly caused the same kind of calamity that had befallen the yacht, and with great reluctance Rees was obliged to leave the unlucky third man clinging to the gunwales of his craft for the time being. But help was at hand.

Ivor and Morgan, knowing Dan would need help, had a small mosquito-class sailing boat anchored offshore, which was normally reached by means of the boat Dan himself had taken. With time being of the essence, Ivor promptly ran into the water fully clothed and swam out to the boat, brought it closer inshore to pick up Morgan, then set a course for the capsized yacht and picked up the remaining survivor of the catastrophe. As they were all rounding Sully Island and making their way back to shore, the local tug *Firefly* arrived on the scene; Dan Rees, believing that it would be safer and quicker for his men to take this vessel, helped transfer them into her for the final leg of their journey.

There were reports that one of the young men rescued was the son of James Rank, the famous flour miller whose business eventually became Rank Hovis McDougall. This may be true but there were conflicting and inaccurate accounts of this rescue doing the rounds in the days afterwards, one of which claimed that Dan Rees had failed to get to the three men, that one had attempted to swim to shore, and that they had been rescued by the tug. Harold Lloyd, the man who had first raised the alarm and witnessed events from beginning to end, felt compelled to send his own account into the *South Wales Daily News* to ensure that Dan Rees and his companions were rightfully recognised

The RNLI wanted Dan Rees to travel to London to be presented with his gold medal (and Ivor and Morgan their own rewards) but this didn't go down well in Penarth, where the Lifeboat Committee wanted a local ceremony. They got their way. On 19 October 1907, five months after the incident, the three local heroes were paraded before the Penarth Lifeboat Committee, where the chairman pointed out that the RNLI's gold medal was a 'rarer honour than even the Victoria Cross', since Dan Rees' medal was the 100th to have been issued, whereas 183 VCs had been given out.[1]

The Lord Mayor of Cardiff then presented Dan with the medal, saying, 'I am glad that God has blessed you with the health you enjoy, and the spirit that is in you towards your fellow men.' To loud cheers, Dan modestly replied that he 'didn't feel deserving of it'. Ivor Rees then received a silver medal for his part in the rescue, and Morgan a 'vote of thanks' on vellum signed by the Prince of Wales, since at that time the bronze medal had yet to be instituted.[2]

Dan's health took a turn for the worse around ten years later, when he was still only in his mid-forties. He was diagnosed with a heart condition in around 1916, and had visited a London specialist who had been able to offer nothing more than the advice to take things easy. The dramatic change in this normally active and athletic man affected him profoundly. It affected his mood, he was sleeping badly, and friends feared he was on the edge of a nervous breakdown. A few days before taking his own life, he had collapsed while on duty in court, and hadn't been able to work since.

---

1. Although this argument might hold up statistically – and even then in a somewhat limited way – I'm not sure even Dan himself would have read too much into the comparison.
2. The other two also received these in addition to their medals.

His body was found at 9.30 on Monday 2 September 1918. His sister, with whom he had been living in Panarth since separating from his wife, called him and received no answer, so she summoned her husband to go into his room. Mr Corbett found Dan Rees still dressed in his nightclothes, his Colt revolver lying by his side, and a small bullet hole just above the bridge of his nose. It was a desperately sad and tragic end to the hero of Lavernock Point.

Part IV

Firsts

Chapter 18

The First Ever Gold Medal Recipient

Charles Howe Fremantle

There was stormy weather all around the coast of Britain on 8 March 1824, particularly along the south coast, leading to the damage or loss of several ships (and three RNLI silver medals, the first to be awarded, are said to have been issued for various rescue attempts).

One of at least eight such losses was the *Carl Johan*,[1] a Swedish brig carrying a cargo of salt and wine from Alicante to Gävle in her home country. Her master was Peter Walroost.[2] Blown towards the then Hampshire coast and unable to fight her way clear, she ran aground on the beach near a place known as White Pits, close to Christchurch. Word was sent to the Preventive Service station at Lymington, and its senior officer, Captain Charles Fremantle, hurried westwards along the coast to investigate.

He found the vessel broadside on to the shore with the waves crashing against and over her, and it was clear that she was rapidly being destroyed by the buffeting she was taking. Her main mast had already gone by the board, and while she carried lifeboats, her crew were seen to be clinging to their disintegrating ship as if paralysed by fear. There was no way to safely get a boat out to her even if one had been available, so Fremantle took the bold decision to swim out in the bitterly cold early spring seas. He removed some of his outer clothing and took the precaution of having a line tied round his waist, before plunging into the frothing surf, battling through waves 'running mountains high'. Somehow, he made it, but once

1. Sometimes mistakenly referred to (even in the RNLI's own version of the story) as the *Carl Jean*.
2. This is also one of several variations on his name in the reports.

he had clambered aboard the crew of nine men and one ship's boy were still either unable to understand what he was trying to tell them or too panicked to act. All he could do without help was to cut the ropes securing her boats, allowing them to drop into the sea, but it was a risky strategy and they were quickly swamped and lost to sight. Seeing that he could do more to help the seemingly stupefied crew of the *Carl Johan*, Charles Fremantle decided it was time to save his own skin before the ship was smashed to pieces. He jumped back into the turbulent sea and tried to fight his way back to shore – but by now his reserves of energy were running out and it proved too much for him. The only thing that saved his life that day was the line he had prudently attached himself to, and, seeing he was in trouble, men on the shore hauled him in as quickly as they could, finally pulling him out virtually unconscious. He was soon revived using 'the usual methods'.

There are some discrepancies in the few very brief accounts of this story as to what happened next (and, in fact, concerning the event as a whole). What is certain is that the crew of the *Carl Johan* all eventually got off safely after all. Some reports say that they made for the broken mainmast as it floated away from the ship, and were washed towards the beach. But one or two stories make tantalising references to them being rescued by 'the boat's crew' without actually saying what boat this was. The assumption must be that it was a coastguard boat. There was almost certainly an anti-smuggling Revenue cutter based at Lymington; the cutter herself couldn't have got close enough to the grounded brig, but maybe one of her boats was lowered and able to reach the wreck.

One uncomfortable fact about this story is that although Captain Fremantle certainly risked his life on behalf of the crew of the *Carl Johan*, unlike almost every other gold medal recipient in this book, he didn't partaken in the actual saving of anyone. Is it at all possible that his illustrious name and parentage, his naval record, played a part in the decision? To be fair, this being the inception of the very idea of awarding gallantry medals (or medallions as they were initially then called) for sea rescues, there were no precedents regarding what constituted a medal-worthy act. Regardless of this, Fremantle's selflessness and bravery is beyond doubt.

Charles Howe Fremantle was a navy man through and through. His admiral father, Thomas, had seen action at the battles of Copenhagen and Trafalgar, among many other naval exploits, and was a friend of Nelson himself. His son Charles was born in the family home called Old House, in Swanbourne, Buckinghamshire, on the anniversary of the battle of the Glorious First of June six years previously, and which led to him being given the middle name Howe in honour of the Lord Howe who had led the British fleet to victory that day.

Charles' naval career began at the age of 12 – a common age for a prospective naval officer at that time – when he was taken on as a midshipman on the warship *Ramillies*, commanded by future Trafalgar hero Captain Thomas Hardy.

His time with the coastguard, during which he became the first person to be awarded the RNLI's gold medal for gallantry, was actually quite brief. By 1822 he had risen to the rank of commander in the navy, but soon afterwards – perhaps as a result of the navy's dramatic reduction in manpower following the end of the Napoleonic wars – he joined the coastguard service and was based at Lymington. But before two years had passed – during which time he had performed his medal-winning act, he was offered, and accepted, command of the navy sloop *Jasper* and sailed to Mexico. In 1829 he was despatched to Western Australia, where the part he played in the establishing of a town and port there led to it being named after him. Charles Fremantle remained in the navy (though not always on active service) till his death, and served in the Crimean War (1852–1856) by which time he was a vice admiral. He died in London in 1869, at the age of 68.

Chapter 19

Man of Honour

William Hutchinson

Thomas Meekins was an angry man. It was August 1861, Queen Victoria was to visit Dublin, and with her (on what would be his last public engagement before his untimely death) was Prince Albert. The clamour for tickets was enormous, and Mr Meekins had applied for a small number for family and friends (he couldn't make the event himself) and he had been unsuccessful. He felt the procedure was unfair; he was not a local (being a Londoner) and strongly suspected that tickets had been allocated to a favoured few locals. It just so happened that he came across the man responsible for ticket allocation – Lieutenant William Hutchinson, RN, a local worthy and the harbour master – and decided to make his feelings known.

He accosted Hutchinson in what witnesses would later describe as 'an excited manner'. Hutchinson, at that time approaching his seventieth year and blind in one eye (the result of being hit by a fragment of snapped chain cable while coming to the aid of a merchant vessel in distress in the harbour) was unable to help – all the tickets had been allocated. Meekins stormed off, but, still fuming, spun round after a few paces, strode back up to Hutchinson and in a 'vociferous manner' called the way tickets had been handed out 'shameful', and a 'disgrace' – the whole arrangements had been mismanaged. Offended himself, Hutchinson angrily replied that what Meekins had asserted was false.

Meekins wasn't backing down – and, in fact, was angrier than ever because he interpreted the word 'false' (or 'falsehood' according to some reports) as meaning that he was being called a liar.

'If you do not retract that expression, I will horsewhip you.'

'I shall not retract anything.'

Meekins then responded in a curious way. For whatever reason, he happened to have about his person a feather (Hutchinson thought it might be a peacock's feather) with which he touched the older man, saying, 'Consider yourself horsewhipped!'

When the case later came to court (mostly as a result of what happened subsequently), Lieutenant Hutchinson was asked, 'And did you?' to laughter in the courtroom.

'No, I did not,' he replied, to further laughter.

However, he did feel that even as a symbolic gesture it was a gross insult. (It must be borne in mind that this was the tail-end of the era of pistol or sword duelling over matters of honour.) Hutchinson contented himself with pushing his antagonist away, at which Meekins lashed out, punching Hutchinson in the region of the bridge of his nose and blind eye. To make matters worse, a ring he was wearing caused a cut, drawing blood. Passing gentlemen intervened and separated the pair, and the case ended up in court. The local magistrates sensibly urged both parties or their representatives to settle the matter between themselves rather than allowing it to become a criminal matter. Meekins, who had issued a counter-summons against Hutchinson claiming that the older man (he was half Hutchinson's age) had struck rather than pushed him, must have sensed that he wasn't coming out of this looking too well, and an arrangement was eventually made where he paid Hutchinson's costs and the matter was ended out of court. This is just one of the incidents that go towards making William Hutchinson one of the more interesting characters in this book, but the main reason for his appearing takes us back to around the time his assailant was born.

On the night of 13/14 August 1829, there was rain and wind off the east coast of Ireland of a 'violence exceeding anything within our recollection' according to the press, and the coastline was 'strewn with wrecks'. Two vessels that almost made it to safety in Dublin Bay were the *Betsey*, a Dundalk schooner, and the *Duke*, carrying coal from Whitehaven to Dublin itself. Almost, but not quite.

The *Betsey* fared worst, with three of the crew and two female passengers drowning when she was wrecked. But there was still a chance for the ten people on board the *Duke*, which went onto the rocks in Sandy Cove to the south of the bay at about 4.30 on the morning of the 14th.

William Hutchinson rendezvoused with the head of the local coastguard, Lieutenant Burniston, and they both came to the conclusion that the only way to save those on board the *Duke* was to see if they could gather together enough volunteers prepared to face the tremendous wind and waves in a lifeboat and try to get out to the collier. There was no shortage of hands willing to go out with them, and soon the two officers and a crew of 'stout fellows', a mixture of Water Guard men, pilots and boatmen, were hauling through the waves.

The more sheltered lee side of the *Duke* offered the best prospect of a successful mission, despite the risk from the rocks on that side: if the boat were to be tossed against them, they would stand little chance of survival. As it was, Hutchinson and the others managed to hold it in position and help the three women, three children, four men and a ship's boy off the brig. The danger still wasn't over. As they were pulling away from the wreck in their now heavily laden boat, the *Duke*'s mainmast gave way and came crashing down into the sea, just missing them. It wasn't long before the combination of wave and rocks smashed the collier to pieces.

The survivors were no doubt traumatised and exhausted, but when the bodies from the *Betsey* began to wash up on the shore they must have realised how fortunate they were. Newspaper reports pulled no punches about the state of the corpses, which were 'shattered literally to atoms ... scarcely a feature discernible'.

Hutchinson was given the lion's share of the praise for the gold medal-earning rescue effort, and he it was who, a week or two later, acted as a collector of donations to support those whose lives he had helped to save.

William Hutchinson was born in 1793 and joined the navy in 1806. Two years later, he was a midshipman on board the brig *Delight* when she ran aground during an action off Reggio, southern Italy. She was pounded by shore batteries for hours, and, although she gallantly returned fire, she was a sitting duck and outgunned. When her captain and two-thirds of her crew had been killed or wounded, she was forced to surrender – but most of her crew, including Hutchinson, managed to escape in boats to another British warship before they could be taken.

Among the other actions he was involved in during the war, in 1813, he and seven men boarded and took a French gunboat which had a crew of forty on board.

Hutchinson became harbour master after leaving the navy – the first one to be appointed in Kingstown. Despite it not being within his remit, he regularly took part in rescues off the coast, and he was still at it in 1861 a few months before his nasty encounter with Meekins. At the age of 68 he earned the RNLI silver medal for his part in saving the crews of two coal brigs just off Kingstown. His career continued into the next decade, and he didn't retire until 1874, aged 81. He died in 1881.

Part V

Multiple Medals

Rescue

Chapter 20

The Day of Three Golds

Philip Graham, William Johnson and William Watts

When Devonian Lieutenant Philip Graham wasn't saving lives off the coast of Kent, he was fulfilling his primary Preventative Coastal Blockade duty – that of intercepting smugglers trying to evade the import duties levied on alcohol and other commodities.

At around midnight on 28 August 1823, one of Graham's Preventive men observed a private boat arriving on an area of beach know to be used by smugglers. The seaman, called Pinner, noticed that the yacht bore some outward signs of being a fishing smack yet something didn't look quite right, and when a sailor left the yacht appearing to be concealing something in his jacket, Pinner moved forward and challenged the man. The sailor angrily refused to allow Pinner to search him, and shouted back to his yacht for help. Before long, the Preventive man was surrounded, so Pinner took out his pistol and fired into the air to alert his colleagues. It emerged that the suspicious sailor, dressed as a 'common seaman', was actually Robert Sherard, the Sixth Earl of Harborough, who was said to had thrown a Preventive man overboard during a search of his boat the previous summer.

The following morning, Lieutenant Graham and his men conducted a search of Harborough's yacht, but when his lordship arrived and found out what was happening, the incident turned ugly. When it later came to court, Harborough would claim that he was 'insulted by Lieutenant Graham and a midshipman in most violent and offensive language', and even that Graham gave him his card and 'demanded the satisfaction of a gentleman', which was the coded language of the day for challenging someone to a duel. Graham denied this, and it seems clear that Harborough was an arrogant and bellicose man who thought he was above the law. Unfortunately for Graham, when Harborough brought an action against him in the courts, the jury sided with the earl.

There was general astonishment when, despite numerous affidavits as to what really happened during the incident and to Graham's own character and professionalism, the Preventive man was sentenced to four months' imprisonment in the Marshalsea prison. To their great credit, the Admiralty made their feelings on the subject clear by pointedly promoting Graham to the rank of commander while he was still serving his sentence.

Deal, November 24 1829 – It has blown a gale at East throughout the day. The Mountaineer, Sheal, from the Cape of Good Hope, is riding with two anchors down, close in towards the shore, off the naval hospital, and has driven considerably during the day.

5 o'clock – The Mountaineer has just come on shore opposite the South Barracks, and it is much feared she will become a wreck.

Half-past six – Still blowing a gale, and a dreadful sea; a boat has reached the Mountaineer but broke adrift, which circumstance prevented getting the crew out, but it is hoped others will succeed. Several have tried to reach her, but all their efforts as yet have proved unsuccessful. Four deal boatmen are on board her.

(*Morning Post*, Thursday 26 November 1829)

The brig *Mountaineer* had departed the Cape of Good Hope on 18 September 1829, bound for London with a cargo consisting mainly of wine. She successfully crossed the Atlantic, only to come to grief on a 'tempestuous night' two months later off the Kent coast near Deal.

People began to gather on the beach, a mixture of the inhabitants of Deal and Walmer, concerned for the safety of ship and crew. With the tide ebbing, Lieutenant William Johnson of the Centre Division of the Preventive Service for the Kent coast took it upon himself to wade out into the surf in the direction of the brig, which had run aground. Two Deal boatmen, inspired by his example, plunged after him. Managing to avoid being swept away by the crashing waves, Johnson reached the *Mountaineer* and clambered aboard, but it soon became clear that he had a job on his hands. The 'wretched men were helpless', and having lashed themselves to the rigging in the time-honoured way, were no longer in a condition to extricate themselves. Johnson created a loop in a long length of rope, had one end taken to the shore, and, helping one of the crewmen down, secured him in the loop, by which means he was hauled ashore. He repeated this procedure three more times, till, exhausted, hands numb from the cold, he could do no more. The Deal men who had come out with Johnson took over, but 'much to his mortification', rather than following his example and lowering the victims over the side of the brig, they were unceremoniously bundled overboard, which, according to the *Morning Post*, 'in all probability injured them against the wreck'. It's possible that the last group were already too far gone anyway, but whatever the cause, a local pilot, one Deal boatman who had boarded earlier in the day, and two (or three according to one report) of the *Mountaineer*'s crew drowned. Her captain, Sheal ('Shiel' in some accounts) had been one of those saved.

Most of her cargo of wine was also salvaged, and, in fact, the brig herself, despite being described as a 'wreck', and having 'gone to pieces', was auctioned off sometime afterwards, although whether this was simply so that surviving timbers, rigging and so on could be recycled isn't clear.

Three naval officers were awarded gold medals for gallantry for their part in the rescue. The accounts are sketchy as to the parts played by Graham and Watts, but it is likely that they commanded the boats that had earlier reached the *Mountaineer* and put four Deal boatmen on board.

Philip Graham we have already met, confined to prison like many of the smugglers he had caught, with only his promotion to comfort him from the burning injustice. There is a tantalising genealogical reference to his nemesis, Lord Harborough, as 'the naughty earl', and a biographical mention in the National Archives, which describes him as being 'notorious for his attitude to the local hunts, to the railway and indeed, to anything that was deemed to encroach upon his estate'. The same belligerently proprietorial attitude clearly applied to his yacht, and it seems highly likely that he was either involved in smuggling or was allowing his crew to do so. Another illustration of the kind of man he was comes from much earlier, in 1801, when he bought a horse from a dealer in Leicestershire and returned it when it became lame a few days later. The dealer refused to accept it back, saying that it had been in good condition when sold and must have been injured while being ridden since. Several 'witnesses of respectability' backed up the dealer's version. Harborough was valuing the horse at £250, whereas another witness said it was more like twenty-five guineas. Typically, the jury found in Harborough's favour, albeit for 155 guineas.

Lieutenant Philip Graham himself had led an interesting and eventful life.

Not long before his unfortunate encounter with the angry earl, he had been publicly praised for his part in the rescue of the crew of the brig *Alice*. Two years previously, he had found himself in conflict with a notorious and violent man called Alexander Spence. He and another man were approached by the Dover gaoler and mayor's sergeant, who had arrest warrants relating to thefts from boats; Spence promptly pulled out a pistol and fired at them. He just missed the gaoler, the ball making a hole in his hat. They sent for Lieutenant Graham, who quickly accompanied them to Spence's location. Graham tried to reason with the man, pointing out that he was making things far worse for himself by engaging in armed resistance. The crook responded by producing another pistol (it later emerged that he was carrying five of them), this time firing at Graham. He missed with his first shot but as Graham rushed him and wrestled him to the ground he was already whipping out yet another gun. Spence fired into Graham's body from point-blank range.

Incredibly, the bullet was deflected by one of his uniform buttons, leaving his coat 'much singed' but his body unharmed other than a graze to the skin, so close did the ball come to hitting him. Spence, a 'noted desperate character', was later hanged.

Lieutenant William Ward Percival Johnson was a protégé of none other than Nelson's mistress Lady Hamilton, and appears to have been on board the *Victory* at Trafalgar – albeit inadvertently. He was serving on board another ship, but because of his connections he had been invited across to Nelson's flagship on the eve of the encounter and his presence was somehow overlooked before battle commenced. (In fairness, there were other, weightier, matters to worry about on that particular day!) He survived a period as prisoner of war when the prize ship he had been put in command of was recaptured, and in a long naval career he reached the rank of full admiral. In 1880 *The Times* listed him as one of only six officers still alive who had been present at Trafalgar. He died in December of that year, aged 90.

Sadly, little is known of Lieutenant William Stephen Watts – other than the fact, of course, that he was one of only a handful of men in the history Britain and Ireland to earn a gold medal winner for gallantry for saving his fellow human beings.

Chapter 21

Always Hope

Samuel Grandy and Thomas Ladd Peake

Terrific and damaging storms lashed Britain in November 1824, and even Portsmouth harbour, where it was declared to have been the worst gale known in thirty years, was no safe haven. In fact on the morning of the 23rd, when the storm reached its peak, the scene resembled the aftermath of a battle. Newspaper accounts spoke of at least twenty-five ships driven ashore, several crashing into each other, leaving 'many of them only presenting heaps of floating ropes and staves'.

One of those ships caught out was the transport *Admiral Berkeley*, 279 tons, which was blown onto the beach below the navy's own Haslar Hospital, on the western (Gosport) side of the harbour entrance, after her anchor chains had parted. On board were 195 people supposed to be bound for South Africa: mostly soldiers of the Royal African Corps and the 2nd West India Regiment, but also a small number of their wives and children.

The power of the waves swamping the stranded ship smashed cabin windows and flooded the decks above and below. Early reports declared that there was 'no hope' for her. However, Lieutenant Samuel Grandy of the coastguard, his Inspecting Commander Captain Thomas Ladd Peake, two more naval officers and a number of men, went into action. With Peake directing operations on shore, Grandy gathered some men together and they put out in a boat, crossing the storm-tossed harbour.

They made it to the *Admiral Berkeley*, but their boat wasn't nearly big enough to carry the survivors. Instead, two officers from HMS *Brazen*, Lieutenants Festing and Walker, together with some of the transport's crew, made a raft from the debris of their ship. In a six-hour operation, with Grandy and his men dispatching people from the ship and Peake receiving them at the other end and sending the raft back, not a single person on board was lost. They were immediately taken to the nearby Haslar Hospital and its barracks to be cared for.

Captain Thomas Ladd Peake was a Dover man who had seen action during the wars with France; in 1812 he was promoted to commander for 'gallant conduct' during a fierce and bloody battle against a French warship. His brother William was killed during a battle with an American sloop during the 1812 war. Like many naval officers, Peake joined the coastguard when peace with France was declared and the navy began reducing its complement. He eventually moved from Portsmouth to the coastguard station at Newhaven, Sussex, where he went on to add a silver medal to his gold during the rescue of the crew of a small fishing vessel, the *John*. He reached the rank of rear-admiral of the blue, and died in 1865 at the age of 80.

The other gold medallist, Lieutenant Samuel Grandy, joined the navy in 1795. He had also fought during the war, serving in a number of ships. He had a varied career, moving between the coastal blockade service, coastguard and periods with other warships, presumably as and when vacancies arose that appealed to him. He finally settled in the coastguard service, where he stayed until 1847. He died ten years later, having reached the naval rank of captain, and Inspecting Commander in the coastguard.

The *Admiral Berkeley*, whose masts had been cut away in addition to the damage to her hull, survived. She was refloated a few days later at high tide, and taken into dock for repairs. Within a few months, advertisements were appearing in the press announcing that she had been fully repaired and restored and was to be sold be auction.

Chapter 22

Joint Effort

Billy Fleming and Jack Swan

A few days before the anniversary of Trafalgar, on the afternoon of Tuesday 17 October 1922, the SS *Hopelyn* sailed out of Newcastle carrying 3,400 tons of coal to help keep the fires in the homes and factories of London burning. Her captain was a man by the name of Gibson, and his ship was just four years old. It was a routine voyage along the east coast, one performed in both directions by ships of all shapes and sizes for centuries, and as the strong north-easterly winds developed into a gale there was still no cause for alarm, especially for a ship the size of the *Hopelyn*. But when the cargo vessel's steering gear broke the following day near the Wold lightship off the coast of Norfolk, things started to go downhill rapidly.

The crew effected a temporary repair with a view of taking the ship into Yarmouth Roads, but their handiwork didn't hold for long and they were obliged to use a manually operated mechanism as they fought to keep the *Hopelyn* on course in the heavy seas. That didn't last long either. The two anchors were let go but it soon became clear that they couldn't hold the ship, which was now at the mercy of the raging seas. The wireless officer sent out an SOS, and it was picked up by the nearby warship HMS *Kennet*, a trawler-class navy vessel. The conditions were already too rough for the *Kennet* to risk going alongside the stricken ship, however; all the captain could do was inform the authorities on shore of the situation.

At 9.20 in the evening the crew of the *Hopelyn*, struggling on deck with the steering equipment, were almost thrown off their feet by a juddering bump beneath them. From that point on, the ship bumped repeatedly on what they would later learn was a treacherous reef called

Scroby Sands, between Yarmouth and Caister, and Captain Gibson could feel and hear his ship 'straining herself'. It was an ominous sign. Great waves washed over the decks, and pretty soon silt and sand 3 feet deep covered her forecastle. The ship's wireless officer stayed at his post, and at just before 11 pm he reported that his vessel was starting to break up. Almost as soon as he had sent the message, a massive wave carried away the radio mast, which, as he commented wryly, 'put an end to my job.' The encroaching sea also flooded the *Hopelyn*'s dynamo, extinguishing all of the ship's lights and making her invisible to the shore and any approaching rescue vessel. Distress rockets were fired as a last resort.

Initially, the Caister lifeboat station was assigned the task of rescuing the crew of the *Hopelyn*, but though they toiled for an hour, the ferocious winds and heavy seas prevented the boat from even being launched. The Gorleston lifeboat, under coxswain Billy 'Jumbo' Fleming, had been on standby all evening and finally launched at about 11 pm, just too late to hear the message about the ship breaking up. Fleming and the crew of the lifeboat *Kentwell* were towed in the direction of the deteriorating ship, having no idea what kind of condition the crew were in nor even whether any were left on board.

Not long after Wireless Operator Shaw sent what proved to be his final message, the *Hopelyn* began to flood below decks. He and the rest of the crew, most of whom were young men under 30 years of age, gathered together and took refuge in the saloon, the highest part of vessel. From there, they could see lights on the shore and also of rescue vessels putting out to sea. These would almost certainly have been those of the *Kentwell* and the screw propeller tug the *George Jewson*, but by the time the lifeboat drew close to them the 30- to 40-foot waves were smashing so frequently and violently into the broken ship that to have left the safety of the saloon would have been suicidal. They could only watch and hope.

It took Fleming and his crew about hour and half to struggle the four miles to the *Hopelyn*. The ship was showing no lights, as we have heard, and from their perspective there was no sign of life. Only her bridge, masts and funnel showed above water, and whenever the sea washed over those parts – which was frequently – even they vanished from sight. The *Kentwell* parted from the *George Jewson* to make her final approach, and Fleming let go the anchor then gradually let the cable out, edging as close as he dared to her lee side. If her crew had escaped in the ship's boats, that was the side they would have chosen, but there was no sign of anyone attempting to get away from the ship. Fleming had never seen worse conditions. Wave after wave poured right over both the tug and the lifeboat, the latter of which had rarely shipped as much water during his time with her. The decision was taken to manoeuvre to a safe distance from the *Hopelyn* and anchor again, where they would ride out the storm till daylight gave them a better idea of the situation.

When dawn arrived, it became clear that the merchant ship was broken in half. What they still couldn't see was any sign of the crew – but Fleming knew that even if they had all been on deck shouting for help, there would have been nothing he could do: it was still just too dangerous to get close enough. Picking up a tow from the *George Jewson* again, the *Kentwell* performed one final circumnavigation of the seemingly deserted wreck. Empty davits showed that all but one of her small boats had gone – but none were in sight. Had the crew taken to the boats and been swamped, or had the storm simply ripped them from their fixings? Fleming feared the worst. At 7 am on the Friday, he and his men realised that there was nothing for it but to run back to shore and return again at low tide.

On the *Hopelyn*, the crew of twenty-four men (and one kitten), all wearing bulky life jackets, were crammed into the ship's 'Marconi' (radio) room, which was beneath the bridge and only about 12 feet square, having been driven there by rising water in the saloon. So tightly packed were they that there was no room to lie down, and those overcome with exhaustion were falling into a fitful sleep while still on their feet. It was a desperate situation, but their spirits weren't crushed. Someone played a mandolin during the night, and the crew all joined in with popular songs of the time. Tishy, the mischievous black kitten,[1] provided some light relief by falling into a bag of flour while exploring, and emerging like a ghost cat. There was a little food. The galley kept flooding and emptying, so by choosing the right time they were able to retrieve whatever hadn't been destroyed or washed away – cold potatoes and onions, biscuits, all washed down with a brew of tea and coffee that had become mixed together. Not exactly haute cuisine, but no doubt as good as a feast to the men on board the disintegrating ship that night.

Their lowest moment was probably when they saw the Gorleston lifeboat finally turn away from them and disappear among the mountainous waves. Their hearts must have sunk – but a chorus of *Will Ye No' Come Back Again* broke out, underlining their indomitable spirit. To help matters further, not long afterwards they were able to see the signalling light of HMS *Kennet* informing them by Morse code that the lifeboat would be returning in the morning.

Jumbo Fleming and his weary men arrived back at Gorleston at around 8 am. Although the search for survivors had proved fruitless and the missing boats was an ominous sign, he 'still had a feeling that there were men imprisoned in the *Hopelyn* somewhere if we could have only found out where'. Fleming requested the local coastguards to telephone their colleagues in Yarmouth and Caister to look out for any signals from the ship while he and his crew went to their homes to recover, grab a quick breakfast, and wait till the time was right for another go. It wasn't a long wait. The Caister coastguard soon contacted Gorleston to say that a 'flag' (which proved to be a strip of mattress from the steward's bed) had been run up the mast of the *Hopelyn*. Fleming asked them to signal to the ship that the lifeboat would soon be on its way. He gathered together his crew, and by 10.30 the *Kentwell* was being towed out to sea once more by the redoubtable *George Jewson*.

They set out on an ebbing tide, and initially in smoother waters than previously, but it wasn't long before the waves were inundating both lifeboat and tug once more. As before, the *Kentwell* let go of the

---

1. The kitten was named after a well-known racehorse.

tow rope once they were near enough to the *Hopelyn*, the lifeboat's crew taking soundings as they cautiously approached. At about 100 yards from the ship the cry was that they were in just a fathom of water. Fleming steered away to southward again and dropped anchor in deeper water while a plan of action was worked out. They decided to explore to the south and the east of the *Hopelyn*, but found that the water was still dangerously shallow, so Fleming took them back to the original anchorage. Someone came up with the idea of pumping their ballast water out, which ought to give them an extra foot of clearance. They decided to try it, but first had to remain at anchor and wait for a change of tide.

'Now, boys,' Fleming said to his men when the time came, 'we will row at her for all we are worth.'

Dropping their anchor and paying out the cable, they pulled as hard as they could, encourage by the crew of the *Hopelyn*, who had gathered at the side of their ship now that the conditions were safe enough for them to emerge from their refuge. But despite their preparations and best efforts, and when they were tantalisingly close to their target, the *Kentwell* ran aground. They were near enough to be able to catch a rope thrown from the ship, but when they began to haul on it, it snapped under the strain. Then a wave sent the *Kentwell*'s stern crashing into the *Hopelyn*, badly damaging the rudder. This was followed by a second collision, this time with a jagged piece of the ship's hull, which sliced through the lifeboat's padding like a surgeon's knife. 'If it had caught our lifeboat's planking,' Fleming later said, 'it would have cut the boat in halves [sic].'

It was time to get off the sandbank before another collision with the *Hopelyn* destroyed the lifeboat. Fleming gave the order to haul away on their anchor cable, which they did 'like tigers' till they were clear. But when they took stock they discovered that their valiant craft was badly damaged and taking in water, and after all their efforts the crew were 'out of wind'. 'We had to have a good blow and a drop of rum to pull us all together,' said Fleming, 'then wait for the flow.' Despite the state of the *Kentwell* they hoped to steer to the northward of the ship and make a rescue attempt from that direction; the drawback was that they would be hampered by the remains of an older wreck just below the surface, whose three mast stumps protruded out of the water. They tried their best, but with a damaged rudder making steering difficult, a tiring crew and darkness coming on, the attempt had to be abandoned. They managed to steer a course towards HMS *Kennet*, still on standby. They passed on a message about their own condition and the need to return to return for repairs or a replacement boat, and requested that the navy vessel signalled to crew of the *Hopelyn* that they would be back in the morning. The drenched and exhausted crew of the *Kentwell* were towed back in to Gorleston by the *George Jewson*. On their way they encountered the motor lifeboat the *Agnes Cross* arriving from Lowestoft, with Gorleston's RNLI Commander Carver on board. Fleming filled him in on their attempts and the damage to the *Kentwell*, and Carver asked him to join him on the *Agnes Cross*, which he did, with his Second Coxswain Samuel Parker taking command of the *Kentwell* for the remainder of the homeward return journey. Fleming was up for having another try at the *Hopelyn*, but after a consultation with Carver it was decided to follow the *Kentwell* and wait till morning brought a favourable tide.

On the morning of 21 October, Commander Carver, discussing with Jumbo Fleming a strategy for the latest rescue attempt, requested that seven of the Gorleston crew join ten Lowestoft men to make up the crew. When Fleming asked for volunteers, 'Hardly before I could speak I might have had a dozen! They all wanted to go and see the thing through.' This combined Gorleston/Lowestoft operation launched at 4 am in relatively better conditions but still heavy weather. They battled against a wind that continually blew water into their faces for an hour and a half before they were in a position to drop anchor to windward of the ship, where they let out the cable until they were abreast of the *Hopelyn*. *Agnes Cross* coxswain Jack Swan said, 'It was a pitiful sight when we drew near the wreck. It was just daybreak. We heard the cries of thankfulness from the men as the boat approached. We let go the anchor, and it was now or never. My men worked like Trojans throughout.'

But before they could even begin to commence their rescue operation, a big wave caught the lifeboat and came close to smashing them into the bigger vessel. Luckily, unlike the *Kentwell* this lifeboat had the advantage of what for those days was a powerful engine, and was able to keep them just steady enough.

In the meantime, the *Hopelyn*'s crew had had time to prepare for the lifeboat's arrival. As soon as she was alongside, several ropes, already made fast to the ship, were tossed down. 'They knew it was their last chance,' Fleming would later reflect, 'and they came at it all in a bunch. I myself had one or two in my arms at a time.' One of the men was, of course, carrying Tishy the kitten. The transfer was performed quickly but without panic. The whole operation, from coming alongside to departing, took no more than eight minutes, and Swan calculated that the actual clambering of the twenty-four men into the lifeboat took only around three.

Even now, though, fate hadn't quite finished with the rescuers or rescued. The *Agnes Cross* narrowly avoided a huge spar from the *Hopelyn* as she was turning away, and then the anchor cable snapped. Luckily, Swan the coxswain was on the ball; he gave the order for the motors to be started, and the lifeboat powered away from the ship, over the sands, and into deep water, heading for home.

The Lowestoft lifeboat, with her cargo of weary but grateful sailors and floury kitten, motored into Yarmouth at around 7 am to cheers and blaring sirens from the crews of the numerous working boats. The rescued men were taken to the local Sailor's Home, where they made sure Tishy got her milk before they themselves were fed.

Captain Gibson of the *Hopelyn*, an Edinburgh man, had been badly wounded by shell fire when on steamer sunk by a German U-boat in the Bristol channel during the First World War, but said this was his worst experience. He had nothing but praise for the conduct of both his crew and the lifeboatmen, however. The rescue was the 'finest peace of seamanship I have ever seen. She let go her anchor, then came down astern, and gradually dropped alongside … They did all that was humanly possible; no men could have done more.' And of his own men: 'No crew could have behaved more wonderfully … My crew were all British, and they were all that in every sense of the term.' (It's interesting that the latter comment is something we would be unlikely to be heard today – I'm not sure that we think, or are even allowed to think, in those terms now. I'll leave it for the reader to decide whether that's a change for the better.)

This was a heavily decorated mission. Fleming and Swan were awarded the RNLI gold medal, in addition to which two silvers and twenty-three bronzes were issued to other crew members.

John Thompson Sterry Swan was born in Lowestoft in 1857. He became the lifeboat coxswain in 1911, and won a silver medal for his part in the rescue of nine crewmen from the wreck of HMS *Condor*, a Royal Navy minesweeper, in the first year of the First World War. His gold medal was only the second to be awarded to a member of the Lowestoft lifeboat crew. He died in 1935 at the age of 77.

Billy 'Jumbo' George Fleming was born in Mutford, near Gorleston, the eldest of nine children. His seafaring career began when he was taken on as a cabin boy on a fishing boat, and he served the lifeboat service for forty-nine years. He was second only to Henry Blogg of Cromer as Norfolk's most decorated lifeboat man. Five years after the *Hopelyn* episode, Fleming won a silver for his part in the rescue of the SS *Georgia* (for which Blogg won one of his golds, as described in the next chapter) and was awarded the Empire Gallantry Medal in the same year as Blogg. Upon retiring, he earned a little money and maintained his connection with the sea by taking holiday makers out in a rowing boat. One wonders whether any of his passengers knew quite what a safe pair of hands they were in. Fleming died in 1954, and in October 2017 a blue plaque was affixed to No. 11 Pavilion Road, Gorleston, the house a short distance from the lifeboat station where he had lived for most of his life.

Chapter 23

Fifty-hour Struggle

The *Rohilla* Disaster

The story that follows stands out in the history of the lifeboat service in a number of ways. Of all the stories featured in this book, it is perhaps the most dramatic and harrowing, involving the greatest loss of life and the largest number of rescue vessels and personnel, the most civilian and military helpers, and the most medals awarded. It also proved to be something of a landmark event as regards the transition from lifeboats powered by oar and sail, to motor lifeboats.

Captain David Neilson, on the bridge of the hospital ship *Rohilla*, had been in command of the vessel since before the Great War but was sailing in what were, for him, unfamiliar waters as he made his way south along the north-east coast of Britain, where there were reports of U-boat activity and the certainty of mines laid to discourage them. These weren't the only hazards. This was October 1914; wartime security measures meant that the lights that would normally be showing from lighthouses and buoys to aid vessels such as his were switched off; he had been unable to obtain the services of a pilot; and the heavy weather he and his crew had been experiencing over the last few hours had developed into a gale.

The *Rohilla* was eight years old and had started her life as a passenger cruise liner before being requisitioned by the military and converted into a fully staffed and equipped hospital ship. She had departed Queensferry, west of Edinburgh, the previous day, the 29th, her a mission to collect injured troops from Belgium.[1] Because of the

---

1. Most versions say Dunkirk, but Captain Neilson himself told the subsequent inquest that Belgium was his destination.

nature of her assignment, she carried a comparatively large 'crew', which as well as the usual sailors and engineers, included doctors, nurses and other ancillary staff.

In the early hours of the morning, Neilson's second officer on the bridge spotted a light blinking in the distance. He soon recognised from the pattern of the flashing light that it must be a Morse code message, but interpreting Morse wasn't his forte and he couldn't keep up with the speed at which it was being transmitted. He sent for a signals officer, as well as alerting the captain. At around this time Neilson received word that soundings showed them to be in shallower water than expected, meaning that they must be uncomfortably close to the shore. He immediately ordered a reduction in speed and change of course that he thought would take them back into deeper waters. The captain had not yet received a translation of the Morse code message, but it wouldn't have mattered if he had. It was already too late.

At just before four that morning, Friday the 30th, a powerful jolt sent everyone on the bridge tumbling to the deck. Neilson cried 'Mine! My God!'; he was convinced – and would always be convinced – that he had hit a wartime mine. In fact, the *Rohilla*, which had it been daylight would have been in sight of Whitby harbour, had struck submerged rocks. In peacetime, the *Rohilla*'s officers would almost certainly have spotted the Whitby lighthouse, the light on the buoy that warned of the dangers, or heard the tolling of its bell; but because of the war the lighthouse and buoy were unlit and the bell silenced. What happened next was to compound the initial miscalculation.

Captain Neilson and his fellow officers made two fatal errors of judgement that would lead to one of the worst disasters of that part of Britain's coast. The first was purely navigational, leading to the *Rohilla*'s current precarious position. But then Neilson decided that having been crippled, as he thought, by a mine, their only hope of salvation was to deliberately turn the ship towards the shore and run her aground at full speed to prevent his crew from drowning should she sink in deeper waters. It is, no doubt, easy to say with hindsight, but until that critical decision was made, even if the *Rohilla* had been sinking there may have been time for many of the crew to lower and man the lifeboats. As it was, a few minutes later she ran into Saltwick Nab, one of the most notorious areas of rock on that part of the coast, in the process carrying away all of the lifeboats on one side of the ship and damaging most of those on the other side beyond use, and the fate of many of those on board had been sealed. Although Neilson wasn't aware of it, the forward part of ship was stuck on a submerged section of the reef about 500 yards offshore, gouging a great hole in her hull; the stern hung over the edge of these rocks with only deep water beneath her, placing a great strain on the vessel's structure. If it had been daylight, Neilson would have seen the foreboding sight of the ruins of Whitby Abbey, one of the inspirations for Bram Stoker's *Dracula*, looming from the cliffs above him.

Albert Jefferies, the clifftop lookout who had attempted to warn the *Rohilla* by Morse code from his post on Whitby's East Cliff, and who had only been able to look on in dismay as the whole appalling event unfolded, fired off maroons and alerted the coastguard's Rocket Brigade. Distress flares from the *Rohilla* also streaked up through the darkness, giving those on shore an idea of her position and thus where they needed to set up their apparatus in order to try to fire a line out to her.

The *Rohilla*'s crew, most of whom had been sleeping below, kept their lifebelts under their pillows as a matter of routine. Shaken into wakefulness by the two impacts, they groggily snatched the lifebelts and headed for the companionways. Captain Neilson had ensured that a lifeboat drill had been carried out shortly before sailing, but the current circumstances couldn't be more different: the ship was already beginning to flood, and the lighting had failed. Not all of the men scrambling for the exits in the pitch-darkness were to make it: the unfolding disaster was already claiming its first victims. Those who did get out in time – some of whom hadn't had time to dress – made for the lifeboat stations as ordered, only to find the boats missing or unusable; worse still, more men were claimed by the waves sweeping over the ship and swept into the sea even as they attempted to reach the boats. It was at around this time that the first attempts to jump ship and swim ashore were made. Two men abandoned their posts at the now useless radio and leapt overboard.

Meanwhile, the rocket brigade, not having the use of a horse, struggled through the fields hauling the cart bearing their apparatus from its station inland on a lane leading to the abbey. It was physically impossible to carry it to the ideal location, but they were able to set up on a headland west of the abbey, to the south of the bay. It was still too dark to make the *Rohilla* out, but at between 5 and 5.15 am they made their first attempt to fire a line towards the area where the distress flares lit up the sky. However, although an elevated position may have been useful in some cases, in this storm the wind played havoc with their aim and the distance they were able to achieve, and the first three rockets fell short. Charles Sutherland, Chief Officer of the coastguard at Whitby and the man in charge of the rocket brigade, realised the futility of wasting any more precious rockets and, with daylight coming on, transferred his equipment down the cliff path to the Saltwick Nab itself.

Thomas Langlands, coxswain of Whitby's No. 1 lifeboat the *Robert and Mary Ellis*, saw the maroons illuminate the dark skies as he rushed to join his crew gathering at the lifeboat station on the West Pier at about 4.45 am, after being notified by the coastguard chief officer of a ship in distress. But it was immediately clear to all that the *Robert and Mary Ellis*, which launched down a chute from the pier-head, wouldn't be able to put to sea in these conditions. Attention now turned to the No. 2 lifeboat, the *John Fielden*, moored in the sheltered harbour; even then it wouldn't be possible to set out from her position, but an ambitious plan was formed to carry her overland in the morning to a point opposite the wreck and put out from there.

Although the *John Fielden* was the smaller of the two boats, she was still 36 feet in length and would probably have weighed three to four tons. Such a feat had never been undertaken before and there were those who, quite reasonably, said it simply couldn't be done; but Thomas Langlands believed it could be. With the help of a crowd of locals and some rope and tackle, she was somehow hoisted out of the water and over an 8-foot concrete breakwater adjacent to Whitby's east pier, then hauled on her carriage for nearly three-and-a-half miles along the wet, slippery, boulder-strewn shoreline until she was in place. At the subsequent inquest, it was put to Langlands that it couldn't have been 'an easy job'. 'It was a tussle', came the laconic reply.

Meanwhile, the rocket brigade had made it down to the shoreline. Even now, though, they were firing at maximum range, and the gale toyed with their attempts at accurate aiming. Sutherland estimated the distance from his rocket position to the *Rohilla* to be 400–500 yards. On the odd occasion when they were able to defy the wind and strike home, the line merely became snagged or was tantalisingly out of reach of the sailors, who could not move freely around the Rohilla's deck because of the damage and the mountainous waves washing over her. He and his men stayed at their posts throughout the whole rescue period; when they had used up all their own rockets they sent to stations at Robin Hood's Bay, Staithes and elsewhere for more.

The crew of the *John Fielden* had better luck. Their gruelling, stumbling journey over the rocks had come at a cost. The boat had sustained damage and would probably let in water – but not, it was decided, enough to prevent an attempt to get out to the *Rohilla*. Many willing hands helped to push her through the surf, and then she was heading out to the ship. Hauling on the oars with all of their might, Thomas Langlands and his crew became the first rescuers to reach the stricken ship. In customary fashion they came alongside in the lee of the vessel to reduce the chances of being blown against her hull.

Waiting to escape the *Rohilla* was a woman who just two years earlier had endured and survived what most would assume must have been an even worse predicament than the one she was currently in. In October 1912, Mary Kezia Roberts had been on board the *Titanic* on that ship's tragic first and only voyage. Liverpudlian Mary, at this time 44 and married with four children, was one of five women whom Captain Neilson had said should be the first to be transferred into the lifeboat, along with the ship's medical officers. Four of the women were nurses, while Mary was a stewardess.[2] Three desperate crewmen also jumped into the lifeboat, an act for which they were later condemned, and branded 'cowards'. To make matters worse for the lifeboat crew, thousands of gallons of water were cascading down on them like a waterfall from the waves that were constantly washing over the *Rohilla*. In all, the *John Fielden* took off seventeen people in this initial foray, but had to land them some way to the north of where she had launched from after being carried by the current. This entailed the fetching of her carriage and yet more manhandling back to the preferred launching place before she could set out again.

After depositing Mary Roberts and the other lucky people, the lifeboat returned to remove eighteen more, but because of her leaking state she was sitting worryingly low in the water on the return journey; and the tide was now coming in, making it much harder work for her crew. 'Come on my bonny lads!' Langlands exhorted them – but he knew it would be the last attempt they dare risk in the battered *John Fielden*.

A growing crowd of onlookers had assembled along the shoreline; these were not rubber-neckers but people willing to lend a hand, and in some cases take rescued crew members into their own homes while they recovered. Surviving footage of the scenes show what appears to be a group of people holding hands and forming a human chain down to the water's edge.

On the wreck, fearing that no more help was at hand, crewmen were now jumping into the sea and trying to swim for it, but distances across water are deceptive; add to that the currents, waves, low temperatures and gale-force wind, and it is little wonder that a good number never reached land alive. Those who survived the swim were helped out by the folk of Whitby, some of whom waded fully clothed into the water to help exhausted men ashore. Others attended to the grimmer task of retrieving corpses washed up by the tide.

---

2. Mary was actually to say later that the *Rohilla* shipwreck had been the worst of her two ordeals. The redoubtable woman was to return to sea once again after recovering from this latest one.

On the *Rohilla*, those left aboard despaired on witnessing a line fired by the rocket men reach the ship, only for it to become frayed by the rocks and sharp edges of the broken vessel and finally snap when tension was applied; it had, perhaps, been partially damaged by the sharp edges of the ship's fragmenting structure. At about 7.30 on that Friday morning, desperation prompted some of those on board to try lowering one of the few lifeboats that hadn't been lost or too badly smashed. It was not just to save their own skins that this was attempted, but the idea was also to secure a rope to the ship and take the other end ashore. This effort was led by Colin Gwyn, the *Rohilla*'s second officer. Despite the launch causing so much damage as to almost sink the boat before they started, and the loss of three oars on the laborious journey, they did make it. Frustratingly, though, the line they were paying out as they went became snagged, and Gwyn could only complete the perilous crossing by cutting it loose.

By this time, with many still left on board the *Rohilla* and the ship in danger of being destroyed completely by the pounding of the waves and the strain caused by the way she was precariously jammed half-on and half-off the rocky ledge, other measures were being considered. The nearest lifeboat was based at Upgang, a mile away; the *William Riley* was just a few miles up the coast, yet frustratingly, like the Whitby No. 1 boat the prevailing conditions meant that she couldn't be launched. But it was figured that if the now unserviceable No. 2 Whitby boat could be hustled for a relatively long distance over land, then so could the similarly sized Upgang craft. A small army of people and horses set to it, hauling the lifeboat from the cove where it had been moored, along the lanes and roads of Whitby to the East Cliff, until it was lowered around 200 feet down the almost vertical cliff-face at a spot best suited for reaching the *Rohilla*. But even now they were beaten by storm and tide and were unable to put the boat to sea, at least not yet. They could only hope and pray that when morning came things would have improved.

The lifeboat stations at Teesmouth to the north and Scarborough to the south were alerted. The *Bradford*, the Teesmouth motor lifeboat, at least twenty-five miles distant, waited out the night and set out at dawn on Saturday, but she sustained storm damage before she could reach Whitby and had to be towed into Middlesbrough. The *Queensbury* at Scarborough put to sea with the help of a tow from a trawler at around 3.30 pm on the Friday, but would take hours to reach the wreck.

As if the situation couldn't get any worse for the shivering and anxious remaining men on board the grounded hospital ship, while all these arrangements were being made, the worst possible thing happened. Up to forty men were stranded on the after-part of the *Rohilla*. Captain Neilson, whose voice could be heard in the darkness calmly issuing orders, had been concerned for the safety of those huddled towards the stern and had sent a direction that they should try to make their way forward – but the broken state of the ship and way the waves were breaking over her made it impossible. But their situation was almost as dangerous as trying to get forward would have been. Despite clinging on as best they could, successive waves swept them off in ones and twos, never to be seen again. At around midday a particularly immense wave crashed over the after part of the ship. When it had dissipated, those watching in horror from the shore could see no signs of life. If any *were* still there, unseen, hanging on grimly, they weren't to last much longer. The fractured ship could withstand the punishment no longer, and the stern section, which had been hanging unsupported over deep water, finally broke off with a sickening shriek of grating metal, plummeting to the bottom and taking with it anyone left on deck.

By 6 pm on Friday evening, after battling through the storm, the *Queensbury* of Scarborough was on scene and ready to see what could be done. As darkness fell, a tug towed the oar-powered boat towards the *Rohilla*; again and again she tried to get close enough to take off more crewmen, but each time the violence of the sea meant that she was forced to withdraw. Finally, they were forced to stand off, securing their boat to the trawler for the night for her own safety. (Even then, the storm was so fierce that the lines parted and a struggle ensued to re-establish the connection.)

In the early hours of Saturday, while it was still dark, Thomas Langlands was able to get the *Robert and Mary Ellis*, the Whitby No. 1 boat, out twice. On the first occasion he rendezvoused with a tug that had arrived from Hartlepool called the *Mayfly*, which took him towards the *Rohilla*; but once the lifeboat was left on her own to make the final approach, she was unable to get closer than a couple of hundred yards and had to be towed back to base. The second launch was to go to the aid of a sailor who had been spotted on a raft; he had made it quite close to shore and was sighted close to the pier – but by the time the lifeboat reached the location he had been lost to the waves. Another lifeboat, from Runswick just up the coast, waited throughout Friday night for an attempt the next day, but it soon became obvious that she would be no more successful than any of the other rowing lifeboats.

After a night when a further two crewmen who had jumped ship made it to safety, the Scarborough lifeboat the *Queensbury* ventured forth again on Saturday morning. But although darkness had given way to daylight it was still blowing a gale, and try as they might, the crew couldn't work their way alongside the *Rohilla*, resulting in yet another disheartening aborted attempt. By the time they had been towed in the Scarborough men were almost as badly affected by cold and exhaustion as some of those who had been carried ashore from the ship itself, and helping hands were needed to lift the gallant crew out of their boat.

Next it was the turn of the Upgang boat, but they met with exactly the same fate as their Scarborough colleagues. The *William Riley* of Upgang was finally able to get out again at around 9 o'clock the following morning, Sunday, but even now the conditions were against them and the crew were unable to get their boat safely alongside the *Rohilla*. The Teesmouth lifeboat, the *Bradford*, had put to sea to add her weight to the ongoing rescue attempt, but she also became a victim of the storm and had to be towed back for repairs. All this time, what was left of the *Rohilla* was still being battered by the waves, and although someone was still able to occasionally signal to the shore, the chilling most recent message was: *crewmen beginning to die from exposure.*

On board the *Rohilla*, Captain Neilson, observing the brave but futile attempts to reach him and seeing the rockets aimed at his vessel continually blown off-target, decided that he and his crew, who as well as being wet and dangerously cold had been without food and water for nearly two days now, could wait no longer. He announced that it was time to abandon ship: those who could do so should attempt to swim to safety, and the rest would build makeshift life rafts and make their bid for freedom at low tide that evening. The captain's signaller sent an ominous message to the shore asking them to have ambulances on standby.

While they waited for the tide to ebb, the crewmen worked on creating their rafts, and when it was deemed that low-water point had been reached there was an exodus from the *Rohilla* – some plunging into the freezing, frothing waves and others on their makeshift craft. They were gambling with their lives, and must have known it. A fair number succeeded, but there was also a new spate of bodies being washed up on shore as a result of this attempt; one man had almost made it but was picked up by a wave and smashed into the rocks, losing his life agonisingly close to safety.

The putting to sea of the rafts was also not a quick or easy task, and when the tide turned and the wind increased in intensity, dozens of men still left on board had to abandon the escape attempt. A small number, though, felt remaining on the disintegrating *Rohilla* was more dangerous than facing the icy waves, and with Neilson's permission they set off anyway. Three out of thirteen made it to safety.

Even though Captain Neilson couldn't have known how few of his men had survived the latest bid to reach the shore, he must have had a shrewd idea that a good proportion of them were unlikely to survive. A consensus was reached among those left on board that if no lifeboat could get to them by 10 am the next morning, they would take to the water whatever the state of the tide and storm.

While this was going on, yet another lifeboat was contending with the gale in an effort to reach the scene. This was the *Henry Vernon*, a motor lifeboat based at North Shields, with Robert Smith as coxswain and carrying Captain Herbert Burton of the Royal Engineers, who was the lifeboat superintendent. She sailed through Saturday night, down the dangerous, unlit coast, finally reaching Whitby harbour at 1 am after a desperate voyage of over forty miles. Her crew needed rest and refreshment and the tide and currents were against them anyway, so any further attempt to relieve the crew of the *Rohilla* was put off till it got light.

Captain Neilson's decision to abandon ship at 10 am was put on hold when a powerful light from the shore began to flash out a Morse message in his direction. A detachment of Royal Engineers had managed to set up one of their searchlights on the clifftop, and were using it as a signalling lamp to inform those on the *Rohilla* of the planned attempt to reach them at daybreak. There was still hope. He dictated a reply: 'The ship is breaking rapidly. Look out for swimmers; low tide tonight. No time to lose.'

Back on shore, Thomas Langlands, the Whitby lifeboat coxswain, discussed the situation with his recently arrived North Shields counterpart Robert Smith. His local knowledge and earlier experiences enabled him to fill Smith in on the task that lay ahead. To further assist him, they decided that Langlands' second coxswain, Richard Eglon, would join the crew of the *Henry Vernon* to act as pilot when she set out later that day. As darkness began to give way to the grey light of morning, the latest rescue attempt got under way in what Eglon was to describe as a 'canny bit of wind'.

Although the storm had abated somewhat, conditions were still rough, and before attempting to close on the bridge of the *Rohilla*, which was just about the only part of her left above water, the crew of the *Henry Vernon* literally poured oil on troubled waters to try to calm the waves.[3] This appeared to have some effect, and they made their move.

The *Henry Vernon* came up on the *Rohilla*'s leeward side at about 7.15 am, with Smith the coxswain using his skills at the controls to keep her nose up against the ship so that they didn't have to risk

---

3. I had assumed this was as much of an old wives/sailors' superstition as whistling up a wind, but apparently it can work!

The Sailor's Farewell. There was a tradition in seafaring families that a wife would hang up a picture of *The Sailor's Farewell* (of which there were many versions) when her husband departed. When he was due home, she would replace it with *The Sailor's Return*. (*Charles Mosely*)

Statue of Dic Evans of the Moelfre lifeboat, Anglesey.

William Fleming of the Gorleston lifeboat.

A breeches buoy in action. (*Originally* London Illustrated News, *courtesy Newbiggin Maritime Centre*)

The sad remains of *City of Bradford II* at Strangford Lough in 2019. Robert Cross was her coxswain during the *Gurth* rescue. (*By kind permission of Nicholas Leach*)

Rocket trials in Cornwall. (*Courtesy Newbiggin Maritime Centre*)

Henry Blogg of Cromer, Britain's most decorated lifeboatman.

Sir William Hillary, founder of the RNLI.

The British Hospital Ship "Rohilla," on Its Way from Leith to Dunkirk to Bring Wounded British and Belgian Soldiers from the Battleground of Northern France, was Wrecked at Whitby on the East Coast of England. The Photograph Shows Life Guards Trying to Get a Line to the Wreck

Whitby folk try to help survivors from the *Rohilla* ashore.

Charlie Fish earned his third gold rescuing the crew of the *Indian Chief*. (*This image appeared originally in* True Tales of Travel, Valour and Virtue)

Caistor lifeboat station a few years before its closure. In 1901 the eight men lost in the *Beauchamp* disaster were laid out here till after the inquest.

Grace Darling's Longstone Lighthouse. Her bedroom window, from where she sighted the *Forfarshire*, is said to be the upper one in the white section.

Grace Darling.

Reunited at last!

securing their wave-tossed boat to the wreck. A rope was thrown down from the ship's bridge, and the remaining fifty pitifully weak and shivering crew began to lower themselves down, helped aboard by the lifeboatmen. Before the last batch of men could be removed, successive waves lifted the lifeboat right over the protruding bridge of the *Rohilla*. Miraculously, both lifeboat and stranded sailors survived the scare and the final part of the operation was put into effect. Naturally enough, Captain Neilson (carrying the ship's cat), was the last to go – but the wind was picking up again, and just as he was about to clamber aboard a wave pushed the *Henry Vernon* away from the ship's side. Luckily, helping hands were already clutching him, and Brownlee, the lifeboat's coxswain, made sure skipper and cat got safely aboard.

Word had spread that what might prove to be a final rescue attempt was to be made that morning, and a growing crowd was assembling on the cliffs and along the shoreline, some standing by with blankets and hot drinks. Even as the *Henry Vernon* turned away from the wreck with the rescued men, the onlookers weren't able to celebrate. Another wave caught her and threatened to overturn her, which even in a self-righting boat would almost certainly have led to great loss of life. For a moment she descended into a trough and disappeared from sight as if lost completely – but there were sighs of relief when she reappeared again, having fully righted herself.

The cheers from the waiting masses as the *Henry Vernon* chugged into the sanctuary of Whitby harbour with sixty-four people somehow crammed inside her became somewhat muted when the condition of the rescued men, several having endured the lengthy and freezing ordeal only partially clothed or in sodden pyjamas, became apparent. Some were unable to walk and had to be helped or carried, and all bore the marks of having been bashed about.

When it was suggested to the crew of the *Henry Vernon* that they could go home in comfort by train, they unanimously opted to return to North Shields the same way they had come. On entering their home harbour they received a deservedly ecstatic welcome from the waiting vessels and crowds of people, including local dignitaries, who had received advance warning of their heroic crew's impending return.

Neilson and officers continued to assert that they had hit a mine, but no one ever reported hearing an explosion, and the coastguard remained sure the ship had hit rocks before her final grounding.

In British Film Institute footage, the tangled wreck of what's left of the devastated *Rohilla* looks more like a scrapyard at sea than a ship. Only the upper section of her mast, broken but still attached and lolling at an angle of almost 90 degrees, reminds us of what she once was. The film also gives us a glimpse of the Whitby No. 2 lifeboat, which has the appearance of a small warship damaged by heavy enemy fire.

Eighty-four men, getting on for a third of the 229 people on board, lost their lives during those nightmarish fifty hours between 4 am on Friday 30 October and early Sunday morning of 2 November. Slightly more than half of the survivors managed to save themselves by taking to the water on rafts or by swimming, and of the remainder, thirty-five, were taken off by oar-powered lifeboats and fifty by the motor lifeboat. Bodies continued to appear along the coast during the weeks to come, but as time passed newly discovered corpses were too decomposed to enable to identification. Around half of the bodies of the drowned were never seen again.

It would be hard to fully do justice to all who were involved in the efforts to save the crew of the *Rohilla*: the numerous lifeboats, tugs, the coastguard and specifically their rocket brigade, the army personnel, the very many members of public, all of whom did what they could during an operation spread over three days and two nights, lasting around fifty hours.

Gold medals were awarded to Whitby coxswain Thomas Langlands, Tynemouth lifeboat superintendent Herbert Burton, and his coxswain Robert Smith. Four silvers were also issued, along with a variety of other non-RNLI awards. For his determination to save the ship's cat even when almost lost overboard during his difficult transfer to the *Henry Vernon*, Captain Neilson was awarded the RSPCA's bronze medal.

Thomas Langlands was born in Seahouses and had been a lifeboatman for nearly forty years at the time of the *Rohilla* rescue. He was attached to the Upgang lifeboat for around twenty-five years before taking over as coxswain of the Whitby boat on the retirement of the previous incumbent of the post. He retired in 1920 and was succeeded by his friend and second coxswain Richard Eglon. When he died two years after his retirement, his coffin was carried through Whitby and laid in a grave close to some of the victims of the wreck of the *Rohilla*.

Herbert Burton, who had lost a son to the war, was from London and had followed his father into the Royal Engineers at the age of 14 as a bugler, rising through the ranks until receiving his commission. He saw action and was decorated while serving in the South African war. 'Bert' Burton retired as a major five years after winning his RNLI gold medal, but briefly came out of retirement at the start of the Second World War, when he was in his mid-seventies, to help organise the Home Guard in Beadnall, where he had settled. Despite being a serving Royal Engineer, his career had been overlapping with that as an active volunteer member of the Tynemouth lifeboat service for some time and the gold medal he received for his part in the *Rohilla* episode (and subsequent Empire Gallantry Medal) wasn't his first such award. Ten years earlier he had been presented with a bronze medal by the Royal Humane Society for plucking someone out of the sea at Tynemouth, and he had earned the RNLI silver medal for a rescue in 1912.

Robert 'Scraper' Smith, the third gold medal recipient, was a non-smoking, non-drinking member of the Methodist church from Cullercoats, just north of Tynemouth. He had joined a fishing boat while still a boy, and a harrowing event he experienced in his teens led to his determination to become a lifeboat volunteer. According to Colin Brittain in *Into the Maelstrom*, his comprehensive account of the *Rohilla* disaster, Smith was an onlooker when a passenger steamer was wrecked off Tynemouth. The only way to save the crew was by breeches buoy, but not all made it. The screams of a group of drowning choirgirls never left him and was one of the major factors behind his decision to become a lifeboatman as soon he had reached the minimum age. Like the other medal winners, he accumulated numerous other awards during his career, and, by coincidence, Scraper Smith retired from the lifeboat service the same year as Thomas Langlands.

The events of the late October 1914 proved to be one of the turning points in RNLI history, since it exposed the shortcomings of the older style lifeboats, which dated back to the age of wooden ships, while highlighting the efficacy of motor-powered vessels. Even the Whitby fishing fleet was turning to powered boats at around this time. At that station, plans had already been afoot before the war to replace oar and sail power, and these were quickly revived after the *Rohilla* affair, although, partly because of the war, it was nearly five years before Whitby had its first motor boat.

The age of men setting out in open rowing boats and battling mountainous waves using muscle power alone in attempting to get alongside big steel ships were coming to an end. A Whitby councillor was reported as commenting, 'Oar-propelled lifeboats are now of very little use.' Lieutenant Hall, the RNLI District Inspector of Lifeboats who had gone out with the *Henry Vernon*, later declared that only a motor lifeboat would have been capable of going down the leeside of the *Rohilla* in the conditions they faced that day. At the inquest, one of the local RNLI officers had to agree that had the Whitby boat been steam powered, they would probably have been able to get everyone off on the very first morning of the incident, and second coxswain Richard Eglon stated that no one would have been drowned if Whitby had had a motor lifeboat.

Chapter 24

The Trials of the *Charles and Eliza Laura*

William Roberts and Owen Jones

The last week of October 1927 was one of storms, rain and floods, affecting structures on land and vessels at sea, and, ultimately leading to loss of life. Phone lines were down, trees fell on houses and across roads. The gales reached hurricane force by the 27th and 28th, and it was, not unsurprisingly, a busy time for the lifeboat service around Britain and Ireland. The Scarborough motor lifeboat experienced engine problems while on operations and drifted fifty miles out to sea; she was feared lost, but an after an all-night struggle her crew got her back to her home port. The north coast of Wales (along with north-west England) was particularly hard-hit at this time. At least twenty-five fishermen and their boats, part of the Irish fishing fleet, were reported lost, and bodies were being washed up on shore in various places.

The 80-ton ketch *Excel* of Poole, Captain Ballance, was carrying coal from Birkenhead to Holyhead and was only about an hour's sailing from her destination – in normal conditions. But the waves were surging over her, and, eventually, sea water found its way below and flooded the engine room. The *Excel* was a venerable old two-masted boat built in 1876; with the engine out of action, sails were her only hope, and John Balance tried to aim for Moelfre harbour. (He had good reason to know Moelfre well, having twice been rescued by its lifeboat in the past.) But the *Excel*'s masts and sails were no match for these extreme conditions, and when the main gaff went by the board the ketch was at the mercy of the raging seas and continuing to take on water. Ballance and his crew of three could do nothing but brace themselves and hope for a timely rescue as their vessel was tossed like a toy boat. Luckily, her plight had been spotted from shore, and the Moelfre lifeboat station was alerted.

The regular coxswain was away, so second coxswain William Roberts (one of two men of that name in the crew) assumed command when the *Charles and Eliza Laura* was launched. She was one of the older-style boats, powered by a combination of sail and ten oars, and put out at 3.40 pm on 28 October. Among the men on board was Captain Owen Jones, not an established lifeboatman but a very experienced sailor who often offered his services when he wasn't away at sea.

A couple of hours later the lifeboat crew had fought their way to within sight of the *Excel*, about seven miles west of Port Lynas, a promontory on Anglesey's north-eastern coast; Roberts could see that she was sinking, and that urgent action was needed. With both vessels being continually storm-tossed it would be difficult and dangerous to try to come alongside her, so Roberts decided upon a drastic measure. He drove the *Charles and Eliza Laura* straight at the ketch, forcing his bows up onto her deck. She remained suspended in this precarious position just long enough to take the crew off, even though one of them was in such as desperate state that he had to be hauled on board as a dead weight. Very soon, the lifeboat was lifted up by another wave and swept back into the sea – but she had been badly damaged, as Roberts and Owen must have feared would happen, and she sat in the sea waterlogged, her mainsail shredded and useless. Roberts managed to work her into a relatively sheltered part of the Menai Straits near Puffin Island and drop anchor, but they were now in a similar state to the vessel whose aid they had come to – an open boat in gale-force winds and freezing rain, helpless, unmanageable, and miles from shore.

Soon, Roberts commented that one of the *Excel*'s crewmen was suspiciously quiet. He was informed by another of the crew that Henry McGuiness, of Kilkeel, County Down, had died from exposure. One of William Roberts' own colleagues, his namesake, was also in a bad way. As well as suffering more than most from the effects of the icy temperatures on men soaked to the skin, he had cracked his head on an iron stanchion during the rescue operation.

The men on board the *Charles and Eliza Laura* had to remain in this state for the rest of the afternoon and all through the night – a total of eighteen hours – but this was too long for Roberts, the 65-year-old father-in-law of the regular coxswain, who died during the night.

Not having heard from their lifeboat since she put out the previous day, the people of Moelfre feared the worst. The Beaumaris motor lifeboat was launched at ten that night and after a search managed to locate the *Charles and Eliza Laura* where she lay at anchor. For reasons unknown, however, it was assumed that the Moelfre crew were safe and simply riding out the storm before making their way home in the morning, so they returned to Beaumaris. But when daylight came the Moelfre boat's flag of distress was spotted and the information relayed to Beaumaris. The lifeboat was launched again, reaching her at about 8.30 am, this time taking her in tow back to Beaumaris.

The following day, Roberts told his tale to a local reporter. The interview was conducted at his home, Crown House, Moelfre, with the hero lying on his couch, his sore eyes bandaged. He and several others in his crew and been temporarily blinded by the effects of the icy salt water. In fact, he was perhaps more badly affected by the events of 27–28 October 1927 than is usually reported, since he retired from the lifeboat service the very next year on grounds of ill-health.

Captain Owen Jones isn't mentioned much in the reports of the *Excel* rescue, but, with Roberts busy at the tiller the whole time, Jones, with his vast experience, assumed a leadership position among the rest of the crew, thus earning his credit. Neither he nor Roberts, both of whom received RNLI gold medals, were young men at that time. Jones was 61, Roberts nearly 50. Owen Jones had served in the navy during the First World War and before, hence the rank by which he was referred to. (He was promoted to captain at the outbreak of war, having served since at least the early 1880s and voyaged all over the world.) The tragic irony of his death was that despite the gallant services he performed for the lifeboat service, five years after gaining his gold medal others were unable to rescue him when disaster struck at sea.

On 27 July 1932, the day he celebrated his golden wedding anniversary, Jones manned one of several fishing boats putting out from Moelfre. A gale came on rapidly and unexpectedly, forcing the little fishing fleet back into harbour. But Jones, manning his vessel single-handedly, failed to return; despite a lifeboat search, neither he nor his boat were ever found.

The sailing lifeboats were crewed by sailing men, and they no doubt had great affection for their vessels and perhaps even felt a reluctance to change and join a world where qualified mechanics assumed positions of importance and petrol fumes masked the smell of clear salty air. But the harrowing trials of the *Charles and Eliza Laura* and her crew served to underline that the days of oar and sail were numbered. The RNLI's annual general meeting in London the year after the *Excel* event (attended by Roberts and Jones), where the medals were awarded, was addressed by its president the Prince of Wales (later Edward VIII, who became the Duke of Windsor after his abdication). In a lengthy and often witty speech, the prince demonstrated that he was no nominal patron but clearly knowledgeable and enthusiastic about the lifeboat service. Towards the end of his speech, praising the bravery of people like the Moelfre men and also the renowned Harry Blogg, he turned to the matter of the lifeboats in the fleet that still relied on wind and oar in order to operate. He admitted that motor boats were much more expensive, but stressed that

> the wisdom of the change is obvious … Except in the case of the Moelfre lifeboat, nearly all the most successful rescues [in that year's report] have been carried out by motor lifeboats. The crews of the sailing boats are just as fine, just as brave, just as ready, but the motor boat can work against wind and tide, can get to the wreck in half or a quarter of the time. That is why we want to replace pulling and sailing lifeboats by motor lifeboats wherever we can.

Chapter 25

Like a Foreign Country

Dic Evans

On 23 November 2004, Prince Charles alighted the royal train at Bangor railway station, North Wales, then travelled by car to the village of Moelfre on the island of Anglesey. There he spent a few minutes talking to local children, and attended a memorial service at Carmel Independent Chapel. But the main purpose for his visit was to unveil a statue in honour of a man whom he described as a 'truly great Welshman'.

The magnificent, larger-than-life (7 feet tall) sculpture depicts Dic Evans, hands firmly grasping a boat's wheel, feet planted resolutely, gazing out to sea from the clifftop. On his left is the Moelfre lifeboat station, where he served in one capacity or another for nearly forty years.

26–27 October 1959

The storms of late October were the worst in years, with winds gusting up to 100mph, flooding, damage from falling trees, boats being sunk. Lives were lost on land and at sea all around Britain. It was a busy night for coxswain Dic Evans and the crew of the lifeboat the *Edmund and Mary Robinson*. Over twenty vessels made for refuge in different bays around Anglesey, but not all made it. The Cardiff merchant ship *Hindlea*, 500 tons and a crew of eight, had left the Manchester Ship Canal in ballast bound for Newport, and had dropped anchor in the bay hoping to ride out the storm, but a sudden change in wind direction caused her to begin dragging shorewards on her anchor despite her engines toiling to keep her away. She was heading for the Swnt Rocks, and her skipper, Captain Roland Chipchase, sent out a distress call by radio.

The stations at Holyhead and Beaumaris were on standby, but it was Dic Evans' *Edmund and Mary Robinson* that answered the call. Just to add to the pressure for Evans, not only was the boat he was taking out that night a 23-year-old relief vessel that he had never sailed in before, but because of difficulties in raising a crew there was one 'pressed' volunteer who had never been in a lifeboat of any kind in his life. The *Hindlea*'s demise wasn't imminent, and it was possible that the wind would either drop or change direction again, so the Moelfre crew stood off, ready to move in if necessary. But, if anything, the weather was getting worse, and after the *Edmund and Mary Robinson* had been standing by and riding out the storm herself for around two hours, Captain Chipchase was inclining towards the view that, 'we had better jump for it before it was too late'.

Evans and his men got to the *Hindlea* when she was little more than 200 yards from the rocks, and getting close was not going to be easy. He took the lifeboat round to the port side, but on his run-in a huge wave lifted her and threatened to pitch her onto the deck of the *Hindlea*. Thankfully as it subsided it pulled her back into the sea. Evans was now able to close on his target, and hold the *Edmund and Mary Robinson* steady long enough for the first crewman to jump aboard. Again and again he repeated this manoeuvre, till, after ten approaches in ten minutes, all eight men were safely accounted for. Dic Evans had acted not a moment too soon, because the *Hindlea* had hit the rocks by the time he had landed her crew. Dic assumed that the *Edmund and Mary Robinson* herself must have been badly damaged, so violent were the conditions. Upon inspecting her, he was amazed and relived to find that she was intact apart from a single scratch. Captain Chipchase, meanwhile, could only look on from the shore as his old ship was dashed to pieces.

Soon, he and the rest of his crew were directed to an empty house in the village that had been commandeered by the locals and turned into a refuge centre. Here, the drenched men of the *Hindlea* were given dry clothes and a hot meal. Only one needed medical treatment – he had broken a bone in his heel when landing in the lifeboat. While the rest of the crew, mostly Cardiff men, spent the night in the temporary shelter, Captain Chipchase was given a room for the night by the mother of one of the lifeboatmen, whose own husband was also a sea captain.

But Dic Evans's labours weren't over yet. Another ship was in trouble, the Greek tanker *Essar I* with a crew of twenty and a pilot from Liverpool. While the grateful men of the *Hindlea* were recovering and eventually getting some well-earned sleep, the *Edmund and Mary Robinson* was taken out again into what Dic called 'the worst storm I have ever known in thirty-six years'. The tanker had experienced engine problems on a voyage from Liverpool but had managed to make it into Moelfre Bay. When Evans and his men arrived at the spot near Port Lynas, the pilot she was carrying informed them that he believed the *Essar I* could see the night out without intervention. The Beaumaris lifeboat arrived on scene, and was prepared to keep watch on the tanker through the night, allowing the Moelfre men to finally return to base and get some well-earned rest, and a tug was able to tow the *Essar I* into Holyhead the next day.

2 December 1966

Lieutenant Commander Harold Harvey, RNR, Inspector of Lifeboats for the north-west, paid a visit to the home in Holyhead of T. B. Roberts, the lifeboat station's honorary secretary, only to find that he had just missed him – he was heading for the boathouse, having been informed that a Greek tanker of 1200 tons called *Nafisporos* was in trouble about twenty miles north of Point Lynas on the northern coast of Anglesey. A lifeboat from Douglas, Isle of Man, had been in search of her when she was in that vicinity, but had failed to find her. Because the storms had cut off the phone lines, Roberts had hurried to Holyhead to alert her coxswain. Harvey set off after him.

When he got to the station, the *St Cybi*, the Holyhead lifeboat,[1] was just about to put out, and Harvey persuaded the coxswain, who was one man short of a full complement, to allow him to take his place among the crew when she launched in a Force 10 gale gusting to Force 11 (one stage short of a hurricane), at 10.30 am. Needless to

---

1. *St Cybi* can now be seen at the Chatham Historic Dockyard.

say, visibility was poor and the going was rough in the extreme. After three hours, a Shackleton search and rescue aircraft that had been tracking the ship guided the *St Cybi* towards her.

Dic Evans and the Moelfre lifeboat *Watkin Williams* had been at sea all morning on another missions, but by early afternoon they were asked to join in the efforts to save the crew of the *Nafisporos*. A Russian ship had attempted to tow her to safety but the storm had reached hurricane proportions and the towing line had proved inadequate to the task. With darkness coming on much earlier because of the conditions, the Greek tanker was heading inexorably towards the north Anglesey coast, yawing dramatically.

The *St Cybi* gallantly closed on the vastly bigger *Nafisporos*, but as the tanker rolled over she crashed down onto the lifeboat, her giant propeller thrashing wildly just feet away from the lifeboat's rudder post, and Thomas Alcock, her coxswain, had to withdraw his damaged vessel to a safe distance. Dic Evans in the *William Watkins* caught sight of the tanker's outline in the twilight, and approached her from her stern. He was able to nudge against her side, but now saw that one of the *Nafisporos*' own boats was hanging loosely from its davit after a failed attempt to launch it, and its uncontrolled swinging and twisting as the ship continued to roll from side to side posed a serious threat to his own boat. He had to abandon the attempt. When he came in a second time, no one on board the *Nafisporos* had the courage to make the big leap in conditions that were, after all, almost as extreme as it was possible to imagine.

Late in the afternoon, when darkness had set in, the *St Cybi* tried again. By now, Harvey, the lifeboat inspector, was at the helm since Alcock, her coxswain, needed to be with his crew on deck. Harvey approached the Greek ship's starboard side, allowing the tide to sweep him towards the ship. A sailor climbed down one of her ladders and waited to time his jump, but the churning sea was lifting and dropping the lifeboat in a dramatic fashion. With patience and perseverance, not to mention great skill on Harvey's part, this sailor and then four others were taken on board the Holyhead lifeboat. Before they could take any more, the ship's loose boat finally came crashing down, first onto the deck of the tanker, and then over the side and into the sea; only quick thinking and skilful manoeuvring by Harvey prevented the lifeboat and all aboard her from being destroyed.

Now it was Dic Evans' turn again. He guided the *Watkin Williams* into position, his crew ready on deck with linked arms to prevent themselves from being swept away. Dic managed to hold station long enough for ten further crewmen to be taken off before he had to pull away. The man at the head of the chain of lifeboatmen helping pull the sailors aboard was Dic's own son David, and he was remembered by the grateful recipients of his aid as a 'bear of a man ... big, strong and powerful'. He grabbed each men and hauled them into the lifeboat 'like sacks of corn'.

But not all of the crew were yet safe: her captain and three of his men remained on board, and were nowhere to be seen when the lifeboats closed with the *Nafisporos* once more. For now, the *St Cybi* and the Moelfre boat, both now damaged, set a course for Holyhead to recover and get their passengers safely ashore. The *St Cybi* went back out, but although she stayed on station just in case, a Dutch tug, in cooperation with rescue aircraft lighting the scene up with flares, got the Greek vessel under tow and was able to get her into Liverpool with the captain and four remaining crewmen still on board.

Dic Evans was 61 at this point and had been at sea since his early teens, yet the events of that day were an eye-opener even for him:

> The sea was like a foreign country. With the leaping and the plunging of the lifeboat, the compass was swinging wildly, I could see nothing. The sea was being blown into clouds of spray and visibility was nil. The waves were like nothing I'd ever been told about. We climbed perpendicularly and we went down the same way. I was afraid every wave was going to send us somersaulting on our back. There would have been no hope for any of us then, we would have disappeared forever.

Dic Evans and his *Watkin Williams* men had been out for thirteen hours, while Lieutenant Commander Harold Harvey had been at it for twenty-two hours. 'Once ashore, the rum came out,' he reported. 'We were all proud and grateful men, speaking little and bound by the experience of such extreme lifeboat drama and action.'

Saving lives at sea was in Dic Evans' blood. It is said that one of his ancestors had helped to save some of the crew of the steam clipper the *Royal Charter*, which ran aground in similar conditions close to Moelfre 100 years almost to the day before Dic won his first gold medal attending the *Hindlea*. Both of his grandfathers had been lifeboat crew, one of them a second coxswain. When Dic himself became a lifeboat volunteer at the age of 16, his father was already a crewman and his uncle, John Matthews, was coxswain. Dic's own three sons served under him while he was coxswain.

The year after winning his first RNLI gold medal, Dic was awarded the Queen's silver medal for gallantry at sea, and the year before his retirement in 1969 he gained the British Empire Medal. Before all that, during the Second World War, he had been awarded the RNLI bronze medal for his part in the rescue of a bomber crew that had ditched in the sea. He became something of a public figure in retirement, appearing on radio and television and using his fame to raise funds for the RNLI. In 1970 he was surprised by Eamon Andrews and dragged into the *This is Your Life* studios, and in 1978 he was made Honorary Bard at the National Eisteddfod, and an ode was written to commemorate his life and achievements.

He lived to the ripe old age of 96, dying in 2001. At his funeral, lifeboatmen past and present from around Wales attended, and two flares were fired out to sea.

Lieutenant Commander Harold Harvey, VRD, RNR, had served on the teaching staff of the navy's Navigation and Direction School at Southwick, Portsmouth. He became an RNLI inspector in 1952, a job he described as having the 'responsibility of an admiral and the authority of a midshipman'. He was promoted to superintendent in 1969, retiring four years later. He died in 1992, aged 71 – the only lifeboat inspector to have been awarded the RNLI gold medal for gallantry.

Part VI

Multiple Medals

Individuals

Chapter 26

From Shipwreck Victim to Rescuer

Henry Randall

January 1812

The frigate HMS *Manilla* was cruising off the Dutch coast, near the Texel, when, partly thanks to an error by the pilot she had on board, and partly due to a gale, she found herself aground. Her captain ordered the firing of guns to alert those on shore to her predicament; the outcome was never likely to be a good one since the Dutch were on the side of Napoleon, but in their position it was the least worst option. HMS *Hero* had been wrecked in the same place only weeks earlier, and most of her crew were drowned. Because of the heavy seas, it took some time to get the British crew off, but it was eventually achieved. The captain and officers were taken to the serve their imprisonment in the fortified town of Verdun. The treatment there was generally good and a great deal of liberty was usually allowed, but the quality and amount of food and accommodation was basic at best – anything more had to be paid for and depended on what the officer could afford. One of those officers was Lieutenant Henry Randall.[1]

The *Devoron*

Randall was released after just under two years, and rejoined the navy on his return to England, being promoted to lieutenant in the same year, 1814. With the end of war with France he found a position within the coastguard in Scotland, serving at stations in Crail and

---

1. A midshipman wasn't technically an officer, more an 'officer in training'; but midshipmen, 'young gentlemen', would have almost certainly have counted as officers in cases like these.

Elie, twelve miles apart in Fife, and also Aberdeen. He joined the ranks of gold medal winners in early 1824.

On the morning of Tuesday, 18 January, there was a strong southerly wind blowing along the east coast of Scotland, accompanied by heavy seas. As was usual in such conditions, the commander of the coastguard, Lieutenant Henry Randall, sent some men to a position north of the River Don to keep an eye out for ships in distress. Once there they were confronted, at about 6 am, with a schooner – the *Devoron* – aground in the breakers about four miles north of the river, being pounded by a heavy surf and with her crew gathered together in the stern.

The alarm was raised, Randall and all available coastguard men hurried to the location, taking with them their 24-pound Manby's mortar. Trying to ignore the sandstorm whipped up by the fierce winds along the beach, the coastguards slipped into their well-practised drill for setting up the equipment, and within a short time the first shot was aimed towards the *Devoron*. But the weather played havoc not just with the line being fired, but the coiled length of line waiting to be paid out, the wind tossing it about and getting it tangled. The first line fired out snapped, and this happened again with the next two shots. Randall decided they needed to close the distance. He and his men waited for the waves to wash back down the beach, then quickly follow them with their heavy equipment. The waves soon returned, of course, and washed around them as they worked, but they had gained about 30 yards. The first attempt from the new position also failed, spoiled by the incoming sea, but, finally Randall had the satisfaction of seeing a line reach its target – actually landing in the schooner's cabin.

Sailors on board the *Devoron* rushed to grab it and then bent a heavier rope to it. This was hauled back across by Randall and his men, and secured in order to keep the schooner stable and with her head to the sea. Four of his men then volunteered to take the coastguard boat out to her, using the same rope. 'I was gratified', Randall said later, 'at witnessing the coolness and steadiness of these men when hauling through a most dangerous surf.' The coastguard men helped the four crew and master aboard, and pulled for all they were worth back to shore. The only casualty had occurred before the attempted rescue – Alex Craig, a husband and father of six and the ship's mate, had earlier been washed over the side and drowned.

The *Devoron* had been transporting a cargo of grain to London, and was reported to have dragged on her anchors into the bay. She was only four years old, and lived to fight another day. The schooner was floated off and taken into Aberdeen harbour; an inspection revealed less damage than was feared, and she continued to ply her trade for at least twenty more years. While Randall deserved his gold, it seems a great shame that no silvers were awarded to his men.[2]

The *Wanderer*

On 2 February 1833, the alert went up when a Stornoway schooner, the *Wanderer*, struck the Vows rocks off the coast near Kirkcaldy, some miles to the south of the Elie coastguard station. She had been carrying a mixed cargo of wines, spirits, seeds and grapes from Bordeaux to Leith, and foundered almost within sight of her destination.

The schooner toppled onto her side, and, sadly, just as with the *Devoron*, one of her crew was lost overboard – this time a ship's boy. The remaining six sailors and McKenzie, the master, took refuge in the rigging. By the time Henry Randall and his men arrived on scene, the *Wanderer* had floated off the rock only to be carried northward along the coast to ground again near the western end of Earlsferry, a 'musket shot' from the beach, with the mountainous waves breaking over heads of crew. Civilians who had converged on the scene volunteered to supplement Randall's crew in their light boat, and between them they got out to the *Wanderer* and brought her crew to shore safely. Lieutenant Randall had earned his second gold medal.

---

2. Most accounts say this incident happened on the 17th, which was a Monday. But in his own words as reported at the time, Randall says it took place on 'Tuesday morning'.

Henry Randall was eventually promoted through the naval ranks to commander and finally captain while still serving with the coastguard. For most of his adult life he lived in Elie just down the coast from Aberdeen, whose station he eventually commanded. He had joined the navy as a midshipman aged 17, serving on several vessels including the ill-fated *Manilla*. Being shipwrecked while aboard her and then imprisoned must have been traumatic – but perhaps his overwhelming emotion was one of gratitude for escaping with his life. When he died in 1864 at the age of 79, he was living in a house ('a large, handsomely built dwelling house') he had had built in Elie – called Manilla Cottage.

Chapter 27

Trafalgar Veteran

Thomas Leigh

On 21 June 1841, thousands converged on the Woolwich dockyard to witness the young Queen Victoria launching a new battleship, the 120-gun *Trafalgar*. Boats of all shapes and sizes crowded the Thames, and newspaper reports claimed that up to half a million spectators were on hand to watch the big ship – one of the last great wooden sailing men o' war – rumble down the slipway to great cheers. Her main deck was crowded with dignitaries, and one of them was given the honour of raising the royal standard.

He was chosen because thirty-six years previously he had actually fought at Trafalgar, on board HMS *Conqueror*. He was Commander Thomas Leigh, and he had recently retired from the coastguard: a double gallantry gold medal recipient.

Two events within four weeks of each other eleven years before that great launching event led to the then Lieutenant Leigh being awarded his first gold.

On 26 November 1830, at his coastguard station in Winterton, around ten miles north of Great Yarmouth, Leigh heard that a collier called the *Annabella* had been wrecked on the outer bank in tremendous gale. He and the coastguards on duty hurried their Manby mortar apparatus to the spot, north along the coast towards Horsey, but the power of the wind was such that shot after shot fell short of the ship until all of their ammunition had been used up. Leigh wanted to go out by boat, but the *Annabella*'s crew were in imminent danger and the lifeboat was too far away. The only vessel to hand was 'an old beach boat, scarcely sea-worthy'. The Winterton beachmen who had converged on the scene refused to risk their lives in that boat in such conditions. Luckily, as well as two of his coastguards, four Horsey beachmen volunteered to go with Leigh. After battling through the waves, the courageous makeshift crew managed to get all seven of the sailors off the *Annabella* and back to dry land before their brig disintegrated.

On Christmas Eve morning, 1830, Leigh was on duty when the brig *Henry*, carrying a cargo of slabs and potatoes, came to grief on the local sand bar known as the Ness. An indication of the conditions prevailing that day is that Leigh and his men had to fight their way through snow that had drifted to waist-deep in places while hauling their mortar equipment to the closest spot to the wreck, which lay nearly two cables' length (up to four hundred metres) from the shore.

Once they were on scene, they could see that the brig's hull was submerged, the crew having clambered up into the rigging and lashed themselves there. Despite the unimaginable cold, biting wind and snow, it was the only place of safety remaining to them, And even when Leigh and the coastguards with him managed to fire a line over the *Henry*, the desperate men on board were too overcome by cold and exhaustion to do anything with it.

Despite doubts about whether a rescue by sea might be possible, Leigh ordered the lifeboat to be dragged over the beach and down to the water's edge. They launched at about 3.30 in the afternoon, but despite the efforts of his own men along with twenty local beachmen at the oars, a powerful flood tide broke over the boat, forcing them to abandon their mission of mercy. Leigh was determined not to give up. He urged the beachmen to go home to change into dry clothes and take some rest and refreshments, then return for another go. There was an air of pessimism, but the men did reassemble at between 7 and 8 in the evening. By now it was dark, and when Leigh discussed the situation with some of the older hands among the beachmen, 'they considered any further attempt not only impractical but unnecessary', since no cries for help had been heard from the wreck for over an hour and it was considered that all hands must have died from exposure or drowning by now.

But Leigh hadn't given up hope. He insisted that at least a few could be still alive but unable to summon up the energy to shout. In desperation, he even promised the beachmen a financial reward if they would go out with him again, regardless of whether of the collier's crew were found alive. Finally, fifteen beachmen and three coastguards manned the lifeboat – now coated in a sheet of ice – and put out 'with considerable difficulty' at about 9 pm. They had to cross the same sandbank that had claimed the *Henry*, and even in their smaller vessel they scraped the bottom on a number of occasions, putting themselves at great risk. But, eventually, they came upon the coaster, and when they hailed her they could just make out feeble cries from across the waters before they were snatched away by the wind.

A line was tossed onto the deck of the ship, but the crew couldn't even summon up the energy to grab it and tie a simple knot. The only remaining option was to take the lifeboat even closer, into shallower water and with the added danger of being dashed against the brig. As they closed with the *Henry* she took on the appearance of a ghost ship, swathed in snow and frost, and despite the darkness Leigh could make out what he described as 'the most appalling sight'. He witnessed the ship

> in a heavy surf rocking fast to pieces … Her master suspended from the main rigging by his heels, a corpse, having bled to death from a wound received on first striking; a lad hanging from main catharpings frozen to death.[1]

The *Henry*'s crew had been stuck in this horrific predicament for ten hours. Two of the Winterton beachmen scrambled up the rigging and cut free both living and dead and got them into the boat with wave and surf sweeping over them. They got off the Ness 'with extreme exertions', and took their casualties to shore. Within an hour of the rescue, both of the brig's masts, in whose rigging the crew had been dangling, went by the board, and soon 'not one atom of her was to be seen'. But the poor surviving four crewmen were in no

---

1. Catharpings are short lines at the lower end of the futtock shrouds.

state to celebrate their escape. They were 'dreadfully frost-bitten in extremities', and a local surgeon predicted that several amputations would be necessary.

Thomas Leigh's second gold came as the result of a rescue on a spring day three years later. The *Crawford Davison*, with a crew of sixteen, was carrying an unusual cargo – forty horses from Hamburg, to be delivered to London. There was a pilot on board as she made her way along the coast of East Anglia, but he wasn't a local man – probably from Harwich, although one account refers to him as an 'overseas pilot' – and what he took to be the lights at Happisburgh were actually those of Orfordness. As a result of this miscalculation, the *Crawford Davison* struck the Haisborough Sands at about 4 am on 19 March, heeling over onto her side and taking in a lot of water. She was then swept back into deeper water, still leaking badly and with her rudder destroyed.

Some of those on board now set off in the ship's own boats, but her captain, George Sandford, stayed on board for the time being. Sandford, though, was worried for his wife and niece, who, along with several other men, had escaped in a boat 'known to be leaky', so when a working boat from Sea Palling just along the coast hove into view, Sandford begged them to go to the aid of the boat his wife was in. They refused, and even when he offered them twenty guineas 'or any sum they might ask' his pleas fell upon deaf ears, 'the wretched thirst for gain thus overcoming the splendid feelings of humanity' as a local newspaper described it. Luckily, there was also a boat from Caister in the vicinity, and this vessel was prepared to divert to rescue the captain's wife and her companions, By now, Leigh and his men were in action too. They came to the rescue of Captain Sandford and the rest of the crew who had remained with him, ensuring that there were no casualties. At least, not human ones.

A sailor from the *Crawford Davison* later reported that

nothing can be imagined more horrific than was the state of the vessel when about to be deserted. Horses which had been secured in slings lost their fastenings ... fighting and kicking ...

the shrieks of the poor animals may be conceived but hardly described.

Every animal drowned, their bodies washing up along the shore in the coming days.

Thomas Leigh won a further silver in 1835, in which year he was both promoted from lieutenant to commander and also retired, having spent twenty-seven years in the navy. He is said to have been in action with the enemy ten times during the war, before commencing his coastguard career, being mentioned in dispatches on four of those occasions. He was also decorated by the Royal Humane Society for both the *Henry* and *Crawford Davison* rescues. He died in 1846.

Chapter 28

Storm Warrior

Charlie Fish

After the Lord Mayor's Show

The Ramsgate lifeboat crew set out at noon in poor conditions, the rain coming down in what was described as a 'pitiless torrent', conditions that were to last all day. Charles Edward Fish, on what was to be one of his last appearances as coxswain now that his health was not so good, led his men as he had many times before – but this was no ordinary mission.

For a start, the Ramsgate men weren't in their own lifeboat, but one loaned for the occasion by the RNLI; there was no one to be rescued, and the lifeboat was driven not by wind or oars, but by horse power. Eight, to be precise, pulling the carriage upon which the lifeboat rested while the Ramsgate men stood to take in the adulation of the cheering crowds as they trundled along the streets of London – for this was the Lord Mayor's Show, 1891.

It was a picturesque affair, despite the depressing weather. The new Lord Mayor, Alderman Evans, was a Welshman, a relatively rare thing, which had attracted large numbers of his fellow countrymen and women. A band played traditional tunes such as *Men of Harlech*, and women in traditional Welsh dress added to the colour.

Charlie Fish and his men had boarded their boat in traditional gear of red caps and guernsey tops, though, as the newspapers wryly pointed out, oilskins and sou'westers would have been more appropriate for the weather. It wasn't just the Welsh who had come to support their own – special train excursions had been laid on from Ramsgate. Charlie Fish's exploits had earned him national fame and the soubriquet of the 'storm warrior'; more than one newspaper said that the lifeboat received the biggest cheer of the afternoon as it passed through the crowds – who, despite the rain, were so densely packed that fainting people had to be carried away for treatment.

The route took the Ramsgate lifeboatmen along streets they had perhaps only previously read about: starting from the Guildhall at noon, taking in Mansion House, Upper Thames Street where the Great Fire had been fuelled by warehouses full of inflammable materials, past St Paul's, along Fleet Street, the Strand, Victoria Embankment. There were displays and floats galore, from the band of the Scots Guards to the banners of the Worshipful Company of Playing Card Makers. The lifeboat itself was drawn by horses belonging to Commissioners of Sewers of the City of London.

No doubt Charlie and his comrades enjoyed their big day, although lifeboats and casualties often go together, and, unfortunately, this was to be the case today. In one place the crowds were so great that as the lifeboat passed by, two young girls were pushed forwards into its path by the surge of people craning for a view. This was no minor incident. They fell under wheels of the carriage conveying the great, heavy craft, resulting in one poor child needing a leg amputation. The report from the hospital later was that both were in a 'precarious condition'.

Indian Chief

The rescue for which Charlie Fish earned his first gold medal had taken place nearly ten years before the Lord Mayor's Show. On the morning of 5 January 1881 news reached Ramsgate that during a gale the *Indian Chief*, a barque of over 1,000 tons, had run onto the Long Sand, towards the mouth of the Thames Estuary and close to Knock lightship. She had been on her way from Middlesbrough to Yokohama carrying a mixed cargo. Constantly pounded by waves, the ship was breaking up; the crew took the usual course of climbing into the rigging, hoping for at least temporary safety. The lifeboats from Clacton and Harwich, to the north of the Long Sand, had both failed to locate the barque, so Captain Braine, Harbour Master of Ramsgate to the south of the sandbank, was contacted and he called out both the local lifeboat and the *Vulcan*, a paddle-steamer tug. Despite the conditions, the latter vessel should be able to tow the lifeboat *Bradford* into the teeth of the wind and on to the site of the wreck.

The gale was, in fact, worsening at this time, but Charlie Fish had every confidence in his self-righting lifeboat. He was later to give a lengthy account to the newspapers, and although the *Bradford* was one of the country's biggest lifeboats, he tried to put it into some sort of perspective for readers. It was, he said,

> ridiculous to talk of bigness when it means only forty-two feet long, and when a sea is raging round you heavy enough to swamp a line-of-battle ship. I had my eye on the tug – named the *Vulcan*, sir – and when she met the first of the seas, and she was thrown up like a ball, and you could see her starboard paddle revolving in the air high enough for a coach to pass under; and when she struck the hollow she dished a sea over her bows that left only the stern showing.

Waves and spray continually washed over the crew, soaking them to the skin despite their waterproof gear. On the way out to the ship they rigged up a tarpaulin sail to give themselves at least a little cover, but it lasted no more than a couple of minutes before being torn to shreds.

> I never remember a colder wind … Old Tom Cooper, one of the best boatmen in all England, sir, who made one of our crew, agreed with me that it was more like a flaying machine than a natural gale of wind. The feel of it in the face was like being gnawed by a dog. I only wonder it didn't freeze the tears it fetched out of our eyes.

For a short time the two vessels were offered some protection by the North Foreland, but as soon as they cleared this they felt the full force of the storm, and seas that seemed 'miles long … like an Atlantic sea'. Charlie noticed that the tug's progress was slowing, and he began to fear the state of the sea was too much even for her. He could see her master, Alf Page, 'coming and going like the moon when the clouds sweep over it, as the seas smothered him up one moment, and left him shining in the sun the next'. However, slowly but surely the

Vulcan inched towards her destination. They passed a collier on her way to Ramsgate, limping along with her foretopgallant yard missing but with the wind behind her and not requiring assistance. Seeing the lifeboat and realising the mission she was on (they had seen the wreck and were on their way to report it) they gave the crew of the *Bradford* a rousing cheer before disappearing into the spray.

A member of the lifeboat's crew suggested a tot of rum might keep their spirits up; Charlie Fish generally liked to keep some in reserve to dish out to the crew of a shipwreck 'who are pretty sure to be in greater need of the stuff than us', but he – a teetotaller – agreed to the request and told crewmate Charlie Verrion to measure the rum out and serve it round.

> And it would have made you laugh, I do believe, sir, to have seen the care the men took of the big bottle – Charlie cocking his finger into the cork-hole, and David Berry clapping his hand over the pewter measure whenever a sea came to prevent the salt water from spoiling the liquor.

Daylight was beginning to fade by half-past four in the afternoon, but out of the gloom they first spotted the flashing light of the manned Kentish Knock lightship, and as they got closer they could make out her name painted on her hull in big white letters on a red background. She too was being tossed about, but Charlie drew as close as he dare and managed to make himself heard above the storm to ask two crewmen who were leaning over her side for the bearing to the wreck. 'Nor' west by north' came the reply, after which the *Vulcan*'s tow took the *Bradford* on past the lightship on towards their target. 'We felt the power of those waves, sir,' Charlie reported of the manoeuvre. 'It looked a wonder that we were not rolled over and drowned, every man of us. We held on with our teeth clenched, and twice the boat was filled, and the water up to our throats. "Look out for it, men!" was always the cry.'

The moon peeped out now and then through scudding black clouds, but otherwise it had grown dark. They were only able to see the tug ahead of them in the glimmer from the waves and foam.

'Bitter cold work, Charlie,' says old Tom Cooper to me. 'But,' says he, 'it's colder for the poor wretches aboard the wreck, if they're alive to feel it.' The thought of them made our own sufferings small, and we kept looking and looking into the darkness around, but there was nothing to be spied, only now and again, and long whiles apart the flash of a rocket in the sky from the Sunk lightship ... Meanwhile, from time to time, we burnt a hand-signal – a light, sir, that's fired something after the manner of a gun. You fit it into a wooden tube, and give a sort of hammer at the end a smart blow, and the flame rushes out, and a bright light it makes, sir. Ours were green lights, and whenever I set one flaring I couldn't help taking notice of the appearance of the men. It was a queer sight, I assure, to see them as green as leaves, with their cork jackets swelling out their bodies so as scarcely to seem like human beings, and the black water as high as our masthead, or howling a long way below us, on either side.

Trying to pick out the wreck of the *Indian Chief* in these conditions was, said Charlie, 'like trying to see through the bottom of a well', and now the crew began to wonder whether there was anything they could achieve – whether they should postpone the search till it got light. After some discussion this was agreed to – not a return to Ramsgate, but lie-to and ride out the storm where they were. They hailed the tug and relayed their intentions. The prospect of spending the next few hours being tossed about on that stormy January night was hardly an appealing one. 'I dare say most of our hearts were at home, and our wishes alongside our hearths, and the warm fires in them,' Charlie wistfully reflected. But he and the rest of them were in complete agreement with crewman Bob Penny: 'We are here to fetch the wreck, and fetch it we will, if we wait a week' and the rest of the crew had concurred 'without a murmur'.

There would be little rest, and certainly no sleep for the crew as they counted down the hours.

The manner in which we were flung towards the sky with half our keel out of water and then dropped into a hollow – like falling from the top of a house, sir – while the heads of the seas blew into and tumbled over us all the time, made us all reckon that … most of our time would be spent in preventing ourselves from being washed overboard.

To replace their earlier covering they were, however, able to wrestle down their foresail, bring it aft and make 'a kind of roof of it' to shelter under. Two men were left on lookout, secured with lifelines to prevent them being thrown overboard. Charlie Fish described their attempts at getting comfortable:

> We all lay in a lump together for warmth, and a fine show we made, I dare say; for a cork jacket, even when a man stands upright, isn't calculated to improve his figure. And as we all of us had cork jackets on and oil-skins, and many of us sea boots, you may guess what a raffle of legs and arms we showed, and what a rum heap of odds and ends we looked, as we sprawled in the bottom of the boat upon one another. Sometimes it would be 21 Johnny Goldsmith – for we had three Goldsmiths – Steve, and Dick and Johnny – growling underneath that someone was lying on his leg; and then maybe Harry Meader would bawl out that there was a man sitting on his head; and once Tom Friend swore his arm was broke. But my opinion is, sir, that it was too cold to feel inconveniences of this kind, and I believe that some among us would not have known if their arms and legs really had been broke, until they tried to use 'em, for the cold seemed to take away all feeling out of the blood. As the seas flew over the boat the water filled the sail that was stretched overhead and bellied it down upon us, and that gave us less room so that some had to lie flat on their faces; but when this bellying got too bad we'd all get up and make one heave with our backs under the sail, and chuck the water out of it in that way.

At about one in the morning, young Tom Cooper suggested they all had another nip of rum, and despite Charlie's humorous description of how they were piled under the sail it was seriously cold and some of the men were 'groaning … pressing themselves against the thwarts with the pain of it'. So, once again, he agreed to the drink being passed round. Charlie himself decided to treat himself to some of the Fry's chocolate, which he always took with him on a shout – but, to his dismay, the locker in which he had stowed it was full of water and his bar of chocolate had disintegrated.

In the grey first light of day, it was the same Young Tom Cooper (his father, Old Tom, was also on board) who sighted their target and excitedly alerted his comrades. All that could be discerned was a tall mast about three miles off, now visible, now hidden as the lifeboat rose and fell in the continuing storm. But hawk-eyed Tom was right – it was the ship the men of the *Bradford* had waited all night to find. It presented a daunting prospect. Charlie could see that

> all about the wreck was the Sand, and the water on it was running in fury all sorts of ways, rushing up in tall columns of foam as high as a ship's mainyard, and thundering so loudly that, though we were to windward, we could hear it above the gale and the boiling of the seas around us.

Still, it was time for the *Bradford* to go into action.

They let loose the tow-rope that connected them to the *Vulcan* and raised a storm foresail, which was soon 'taut as a drum-skin' and they were underway, all the time being battered from behind by huge waves 'flying a dozen yards high over us in broad solid sheets', falling 'with a roar like the explosion of a gun ten and a dozen fathoms ahead'. Soon they were close enough to catch glimpses of the vessel's hull, but Charlie knew that if any of the crew had survived that terrible night they would be somewhere up that mast, clinging to yards and rigging. At first, the signs didn't look good; not a soul could be made out. But as they neared the stricken ship, Charlie caught sight of a strip of canvas fluttering in the wind from near the top of the mast as if being used as a signal. The whole crew of the *Bradford* shouted at the tops of their voices, and then they began to make out figures whose pale oilskins, a similar colour to that of the mast, had previously made them hard to pick out.

One of the *Bradford*'s crew cried 'All hands are there, men!'

'Aye,' Charlie confirmed, 'the whole ship's company, and we'll have them all!'

They could also now assess the state of the barque. She had lost her main and mizzen masts, her bulwarks had been washed away, and even as they looked on they saw, 'great lumps of timber and planking ripping out of her and going overboard with every pour of the seas'. As the *Bradford* dropped anchor, their crew saw the *Indian Chief*'s survivors unlashing themselves from the mast and allowing themselves to drop into the rigging beneath them. The lifeboat's anchor cable was let out, allowing them to drift closer till they were beneath the stem of the barque. Charlie called up for someone to tie a line to a piece of wood and throw it over the side for them to take hold of. He could now see the 'horrible muddle of spars and torn canvas and rigging under her lee' but it was only when they had taken the line and fastened themselves to the ship that they witnessed what a 'fearful sight' she presented. Charlie, for all his experience, was not prepared for what he saw next:

We hauled the Life-boat close under her quarter. There looked to be a whole score of dead bodies knocking about among the spars. It stunned me for a moment, for I had thought all hands were in the foretop, and never dreamt of so many lives having been lost. Seventeen were drowned, and there they were, most of them, and the body of the captain lashed to the head of the mizenmast, so as to look as if he were leaning over it, his head stiff upright and his eyes watching us, and the stir of the seas made him appear to be struggling to get to us. I thought he was alive, and cried to the men to hand him in, but someone said he was killed when the mizenmast fell, and had been dead four or five hours. This was dreadful shock; I never remember the like of it. I can't hardly get those fixed eyes out of my sight, sir, and I lie awake for hours of a night, and so does Tom Cooper, and others of us, seeing those bodies torn by the spars and bleeding, floating in the water alongside the miserable ship.

But there were still the living to be saved. The *Bradford* had positioned herself close enough for the eleven surviving crew of the *Indian Chief* to scramble on board, from where they were transferred to the *Vulcan* tug for the voyage back to Ramsgate. By the time everyone had disembarked, Charlie and his men had been at sea for around 26 hours. Coxswain Charlie Fish was awarded not only the RNLI gold medal, but also the silver Board of Trade Sea Gallantry Medal, and the silver Liverpool Shipwreck & Humane Society Marine Medal. Board of Trade and RNLI silver medals were also awarded to Charlie's crew of eleven, as well as to Alfred Page, master of the *Vulcan* tug, and his six crewmen. The following month the Duke of Edinburgh visited the Ramsgate station wearing the full uniform of the Admiral of the Fleet. With a guard of honour formed by coastguards, Charlie and his men strode across the lawn to be presented with their RNLI medals by His Royal Highness.

As we have seen, Charlie bowed out ten years later, in 1891, when he was in declining health.

On 22 December 1891 an appeal was launched in the press to raise funds for a testimonial for him once news of his resignation became public. A concert and other events were held, raising £100 for the famed Ramsgate coxswain. He had announced his decision to retire at one of the periodical dinners that were held for in the town for the lifeboatmen, paid for out of a bequest left by Admiral George Back.[1] At this dinner he was presented with a gold service clasp to go with his RNLI medal, along with a cheque for £100. All present drank a toast to his health enthusiastically. At this or one of the previous dinners, 'beers all round' were laid on for the men, and it was only later in the evening that those present learned it was the non-drinker Charlie himself who had paid. 'It is not surprising,' said a newspaper account of the event, 'that a man of his type and temperament was universally liked and respected among his fellow citizens.'

---

1. As a young man, Admiral George Back had ventured the Arctic with the renowned explorer Sir John Franklin.

Charlie seems to have led an 'interesting' private life. He married Mary Ann Packer in 1860, but she died around ten years later, and in less than six months he had married another Mary Ann, this time Austen. But over the next few years three children with the surname Picton were born and were living under his roof, and the impression from genealogists is that they were his.[2] They are referred to as 'adopted' in some family trees, although formal adoption in the way we know it today did not exist then. And during this marriage, in 1875, he felt the need to place the following notice the *Thanet Advertiser*:

Caution to Tradesmen and others
I Charles E Fish of 86 Harbour Street Ramsgate will not be responsible for any debts contracted by my wife Mary Ann Fish after the above date; and any tradesmen having any demand on the said Charles Fish are requested to send their bills at once to the above address.

On his death, another notice appeared in the local press giving details of who his creditors should apply to. This may have been routine, but it does give pause for thought.

Charles Edward Fish was living with his daughter when he died, at her home on a street called 'The Plains of Waterloo' in Ramsgate. He died a hero both in his home town and nationally. Obituaries point out that his activities weren't confined to the sea and the lifeboat service. One article said that the local Co-operative Society 'practically owes its foundation' to Charles Fish. It had started in 1891 with Charlie as its president, and many of its meetings were held at his own house.

He had attended 369 shouts, going to the aid of 95 vessels, during which he helped to save 877 lives – a true 'storm warrior'.

---

2. In the census returns they are listed as son/daughter of the head of the house.

Chapter 29

Hero of Spurn Point

Robert Cross

Early on morning of 5 February 1909, the weather off Flamborough Head was worsening to the point that many of the offshore fishing vessels on that part of the coast thought it unwise to put to sea, but the inshore men felt that their fishing grounds should be safe enough, and up to fifty of them put out in their cobles. Forming part of this fleet were the *Gleaner*, carrying John Cross and his sons Robert and Richard, and the *Two Brothers*, crewed by Melchior Chadwick, Tom Leng Major and George Gibbon.

It wasn't long before the wind reached storm-force and changed direction, signalling danger for the little cobles. One by one they began turned towards the safety of the North Landing, a small bay to the north of the Flamborough lighthouse. They had already reached safety when disaster struck. A sudden huge sea turned the *Gleaner* over, sending her three crewmen tumbling overboard. The *Two Brothers*, which had been following the *Gleaner* towards the haven, steered for the scene, coming alongside the upturned boat. Despite being violently tossed by the worsening sea conditions, Chadwick, Major and Gibbon managed to haul the father and sons Cross out of the water.

The drama had been witnessed from the shore, and while this was going on the Flamborough rowing lifeboat *Forrester* had been launched. Despite being double-manned to cope with the ferocity of the storm, her twenty crewmen could fight their way only fifty yards from the beach before being beaten back. Many of the experienced fishermen had, by now, landed their own cobles and were looking on with a growing sense of apprehension. The *Gleaner* had been unlucky to be hit by a freak wave, and it was clear that the *Two Brothers*, now overloaded and struggling to get home as wave after wave washed over her, could have safely made it back had she not courageously remained on station to save the lives of their fellow fishermen. Then, the worst happened. Onlookers saw the *Two Brothers* swamped one time too many, this time no longer to be seen.

Five of the men lost that day were buried in the local churchyard, but the sea never gave up the body of Robert Cross. It was a tragedy the village never forgot. A monument was erected to mark the loss of the local men, and in 2009 an event was held to mark the centenary, and was attended by then current lifeboat volunteer Stewart Cross, great-grandson of John Cross of the *Gleaner*.

And it was also a tragedy one member of the Flamborough lifeboat crew, a namesake of one of the men lost that day, never forgot. His brother and two nephews had been on board the *Gleaner*, and what he witnessed motivated him to devote his life to saving those in need on the sea. His name was Robert Cross.

The *Gurth*

The distress signal came at a bad time. The Humber lifeboat station on Spurn Point was Britain's only full-time one, and when the boat put out it normally carried a crew of seven. But when an SOS from the Grimsby trawler *Gurth* was received at 6.30 on the evening of 12 February 1940, coxswain Robert Cross had two men on the sick list, one man away from the boathouse, but an urgent need to set out immediately. The assistant motor mechanic was one of those ill, but he climbed out of his sick bed and begged Cross to let him go with the rest of the men. The coxswain wasn't keen, but probably had little choice. The lifeboat launched two men short, and it would prove to make a difficult job even harder.

The *Gurth*, with a crew of nine, had been returning from a fishing trip when disaster struck. She found herself being pushed towards land by the gale until, finally, she struck the shore bow-first, her stern submerged beneath the waves. Before the impact, the *Gurth* fired distress flares, and these were seen by a Royal Navy signal station. The news was relayed to the Humber lifeboat station via the Donna Nook coastguard to the south of Spurn Point.

Robert Cross guided the *City of Bradford II* lifeboat southwards for around an hour until he saw a distant light near the Hall Buoy. It was indeed the *Gurth*, but he could see her drifting inexorably towards the shore, and by the time they arrived on scene they saw through the darkness that she had grounded and only the fore part of the ship remained above water. Cross motored round to the relatively sheltered leeward side of the trawler, where the *Bradford*'s anchor was dropped and the lifeboat approached stern-first. But all the time Cross was having to fight the conditions. The gale-force wind was driving snow into the crew's faces, and whenever a big wave approached the *Bradford* he had to ride it by putting on full-power towards it before resuming his stern-first approach to the *Gurth*. The shortage of crewmen meant he was working almost blind, because no one could be spared to work the searchlight as would usually be the case. His crewmen were also taking a buffeting, being swept off their feet time and again by the waves washing over their boat, clinging to the rails to avoid being washed overboard. When they got close enough, the only two men who could be spared were sent forward to be ready to receive the men escaping from the wreck.

The *City of Bradford II* had almost completed the 160-yard approach when she was lifted by a big sea and carried almost the same distance along the coast away from their target. She was left broadside on to the waves, the worst possible position, with seawater rushing in and flooding her engine room. Within moments, Major, the lifeboat's mechanic was up to his neck in water – but the engines themselves were unaffected and the brave mechanic stuck at his post, operating the controls by feel alone.

Once his crew had gathered themselves, Cross was able to direct the lifeboat back towards the *Gurth*. It was much too dangerous to try to stay alongside her; at times the raging sea was lifting the little lifeboat higher than the trawler, before dropping her again with a crash. There were times when the *Bradford* was in danger of being swept onto the deck of the *Gurth*, and full power astern had to be quickly applied to get them clear. The only choice was to nudge the *Bradford*'s bow against the *Gurth*'s forecastle, where the crew had gathered, long enough to allow one man to jump in, quickly retreat, then return as many times as necessary. The *Bradford* had been out for about two hours when the first grateful man was helped aboard. It took Cross no less than twenty such perilous attempts over the course of an hour to get just six of the nine men off the *Gurth*. Then, before he could drive at the trawler once more, there was a spluttering from one of the engines, followed by a sudden loss of power.

When the crew investigated, they found that in the furious conditions a rope had been washed overboard and become fouled in one of the propellers. Unsure whether it could be cleared and not having anyone free to attend to it anyway, Cross decided the operation could just about continue using the remaining working engine, and in this way the final three crewmen were taken off the wreck. But the *Bradford* had been operating in very shallow water, and as Cross turned away from the trawler there was a violent tremor. They had struck bottom, damaging the rudder, stern post and other parts of the boat. Fortunately, Cross found he was still able to steer. Once safely clear of the trawler, one of the crewmen opened the scuttle above the fouled propeller and was able to cut the rope away,[1] and at long last the *City of Bradford II* was heading for Grimsby on two engines.

It had been hard work for the lifeboatmen, and as well as the battering they had taken from constantly being knocked off their feet by the waves, some were suffering from exposure. When they arrived at just after 10.30 pm after three-and-a-half hours at sea, one onlooker at Grimsby declared that the crew of the *Bradford* appeared to be in a worse state than the men from the *Gurth*. Another said that the lifeboat itself looked like 'a battle-scarred warrior'. Robert Cross duly received his first RNLI gold medal, and subsequently the George Medal. But if ever there was a case for a second gold it must surely be that of Major, the lifeboat's mechanic, for staying at his post almost submerged in freezing water and working the engines 'blind', by feel alone. As it was, he was awarded the silver, and the rest of the crew received a bronze medal.

---

1. The crewman used a special knife invented by Cross himself, according to the RNLI archives.

The *Almondine*

The night of 6 January 1943 was a busy one for the crew of the *City of Bradford II*. At just before 8 pm they were called out to go to the aid of Phillip's Defence Unit No. 1, which had broken free of her moorings in a gale and drifted ashore near Trinity Sand in the Humber Estuary. These units were manned floating gun platforms, anchored offshore ready to intercept enemy attacks. Robert Cross and his men were soon on their way, ploughing through the waves, wind and snow to see what they could do. This being wartime, there was a boom defending the estuary, and vessels coming and going had to go through a 'gate', next to which a 'defence-boom vessel' kept watch. As the *Bradford* drew near to the vessel, they were hailed by megaphone: a tug had attended the troubled defence unit, and the lifeboat's services weren't required. They were back at the lifeboat station within about half an hour and in the process of rehousing the *Bradford* when a second call came in. Another vessel was in trouble, having grounded on what is known as the Stony Binks, just off Spurn Head and close to where the lifeboat station had been located exactly because so many ships came to grief in that area.

Cross couldn't take the *Bradford* out immediately because of the ebbing tide, so all they could do for now was wait. But before they had a chance to put out, a third shout came through. This time it was to another defence unit, No 3 with five men on board, which like the previous one had parted from her mooring and drifted helplessly away. Robert Cross and his men were close enough to see the red distress flares soaring into the night sky. This Phillips unit had ended up snagged against the boom defence, but there was the risk that at any time it could be ripped away by the pounding waves and swept out to sea.

Shore searchlights guided the *City of Bradford II*, although they were so powerful that every now and then the crew would be blinded by them. As with the *Gurth* rescue, Cross went in bow-first, got one man aboard, backed off, then repeated the procedure until all five men were safely in the lifeboat. But also like the *Gurth* rescue, the *Bradford* didn't come away unscathed. The boom, was, after all, a defensive measure and as such it bristled with steel spikes. It was impossible to avoid them completely – which was the whole idea – and they left their mark on the boat. It wasn't enough to prevent her from returning to the station, however, and at 11.20 pm the men from the defence unit were transferred to dry land. Cross and his men remained on stand-by till the tide changed – there was still the vessel stranded on the Binks.

After around four hours had passed, Cross and his men were able embark on their third mission of that eventful night: HM Trawler *Almondine* lay on the sands with her port side under water and the sea washing over her exposed starboard side. It was pitch black and still snowing heavily when the *Bradford* closed on the wreck and saw her signals for help. Cross brought the lifeboat abreast of the *Almondine* and a sailor on board caught a rope that was thrown up to him, securing it to the ship. To complicate matters, there was a fast-flowing spring tide, and before the lifeboat men could get to work the *Bradford* was swung into a collision with the trawler; the rope parted, but not before the impact had destroyed the lifeboat's radio mast, cutting off communications with the shore.

The *Bradford* was still seaworthy, however, and Cross brought her close again. This time, rather than try to hold her steady in the almost impossible conditions, he ran back and forth alongside her like a jousting knight, veering away at the end of each run and returning for another charge, on each pass pausing just briefly enough for a sailor (sometimes more than one) to drop into the boat. This was repeated twelve times, and nineteen men were rescued. But this wasn't as smooth an operation as it might sound. Not all of Cross's runs were successful – he had to make far more approaches than there were crew on the ship – and *City of Bradford II* sustained yet more damage because of the inevitable contact with the *Almondine* on a number of these runs. Her hull was splintered and broken in several places, and eventually holed. The breach was just above the waterline, but in these seas that was only of marginal comfort, and there were still crewmen to be extricated.

By 4.20 on the morning of the 6th, the incoming tide was starting to lift the *Almondine* and it seemed she might soon refloat. Her captain hailed Cross for advice on whether he and his officers should stay on board, presumably with a view to steering her at least away from other shipping if not to a place of safety, or whether they should join their shipmates in the lifeboat. But just then the *Almondine*'s batteries must have finally failed, because her lights blinked out. Such was the darkness of the night that despite the trawler having been within hailing distance of the *Bradford*, she disappeared from sight. The ship must at around this point have been picked up by the rising tide and carried away, because even though both the *Bradford* and the observers on shore swept the area with their lights, the *Almondine* had vanished as if by some illusionist's trick. When no trace of her could be found after well over an hour's searching, there was nothing for Cross to do but transport his rescued sailors to the lifeboat station, where he landed at 6.15 am.

Once ashore, Cross was informed by phone that a local tug had the *Almondine* and her remaining crew safely under tow, having come across her drifting in the entrance to the Humber.

This actually wasn't the first time the *City of Bradford II* had come to the aid of the *Almondine*. Five years previously, before she had been commandeered by the navy and was still a fishing trawler, she had run aground on Trinity Sand. On that occasion Cross's crew didn't need to intervene, merely advising her captain to drop anchor so that she couldn't be carried any further onto the Sands. When the tide turned and the trawler was afloat again, the *Bradford* acted as her pilot and guided her to safety. For his part in the later 1943 rescue, Cross received his second gold, and the rest of his crew were also suitably rewarded.

Surprisingly, the *City of Bradford II* was still seaworthy, and was in action again just four days later. In fact, the boat continued in active service until 1960, and then remained as part of the relief fleet for a further eight years. She survived into the present day, and came to light in 2018 moored in Strangford Lough, County Down, 'free to a good home' but in need of extensive repairs. Sadly, it appears that no one was prepared to spend the requisite amount of money, because there is a reference online to her having been subsequently broken up.

Robert Cross was born in Flamborough in 1876. He was the son of a fisherman, like so many of our lifeboat heroes of that age when there still a huge British fishing fleet. His lifeboat career began in 1902, and he became coxswain in 1911. Before his gold medal exploits he had already won the silver. In 1916 a steamer ran aground on the Binks; the storm was so bad that he couldn't bring the lifeboat close enough to take anyone off. No one responded to his call for a volunteer to get a line to the ship, so he tied it round his body and went in himself. He succeeded in reaching the vessel at the second attempt, and eight lives were saved. In all, Robert Cross received seven RNLI medals: two gold, three silver and two bronze, putting him in the same league as people like Hillary and Henry Blogg. Cross was 66 at the time of the *Almondine* rescue, and retired soon afterwards. Known locally as a modest hero, he died in 1964 at the age of 88.

Chapter 30

A Family Affair

Henry Blogg

Last Hurrah

It was 5 June 1953, a few days after the coronation of Elizabeth II. Union Jacks and red, white and blue bunting still garlanded the small fishing town of Cromer in honour of the accession of the young queen. A crowd of locals and holiday-makers, idling on the esplanade, observed the arrival of three crab boats returning with their catch. These were crewed by experienced men – in one of the boats was Jimmy Davies, 44, coxswain of Cromer's No. 2 lifeboat as well as being a town councillor, and his brother and fellow lifeboatman, Frank. The sea was calm and smooth when the little boats came in. Calm, that was, until seemingly out of nowhere a great wave surged up from astern and caught them unawares when they were just a hundred yards from safety. All three vessels were pitched and tossed violently and took on water as the crews tumbled around inside. Moments later, with the wave dissipating on the beach, only two of the boats remained afloat, their crews frantically bailing. The one carrying the Davies brothers and a third crewman, Ted Bussey, was completely swamped and sinking quickly.

Cries of alarm quickly went up from the shore, rapidly spreading along the promenade and further inland. The cacophony of distress soon reached the ears of the coxswain of Cromer's No. 1 lifeboat, Henry Davies – brother of the two stricken men.

While he gathered his crew and ran to the lifeboat station at the pier head, local fishermen scrambled to haul out their own craft.

With the crabbing boat rapidly disappearing beneath the waves, the three crewmen had tumbled into the cold waters, the weight of their oilskins pulling them under. One was briefly spotted trying to swim for it, but within seconds he, too, had vanished from view. The horrified observers caught occasional, fleeting glimpses of the empty boat breaking the surface, and more worryingly began to make out pieces of timber floating in the vicinity, but there was no further sign of the three men.

The fishing vessels soon reached the spot and began their search, and there was a great splash as the motorised lifeboat, named the *Henry Blogg* after Cromer's – and Britain's – most decorated lifeboatman, slid down its ramp into the murky sea. Seeing that there was little for them to do at the site of the sinking, the lifeboatmen focused their efforts on preserving the lives of crews of the remaining two boats, shepherding them towards the shore.

But until bodies were found, there was always hope. One elderly local man had been alerted to the unfolding drama by the cries and commotion along the seafront and began to make his way there. Perhaps it wasn't wise – he was 77 years old and had a recent history of heart trouble. But he had his reasons. Not only were Jimmy and Frank Davies his nephews, but the old man was the former coxswain of the Cromer No. 1 lifeboat. He had retired seven years previously, but it was in his blood. It was what he did.

As he hurried down from the esplanade he must have heard the wails of the womenfolk, and perhaps passed the old fisherman trudging away from the sea ashen and breathless, who was heard to moan disconsolately, 'They've gone ...'

The effort of rushing to the seafront and the strain of fearing the worst for his colleagues and relatives proved too much for the elderly man. He had barely reached the water's edge when he collapsed. The search continued for two hours without success, but later in the evening the body of Jimmy Davies was washed ashore two miles along the coast. He was a father of four, and his brother Frank left three children behind; Ted Bussey was 21 and his wife was expecting their first child.

The coronation bunting was taken down in Cromer that night, and the flags lowered to half-mast. Long before that, the prostrate man who had tried to do his bit had been tended to and then gently carried back to his cottage on New Street.

His name was Henry Blogg.

Henry George Blogg, known to locals as Harry, was a Cromer man through and through. He was born in the little Norfolk seaside town in a cottage close enough to the sea to be able to hear the waves lapping up the beach. Although some accounts of his life are somewhat coy about it, Harry was an illegitimate child and the identity of his birth father is unknown. He was born on 6 February 1876 to 20-year-old Ellen Blogg, a domestic servant still living with her parents. Like many men in Cromer at that time, Ellen's father earned his living on the sea. When Ellen got married five years after Henry's birth, it was to another fisherman, John Davies, who lived with his family just a short distance away on Garden Street. His father was in the same line of work, and was coxswain of the Cromer lifeboat the *Benjamin Bond Cabbell*, named after a local worthy. James, who would become Henry Blogg's step-grandfather, had guided the Cromer lifeboat to the rescue when the Middlesbrough brig *Emulous* got into difficulties during a gale in 1870. (Henry himself would cox a lifeboat of the same name, the successor to the one in question.)

Ellen Blogg married the hero's son James in in 1881, and had four further children by him.[1]

They obviously took their birth father's surname, while Henry continued to go by his mother's maiden name. Ellen died at the age of just 44, when Henry himself was only 24. John Davies, his step-father, married again (in fact, it was to Ellen's cousin, Martha Blogg); but by then Henry was making his own way in life and in that same year he took a wife of his own: a local woman called Anne Brackenbury, whose father was yet another a fisherman. Henry and Anne set up home in South Cottages on New Street, the same street in which he was born (possibly the same 'Swallow Cottage' in which he was living in as recorded in the 1939 Register). Relatives later described Annie as 'the beauty of Cromer', a frail woman but witty and talkative; Harry didn't like talking of his exploits and honours, but a proud Annie made up for his reticence. She was a 'good coxswain's wife', who used to take phone and other messages and

---

1. The Davies family continued to serve the Cromer lifeboat. In 2018, John Davies, representing the eighth generation of continuous service, retired as coxswain.

keep other crewmen's wives and families informed of the progress of a mission.

Henry and Anne had two children, but sadly neither were long-lived. Son Henry James died in infancy, and daughter Annie (known as 'Queenie') passed away at the age of 27. Harry was close to Queenie, and her death hit him particularly hard – in fact, his nephew 'Shrimp' (see below for the origins of his nickname) would later say that he was a changed man afterwards. Harry had always sworn a lot, in 'almost every sentence', in fact. But after Queenie's death he never swore again and was more subdued and less talkative.

All of the men mentioned above, and many others like them, would have had an intimate knowledge of the sea, especially the coastal waters off Cromer, and how to work small sailing boats in all conditions.

Harry was said to have been a bright scholar, but by the age of 11 he was already putting to sea with his step-father in pursuit of the famous Cromer crab, and by 1894, when he was 18, he volunteered to man the Cromer lifeboat. There had been a lifeboat operating out of Cromer since 1804, originally under the auspices of the Norfolk Shipwreck Association before being absorbed into the RLNI about twenty years before Harry's birth. Harry started in the *Benjamin Bond Cabbell*, which we've already seen in action with his step-grandfather in charge, but it wasn't long before this was replaced by the *Louisa Heartwell*, in which Harry became second coxswain. One of the first missions in which his name features is the rescue of three tourists in difficulties, rowing to their aid and helping to haul them out of the water. Three years later, in 1906, he and the rest of his crew (he appears to have been acting-coxswain on this occasion) were watched by crowds on the shore as they rowed to the assistance of a schooner called the *Zuma*, flying a flag of distress in heavy seas. It took the men of the *Louisa Heartwell* about an hour of strenuous hauling to reach her. Members of his crew were able to board her and work the ship into Yarmouth.

Harry becoming Cromer's coxswain was not a foregone conclusion by any means, as a family member revealed. In the 1960s a documentary about Harry Blogg appeared on Anglia Television and featured interviews with two men who had served with him: Jack Davies, his half-brother, and Harry's nephew, Henry Davies. Henry was named after his uncle, but because when he was a baby Harry remarked that he looked like a shrimp, 'Shrimp' became the nickname by which he was known throughout his life. And it was Shrimp who explained that the position of coxswain was decided by a vote among all the lifeboatmen – and Harry Blogg got in by just one vote.

The Longest Day

First Gold Medal

The alarm was raised in the early hours of 9 January 1917. The Greek steamer *Pyrin* had come adrift from her moorings and was being tossed and carried at the mercy of the wind and currents with her crew on board. This was, of course, at the height of the First World War and Cromer, like many other places, was depleted of young men. So it was that Harry Blogg's crew that day had an average age of around 50; Harry himself was 41, while one crewman was said to have been nearly 70. The conditions would have been testing for men of any age. It took a group of soldiers from the town, standing waist-deep in the freezing and choppy water, to keep the lifeboat steady and prevent her from capsizing while she was being launched. Then, fight though they might to reach the *Pyrin*, before they could make any real headway Harry and his men were carried west along the coast for up to a mile till they were in danger of being dashed against the pier. Eventually, however, they managed to work the boat far enough out to allow them to safely set sail, after which it was a relatively simple task to make for the Greek ship, which they came alongside at around 2 pm after a four-hour slog. An hour later they had landed the grateful crew ashore, but Harry's men had barely had time to relax and get warm when there was another reminder that this was a time of war – the sound of a violent explosion echoed across the water.

The SS *Fernebo*, laden with timber, had struck a mine. It had detonated with enough force to completely split the ship in two.

Incredibly, there was only one fatality, and the rest of the crew huddled together in the after part of the vessel as it wallowed in the heavy seas. The weary Cromer lifeboatmen didn't hesitate to launch the *Louisa Heartwell* once more. This time it was even harder to get the boat beyond the breakers. They fought with aching muscles for half an hour, but Harry finally had to call a halt to the attempt and the boat was returned to shore for the time being.

By early evening the two halves of the *Pyrin* drifted independently of each other towards the shore, and the stern section with the crew still clinging to it came to rest alongside a long wooden groyne that reached about 400 feet into sea to the east of the lifeboat station. It was decided to attempt a rescue using rockets to fire a line to the remains of the *Pyrin*, employing some of the powerful army searchlights positioned on the clifftop for the detection of airborne enemy attackers. But when this effort failed, too, Blogg and his men felt they had no choice but to face the biting winds and put to sea in the *Louisa Heartwell* again. This they did at about 9.30, but the heavy seas hadn't abated and, five broken and three lost oars later, Harry was obliged to take the boat back to shore yet again. But the Cromer men weren't beaten. They rested briefly, found new oars, and after a fierce battle with the elements finally reached the remaining eleven cold and bedraggled men on what was left of the *Pyrin* and helped them into the lifeboat. Six others had almost made it to the beach in their own ship's boat when it capsized, but they were helped onto dry land by soldiers and townsfolk. Only one man, the ship's chief engineer who went missing just after the explosion, lost his life that day thanks to Harry Blogg, his crew and the people of Cromer.

'And so a wonderful day and night's work ended', said one newspaper account.

This was a historic event in the history not only of the Cromer lifeboat, but the RNLI itself. Harry Blogg was awarded his gold medal for gallantry the following month, and the second coxswain a silver. But that wasn't all. The herculean efforts, courage and refusal to be beaten displayed by the whole crew during this rescue was directly responsible for the RNLI deciding to introduce a new bronze award, and the Cromer men were the first recipients. Commander Basil Hall RN, an inspector of lifeboats for the RNLI and a gallantry medal recipient himself, declared that he had never, in all his experience, seen greater gallantry shown by any lifeboat crew.

The *Georgia*

Second Gold Medal

At 7.30 on the night of Monday November 21 1927, some wreckage and a ship's lifeboat bearing the name SS *Georgia* washed up on shore at Mundesley, a few miles south of Cromer, and was found by the coastguard. Although it was later to emerge that the boat had never been used but had just been dislodged from the ship in a gale, it was still a sign that all was not well.

The *Georgia*, transporting crude oil from the Persian Gulf to Grangemouth, had hit the Haisborough Sands at around midnight on the Sunday. By 2.30 am the following day, a distress call was sent by a Dutch steamer called the *Trent* (relayed via a British ship, the *Corsair*) to the lifeboat station at Cromer: the *Georgia*, also Dutch, was showing red lights and in a 'sinking condition and a danger to shipping'. In fact, such was the force of the collision and the subsequent pounding by the waves that the 5,111-ton steamer had broken in two, the sections floating away from each other as had happened with the *Pyrin*. The *Trent* had arrived on scene and managed to rescue sixteen men from the stern, but the fore part of the ship, where another fifteen had taken refuge in the wheelhouse, drifted away and out of sight. The only good news was that, this being an oil transport ship, she was divided below decks into numerous sealed oil storage compartments, and this design was helping keep her two halves afloat despite the catastrophic damage.

These survivors were packed into the small space, talking in muted voices, smoking and hoping that the gale-force seas and the sands beneath them wouldn't destroy the only thing that was keeping them alive. Unknown to them, they were in for the long haul, with no food or drink to sustain them. For the time being, they were helpless.

Harry Blogg and his crew responded to the SOS and put out in the *HF Bailey*, the latest design of RNLI motor lifeboat, but soon returned to within sight of the station to convey by semaphore message that there were no crewmen on board the section of the vessel they had encountered. Fortunately, this did not mean that the remaining *Georgia* crewmen had been washed overboard: Harry and his crew had happened upon the after part of the ship, unaware that this had already been evacuated by the *Trent*. Rather than returning to land, the *HF Bailey* stayed near the stern section to warn off approaching shipping.

As the new day dawned, crowds of concerned spectators began to gather along the cliffs of Cromer and watched as attempt after attempt was made to get to the stranded fifteen men on the forward half of the wreck. The Gorleston lifeboat put out from Yarmouth but was beaten back by the brutal seas every time. The Southwold boat appeared late in the afternoon, but like the one from Gorleston was tossed about like a cork and no more successful. By now, more help was on hand in the form of the navy destroyer HMS *Thannet*, which had been sent to relieve the *Trent* and allow her to take the crewmen she had extricated to safety.

There was a scare later in the evening when the Gorleston lifeboat, on her way back to base, was reported missing by the coastguard – but to everyone's relief a later message announced that the boat and her exhausted crew had 'just hoved into sight'.

There was an unusual development during the afternoon. Concerned by dangerous and ineffectual attempts to save the men in the wheelhouse of the *Georgia*, the Cromer coastguard contacted the Board of Trade's coastguard section in London with an urgent request for a new type of equipment: 'a special pistol which will hurl a line 150 yards'. In something reminiscent of a scene from a thriller, a speedy Daimler was hired to race the device from the East India Docks, through the streets of London and north to the location of the drama. 'It will be a race against time,' a Board of Trade official told the press. As it happened, the special pistol was not needed – for Harry Blogg and his men were now about to take their turn.

It was getting dark, but HMS *Thannet* was using her powerful searchlight to illuminate the scene for the *HF Bailey* as she made her approach. Although the conditions were improving somewhat, it still it wasn't easy, and it took Harry three goes to manoeuvre her into the right position. The Cromer boat nearly overturned and sustained damage when she was thrown by a wave on to the bulwarks of the wreck, and all the time the crew were breathing in vapour from thousands of gallons of crude oil leaking from ship. But on the third attempt, Harry Blogg (who was still unaware that half the crew had already been saved) was able to get his boat alongside the remains of the *Georgia* and just about hold her steady. The wet and shivering men quickly emerged from their hiding place and caught a rope thrown up to them by one of the *HF Bailey*'s crew. Harry called to those waiting above to keep calm and come one at a time, and, after thirty-nine trying, hair-raising hours, the men began to make the descent of around 10 feet to safety. They had taken it upon themselves to come off in order of age, youngest to the oldest, with the exception of the captain who, according to custom, stayed until last. They later reported that they had all but given up hope of being rescued before what was left of the ship disintegrated around them. Once they were all on board the lifeboat they were given bread, cheese and cakes, which must have felt like the finest banquet imaginable after what they had been through.

At the end of this ordeal, not a single life had been lost and the final fifteen survivors were all 'loud in their praise of lifeboatmen, who handled their boat splendidly'. Henry guided his battered boat towards Yarmouth, where the seamen were landed sometime between 7 and 8 pm and provided with clean, dry clothes at the Sailors' Home.

It transpired that the special pistol that had been raced from London had been put on board the Gorleston lifeboat, but Harry had effected the rescue before they could join the effort. As they had departed the *Georgia*, the Cromer crew had seen their Gorleston comrades in the distance heading to the wreck and tried to signal them that all were now saved, but this wasn't seen and the unfortunate Gorleston men were out all night.

Harry and his men spent the night in Yarmouth, but the next day, Thursday 24 November, hundreds of people lined the Cromer cliffs and filled the beach and pier, waiting to welcome their returning heroes. Rockets were fired, church bells tolled and there was a sort of semi-official reception committee of district councillors on the pier. The chairman of council declared 'Cromer is proud of you, Norfolk is proud of you, England is proud of you', and many of the spectators were moved to tears. However, the *HF Bailey* crew hadn't expected all this and were somewhat taken aback, especially Harry himself who was a notoriously publicity-shy, quiet, taciturn man. When he was ushered forward to have his hand shaken, it was noted that he appeared 'more disturbed by the warmth of the reception than by the danger of his rescue task'. And when asked to make a short speech in reply, the only contribution he could muster was 'What's all this fuss about? I would rather be home out of this … It was all in a day's work and we have done our duty.'

It was left to one of the rescued crew of the *Georgia*, Leslie Kaye, to put it into perspective:

'It was the most wonderful piece of navigation any of us have ever seen. It seemed an impossible task … Our crew nearly caused a disaster in their panic to get off, but Coxswain Henry Blogg … steadied us … with his warning shout of "Steady now, boys. One at a time."'

The following month, Harry received a gold bar to be added to his original medal. The rest of the crew got bronze medals, and they included the brothers R. and W. H. Davies; father and son J. and J. Davies; and another father and son, W. and Jim Davies. Harry, as an adopted member of the Davies family almost from birth, was thus one of seven representatives of the same family taking part in the rescue – a situation not untypical of the whole of his lifeboat career.

Harry at War

The Third Gold Medal
Despite Henry Bloggs' third gold medal-winning achievement being a landmark in the history of the RNLI, it barely caused a ripple in the national press. The reason for this is clear when the date is borne in

mind: August, 1941. The war was now in full-swing, enemy fighters and bombers were over Britain, and British merchant and naval vessels were being sunk on a daily basis.[2] And outstanding though this particular rescue was, it was one of many being undertaken by the RNLI at this difficult time. It was the organisation's busiest year since the previous war, with the RNLI rescuing more people in one wartime year than during the five years of peace leading up to the conflict, one result of which was the need for a national campaign to appeal for more donations.

Early on the morning of 6 August, Harry's station got news of a number of vessels on the way from London to Newcastle having round aground during the night. Seven ships of a merchant convoy, steaming under a Royal Navy escort, had come to grief on Haisborough Sands at just before 4 am.

There is some doubt as to the cause of the disaster. A thick sea mist has been mentioned, but the weather is also said to have been stormy and the two things could hardly have obtained at the same time. It's said that the lightship marking the Sands could only show its light for ten minutes when the convoy was approaching because of the blackout regulations, but there are even rumours of an E-boat attack causing a change of direction, as well as allegations of pure and simple navigational errors. Whatever the primary cause or causes, the leading convoy escort – HMT *Agate*, a trawler converted into an anti-submarine vessel – was the first to become stranded, followed by the *Oxshott*, *Afon Towy*, *Deerwood*, *Betty Hindley*, *Aberhill*, *Gallois* and *Taara*.

One of the escorting naval destroyers had already lowered a boat to see what help it could provide, and Henry and his men launched the *HF Bailey* immediately, reaching the Sands at about 9.40. Sadly, by the time the Cromer boat came on scene the attempted naval rescue had turned into disaster. Twelve of her crew had been washed overboard in the stormy conditions and had drowned.

With RAF planes circling overhead to offer protection from any enemy attack, Harry initially steered for the *Oxshott*, the first of the

---

2. It could also be that there was a reluctance to publicise the loss of cargo ships.

merchantmen to have hit the sandbank. He performed the risky manoeuvre of deliberately running the *HF Bailey* onto the *Oxshott's* almost submerged deck, allowing his crew to get sixteen men off that ship, after which Harry turned his attentions to the *Gallois*. There, the coxswain turned the *HF Bailey's* head into the wind and kept her on station while a further thirty-one crewmen either jumped or descended by rope into the refuge of the lifeboat. There was almost a calamity when one sailor tumbled into the sea, but Harry's men managed to get hold of him and pull the bedraggled man aboard to join his shipmates. The overcrowded lifeboat now turned away from the Haisborough Sands and delivered the rescued men to one of the two escorting destroyers, before heading back to see what else could be done.

In the meantime, Comer's second lifeboat, the *Harriet Dixon*, had made her way to the scene. Harry, deciding she needed an experienced man at her helm, moved his own nephew and second coxswain, John J. ('Jack') Davies over to her to act as her coxswain. Taking the *HF Bailey* back into the action, Harry Blogg oversaw the removal of forty-one men from the *Deerwood* and the *Betty Hindley* and once again handed them over to one of the destroyers. There were still more men to be saved – but by this point the *HF Bailey* had taken such a pounding that Harry had to pull her out of the action. There was no shortage of lifeboats on hand, however, since the Gorleston boat had joined the *Harriet Dixon*.

Because of the paucity of contemporary reporting of the day's events, statistics on the saved and the lost tend to vary from one account to another. There were said to have been 147 men rescued altogether, over a hundred accountable to the two Cromer boats, of which Harry's *HF Bailey* claimed the lion's share. In addition to the men from the destroyer's boat who had drowned trying to effect a rescue, approximately sixteen men of the *Agate* were lost.

It's worth mentioning here that another area of confusion is the actual name of one of the ships Harry attended to that day. She is often called the *Paddy Hendly* (even in the RNLI's own magazine at the time), and Edward Wake-Walker, in his book *Lifeboat Heroes*, alludes to the fact that when the RNLI went to check on the ships involved there was no vessel of that name in the Lloyds list. He even conjectures that her crewmen deliberately gave their rescuers the wrong name for some reason. The truth is probably simpler and more innocent. With *Betty Hindley* and *Paddy Hendly* being so similar, I suspect the misunderstanding was due to different accents and pronunciations (perhaps Northern Irish?) – not to mention exhausted crewmen with bigger things to worry about than whether they had been understood correctly.

Harry Blogg and his crew attended a ceremony at Cromer's Regal Cinema to receive their medals – only for them to all rush off to answer a distress call before the presentation could take place. Thankfully, this shout proved to be a false alarm. Harry returned to receive the second gold bar to his original gold medal; Jack Davies got a silver, as did the Gorleston coxswain Charles Johnson. Other lifeboat men received bronze medals.

The *English Trader*

Harry Blogg's three gold medal tally was matched by only one other man – Sir William Hillary, founder of the RNLI (who earned three in addition to an honorary one). Blogg also won the silver medal four times, the George Cross and the British Empire Medal.[3] Oddly enough, one of the rescues for which Harry is most famous, and the one in which he came closest to losing his life, did not earn him a gold medal. (Perhaps handing out two gold medals to one man in the space of three months was considered too much, no matter how great the courage shown!)

At the end of October 1941, the *English Trader*, sailing north from London, began to lag behind the navy-escorted convoy of which she was a part because of engine problems. After fending off an attack from a German bomber but still struggling to maintain speed, she ran aground on Hammond Knoll, twenty-five miles off Cromer in the early hours of Sunday 26 October.

---

3. But not the Victoria Cross. He is sometimes referred to as Henry Blogg, VC, but this is due to the way in which the RNLI gold medal is sometimes informally called the lifeboat service's 'VC'.

The lifeboat crew were called out at just after 8 am, and the *HF Bailey* had reached the *English Trader* just before noon. According to Shrimp, Harry Blogg described his first view of the ship as 'the most appalling sight he had ever seen'. Her back was broken and the crashing waves were smashing her into bits. Unknown to them yet, five of her crew were already dead. Shrimp explained that on sandbanks, 'the sea doesn't obey the rules … the tide as much as anything causes rough water'. Harry couldn't get closer than a quarter of a mile from the wreck, and decided to lay off her in deep water and wait for 'slack water'. Several of his younger crewmen were itching to take their chances and give it a go, however. At first Harry was insistent that it was too dangerous, but eventually, at almost 2.20 in the afternoon, he gave way to their pleas. They got to within a quarter of a mile once more, when disaster struck. What Shrimp described as the biggest sea he had ever seen caught the *HF Bailey* on the port side, and the next thing he knew, he, Harry and three other men were floundering in the raging sea. Harry and the second coxswain were the first to be pulled out, and Harry immediately resumed charge of the vessel and managed the rescue of the other men. Despite this, Harry Blogg and the others who had gone over the side were 'all pretty well done for' and the *HF Bailey*'s propellers were snagged with ropes, so it was decided to head for Yarmouth. Edward Allen, the lifeboat's signalman, had been the last to be rescued and was unconscious when brought aboard. He rallied briefly and managed to speak, but it was a false dawn, and before they could reach port he had died.

The lifeboat got to Yarmouth at about 6 pm and the crew reported to the Sailors' Home for a change of clothes and something to eat, and from there went to Yarmouth Hospital suffering from exposure. A hospital spokesman told the press that Harry was too weak to undress himself. Yet, incredibly, he and the others were away again at 5 the next morning for another attempt.[4] This time the conditions were not nearly so bad, and Harry and his crew were able to take twelve of the remaining crewmen off the wreck, while the Gorleston boat

---

4. The Gorleston lifeboat had taken over from the Cromer one, but had been equally unsuccessful.

rescued the remainder. The Cromer second coxswain, John James Davies, described the rescue as 'one of the roughest we have ever had to perform', and years later Shrimp wistfully commented, 'I've always believed that if we'd listened to Henry and waited till slack water, then we would have rescued that crew'. For his part in this operation, Harry was awarded the silver medal, and the rest of the crew bronzes.

Harry Blogg's four silver and three gold medals made him the most decorated lifeboatman in history, but he remained a modest and reserved man. Shrimp spoke of how difficult it was to get to know him properly, even adding 'I don't think anybody ever *really* knew him.' He hated retirement from the lifeboats and fishing, and spent a lot of time at the beach, still supervising the hire of deckchairs as he had from an early age (there were still bathing machines on wheels when he had first started). But Shrimp also thought that in old age Harry secretly enjoyed his fame; he was something of a celebrity in his later years, and people would seek him out to hear his tales and have their pictures taken with him. After his retirement, the Cromer No. 1 lifeboat was named after him.

Harry suffered from heart problems in later life. He died in 1954 at the age of 78, almost exactly a year after his collapse during the tragic drowning of his nephews. Harry was a national figure by this time and there were obituaries in most of the newspapers of the day – but this one in *The Times*, written by a woman called Joanna Orr, has a nicely personal touch and its charm owes something to the fact that it is less about lifeboat heroics and more about Henry the man:

The passing of Coxswain Henry Blogg brings back a flood of memories of my childhood. Each summer my parents would take a furnished cottage near the old lifeboat house, and many a storm-tossed August night I have watched my father strain and push with other helpers to run the lifeboat down into the surf. Henry Blogg was a wonderful figure to watch, standing balanced and commanding as the boat was sent sideways and tossed back so many times through the breakers.

In his ordinary occupation of letting out bathing huts, deck-chairs, and costumes, Henry Blogg was a favourite with us children, He was a great tease, but always good tempered and extraordinarily modest. Each year, at the end of our long holiday at Cromer, we were invited to Swallow Cottage, and received chocolates and sweets from Mr and Mrs Blogg and their daughter Queenie as parting gifts, and Mrs Blogg would show us with pride her husband's many cups and medals.

I still see Henry Blogg as a wonderful, rugged, heroic person, with the quietest voice and most modest bearing I have ever encountered.

Part VII

In the Line of Duty

Chapter 31

Coincidences

Robert Patton

On the morning of Wednesday 7 February 1934, Albert Thompson, a 30-year-old South Shields man and master of the tug *Trover*, manoeuvred his vessel into position to attach a towing line to the salvage ship *Disperser* (the former Royal Navy gunboat HMS *Bonetta*). The two ships left Whitby bound for Ramsgate, but, after a time, when they were about eight miles off Flamborough Head, Thompson received a message from the *Disperser* informing him that she was 'having trouble with water' and requesting that they put into nearby Bridlington Bay. He duly changed course, and once at Bridlington he received orders to turn back north and tow the *Disperser* to Hartlepool (her home port). They had only made a few miles on the return journey when, close to Scarborough, the conditions began to change. The wind strengthened and the seas got heavier, becoming 'mountainous' according to the *Trover*'s own log. Soon, the tug was 'just keeping steering way on her'.

It was now the early hours of Thursday 8 February and dark; the height of the waves and the rising and falling of the two vessels meant that the lights of the *Disperser*, at the end of a '130-fathom' (260-yard) rope, were only visible intermittently. The ship herself was invisible.

At 3.30 am, Thompson received a message from Captain Doran of the salvage ship: 'In distress; want immediate assistance.' He immediately ordered the releasing of the tow rope and turned his tug to go to the *Disperser*'s aid. Before he could get there, another communication arrived: 'Take us off – we are sinking fast.' This was accompanied by the firing of distress flares.

Despite his tug being thrown around by the stormy seas, by 4.30 Thompson had managed to get the *Trover* close enough to attempt to get the eight crew from their sinking salvage vessel. After the second man had been taken on board, Thompson's tug was swept away from the *Disperser*, and it took several attempts in the horrendous conditions before he was ready to extract any more. Thompson described the sea as being at times 'like a cliff'; both rescuers and rescued were in grave danger at every moment, and it was an operation that required nerves of steel. But eventually, at around 5.30 am, five more men were able to leap into his tug. This left just one more – but now there was a problem.

This last member of the *Disperser*'s crew, the ship's cook, was not only young (possibly no more than a boy – see below) but disabled and not nearly as capable as making the leap between the two vessels as his colleagues. Fortunately, help was at hand.

The distress flares had been sighted by coastguards at around 4 am, and the Runswick lifeboat station a few miles up the Yorkshire coast was alerted. Coxswain Robert Patton was soon mustering with his crew, ready to launch the appropriately named *Always Ready* motor lifeboat. By 4.25 they had put out to sea, and they were on the scene, about two miles offshore, an hour later – almost at the same time that the last men but one had boarded the *Trover*.

The smaller *Always Ready* was able to get a little closer to the *Disperser* than the tug had. Most reports of what happened next are at variance in some of the detail from the following account – but this is put together from the words of the *Always Ready*'s second coxswain George Taylor, as given in an interview soon after the event, so is likely to be the most accurate version even though it diminishes Richard Patton's part to some small extent.

Several of the lifeboat's men assembled ready to grab the final crewman, the ship's cook, Richard Eglon. But at the crucial moment, when Eglon was about to jump and the lifeboatmen were reaching out to catch him, the lifeboat didn't quite close the gap as much as expected – and the consequences proved calamitous. Patton, making a grab for Eglon, overbalanced and fell overboard but managed to grasp the side of the *Disperser*, and was left dangling over the side. Sea-swell then carried the lifeboat about thirty yards away from the ship. Second Coxswain Taylor gave the order to close the gap, but as the *Always Ready* neared the salvage ship she was washed against her; Eglon took the opportunity to jump in, but Patton was crushed between the two vessels. He was quickly hauled in, and Taylor made full speed for home.

(Just as an example of the conflicting reports of the event, one describes Patton being somewhat saved by his lifebelt, while another reports him as saying that he kept a determined grip on the *Disperser* to avoid dropping into the sea because he *wasn't* wearing a lifebelt.)

The *Always Ready* reached Runswick at 6.15 am, and the *Disperser* finally sank around three hours later. When the news first broke, all of the attention was on Thompson and his heroic saving of the majority of the crew; the rescue of Eglon and Patton's adventure and injuries, which appeared to be minor, were a footnote to the main story. However, upon being examined on shore, a concerned doctor had the coxswain immediately sent to the Whitby War Memorial Cottage Hospital. There, further investigation revealed that as well as broken ribs, Patton had fractured his pelvis in three places (something that at worst can cause catastrophic internal bleeding), at least one of his vertebrae, along with other injuries. Two days later he was able to provide details of what had happened to an RNLI official, but a week after that he succumbed to his injuries.

Bob Patton, 46, was a fisherman who had joined the lifeboat service in 1904 as a 16-year-old, and had been Runswick Bay's coxswain since 1931 (his father had been second coxswain for twenty-seven years and had won the RNLI bronze medal ten years earlier). The only gap in his career came when he served on navy minesweepers during the First World War.

In 1914, he had been among the crew of the *Henry Vernon*, one of several lifeboats fighting to save those on board the wreck of the *Rohilla* (see Part 5, Chapter 21). Building coincidence upon coincidence, Richard Eglon, who returned to his Whitby home having suffering no adverse effects from his ordeal, was the son of the Richard Eglon who had been Patton's coxswain on that mission and who had been awarded the RNLI silver medal for his efforts. Eglon junior's disability isn't known, but is described as a 'leg problem' in one report. And he may have been very young indeed. He is referred to as a 'youth'; the only Richard Eglon I have been able to trace who comes close to fitting the bill was born in Sunderland in 1924 – which would mean he was only 10 at the time of the *Disperser* drama.

Patton's posthumously awarded gold medal was presented to his widow by the Prince of Wales at the RNLI's annual meeting in London a couple of months after her husband's death. Mrs Patton herself was generously cared for. The RNLI provided her with a pension at a level normally issued to Royal Navy petty officers killed in action, and paid for the funeral (attended by 4,000 people). She was awarded a further pension by the Carnegie Hero Fund Trust, which also contributed towards the education of her daughter.

Another honour was bestowed upon her husband in September 1934, when the Runswick lifeboat was renamed. The original name was quite correctly retained, since the lifeboat had been bought on the understanding that it would be called that by the recently deceased Elizabeth Brown, the benefactor who had paid for it. Thus on 20 September, at a well-attended ceremony, the Princess Royal broke a bottle of wine against the bow of the lifeboat with the words 'I name this lifeboat *Robert Patton – The Always Ready*, and I wish her all success in all calls that are made upon her.' A rocket was fired into the air, the national anthem was sung, and the newly named boat sailed out into the bay with an escort of three other local lifeboats.

She served until being sold off in 1954, when she became a pilot boat for the Bristol channel. Later, after a restoration, she was relaunched and put on display in Gloucester docks.

As in the case of Charles Fremantle (Part 4, Chapter 18), it's a painful but not unreasonable course to query the award of the RNLI gold medal to Bob Patton. That his ultimate sacrifice in attempting to save a life should be marked can't be questioned, and the same goes for the support offered to his family. Emotionally, the gold medal feels right; but examined in the cold light of day, he did what hundreds of lifeboat men had done before and have done since without receiving the ultimate award: put to sea in stormy weather and attempted to save life. Does the fact that he suffered the great misfortune of falling overboard and being fatally injured elevate his actions to that of a gold medal achievement? Surely, if anyone deserved that honour it was Albert Thompson, the master of the tug, who was not recognised at all by the RNLI: not so much as a silver or bronze medal. One of the crewmen of the *Disperser* said after his ordeal: 'We owe our lives to this gallant little tug and to the wonderful seamanship of her skipper. His handling of the boat in one of the worst gales I have ever experienced was superb.' Let us remember brave Bob Patton, while not forgetting the seven lives saved thanks to the skill and courage of the master and crew of the *Trover*.

Chapter 32

I Don't Think We'll Make It ...

William Gammon

On Tuesday 29 April 1947, a long, snaking funeral procession made its way through the fishing village of Mumbles, South Wales. Shops and businesses were shut, curtains were drawn; umbrellas were raised among the people lining the route against the heavy rain, water dripped from the capes of the policemen, and the lifeboatmen heading the cortege were dressed in the full gear of their voluntary trade, including waterproof coats, life jackets and sou'westers. The eight coffins they escorted were draped in Union Jacks. These caskets contained the men who, as one newspaper put it, 'died with those they could not save', and chief among them was coxswain of the Mumbles lifeboat, William Gammon. His last known words were said to have been 'I don't think we'll make it, boys, but we'll try anyway ...'

Six days earlier, The SS *Samtampa* had found herself in trouble during a storm in the Bristol channel. She was just four years old, and a 'liberty ship'. These were built in the US and sold to Britain to help replace merchant vessels lost to enemy attacks – but because of wartime necessity they were built cheaply and quickly, and their construction was of dubious quality. She had set sail from Middlesbrough, on her way to Newport for dry dock repairs, and was 'in ballast', so sitting higher in the water than if she had been carrying a cargo. Her captain was Neale Sherwell, from New Zealand; most of her crew of thirty-nine were from the north-east of England.

When, by the 23rd, the wind increased in ferocity and the seas became rougher, the *Samtampa* became increasingly hard to handle, till eventually she found herself being carried towards the Welsh coast near Porthcawl, and the vicinity of the Nash Shoal. Sherwell ordered the dropping of the anchors, which slowed but didn't halt his vessel's progress towards the shore. His radio operator was instructed to call for assistance. Finally, the strain became too much for the ship's anchor cables, and the SS *Samtampa* was completely at the mercy of the sea and wind, which duly drove her onto the rocks at a place called Sker Point near Porthcawl, about thirteen miles north-east of the Mumbles lifeboat station as the crow flies and 300 yards from shore. It's highly likely that the impact would have badly damaged any ship, but liberty ships were notorious for having been welded together rather than riveted, and this may have played a part in the fact that she was soon in three pieces. The bow was carried hundreds of yards out to sea, but most of the crew are thought to have taken refuge in the mid-section or stern.

At 6 pm, William Davies, the Mumbles lifeboat mechanic, fired the maroons into the air that would summon the crew.

The initial plan was for tugs to be sent out, but their skippers decided that the seas were too high for them. Instead, William Gammon and his Mumbles lifeboat were asked to launch.

When volunteer William Howells got the summons, the conditions were so bad that a relative urged him not to go. But Howells had been a recipient of such aid himself after having been torpedoed during the First World War. 'I must go,' he replied. 'They came to me when I was shipwrecked. I could not leave them out there.'

Because it was likely to be an arduous mission, coxswain Gammon decided not to take veteran crewmen Michael and Charles Davies. The latter was a survivor of the 1903 Mumbles lifeboat capsize when six crewmen were lost, and it was a decision that would spare his life once again, but was not such good news for his replacement Richard Smith, who was due to be married at the end of the week.

The *Edward, Prince of Wales* herself was also a veteran, being of an old open design with neither cabin nor radio. She was due to be replaced in time by a more modern vessel, but this proved to be her final voyage.

Gammon and his crew set off shortly after mustering, in winds gusting at times to eighty miles an hour, causing chaos on land as well as it sea, but they were soon back. Gammon had seen an Aldiss lamp signalling to him from the shore, but because of the height of the waves none of his men were able to discern what the message was. In fact, it was a member of the coastguard trying to relay the *Samtampa*'s location, which had been passed to them a few minutes after the lifeboat had set off; when the *Edward, Prince of Wales* approached the lifeboat station this information was hailed to them, and they turned and headed back out to sea. It was the last time the eight crewmen of the lifeboat were seen alive.

Many members of the public and emergency services had spent the night peering into the darkness, some even using car headlights to try to illuminate the scene, hoping to see survivors struggle ashore, hoping for news of the return of the lifeboat. It is said that for a time after the *Samtampa* had hit the rocks, the cries of the crew could be heard echoing across the waters above the howl of the wind. A rocket brigade made attempts to fire a line out to what was left of the ship, but the distance and the force ten or eleven winds made it an impossible task.

As soon as it began to get light the onlookers were able to pick their way among the debris and oil from the broken ship that was being washed ashore. And then, 400–500 yards along the coast a sickening discovery was made: *Edward, Prince of Wales*, upside down, empty.

As the day advanced, searchers started to come across oil-soaked bodies. Four were discovered in the morning, completely black with oil, and by mid-afternoon twenty corpses had been found, including seven of the eight lifeboatmen, still wearing their life jackets. The bodies of at least twenty-five men were eventually recovered. The majority appeared to have choked on the oil rather than having drowned, which might go some way towards explaining why the lifeboat crew lost their lives despite wearing buoyancy aids.

Exactly what happened to the William Gammon and the men of the Mumbles lifeboat was never established, but the most obvious theory was simply that a sudden great wave capsized her, flinging the crew out, perhaps even trapping some beneath her. Damage to the upper part of the boat showed that she had been thrown violently onto the shore, but this may have happened after the crew had been ejected.

HMCS *Chebogue*[1]

Mumbles didn't only lose a lifeboat coxswain, but a decorated one. In March 1941 William Gammon had won the RNLI bronze medal for his part in the rescue of ten sailors from the SS *Cornish Rose* in Swansea Bay, and three years later he became Mumbles' first, and so far only, recipient of the gold.

In October 1944, the Canadian frigate *Chebogue* was performing convoy duty on a voyage from Canada to Britain when, in mid-Atlantic, she came into the sights of *U-1227* and was badly damaged, but not sunk, by a torpedo. She was taken under tow by other convoy escorts until a tug rendezvoused with them and took over. They had almost reached Swansea Bay when, in stormy conditions on the 11th, the towing cable parted and the tug was obliged to head for the safety of deeper water while the *Chebogue* was carried into the bay till she struck bottom stern-first.

At around 7.30 pm William Gammon met up with Tom Ace, one of the Mumbles lifeboat volunteers.

'Tom, we've had no official intimation, but the WRNS [Women's Royal Naval Service] in the signal station have phoned to say there's a vessel in distress off Port Talbot.' Problems with other telephone lines being down meant that the Mumbles men weren't officially called out, but the pair decided to take the initiative and 'went round the various clubs to pick up the old stagers'. Because of the war, a lot of the younger men were away serving, so it would be a veteran crew. Two of Gammon's men were in their late sixties and two more in their early seventies. (In his subsequent account of the night's events, Tom Ace claimed that they had an 80-year-old among their crew.) They set off into the dark and stormy night, and reached the warship

---

1. HMCS = Her Majesty's Canadian Ship.

on a part of the coast that Ace said was known as 'the lifeboatman's dread'.

When the *Edward, Prince of Wales* got within hailing distance of the *Chebogue*, Gammon cried, 'Do you want to leave her?'

Eyeing the relatively tiny lifeboat standing off his frigate, her captain, Lieutenant Commander Oliver, replied, 'Can you save the lot of us?' There were forty-two sailors on board.

'Yes,' replied Gammon, 'if you keep your heads.'

Gammon worked out that, because of her position, the best plan of action would be to run around the stern and then alongside, pause just long enough to take what men he could, get quickly clear then repeat the whole operation as many times as it took to get them all off.

And although it took him twelve runs, he did just that, taking off three or four men at a time. It wasn't without incident. One officer missed the lifeboat and landed in the water, but was safely hauled out, and a sailor broke his leg when he landed awkwardly in the lifeboat. But the mission was completed, and a course set for home.

By the time Gammon deposited the rescued men safely on shore, the storm was still so bad that the lifeboat couldn't be returned to the boat house and had to be run into Swansea River till the winds died down. She was pretty battered, and was out of action for four months while repairs were made. The *Chebogue* was eventually taken clear of the rocks and also repaired, but never left Wales or saw action again, and was scrapped a few years later.

When William Gammon lost his life along with his friends and colleagues three years later, he left behind a wife and 18-year-old daughter. Mumbles was presented with a new lifeboat to replace the *Edward, Prince of Wales*; she was called the *Manchester and District XXX*, but *William Gammon* was added not long afterwards, and *William Gammon* was how she was referred to thereafter.

Chapter 33

Shepherd's Warning

Trevelyan Richards

At some point during August 2016, a person or persons unknown managed to evade multiple levels of security at the headquarters of the RNLI in Poole, Dorset, to commit a theft that shook the whole organisation and made national headlines. Only one item was removed: the gold medal for gallantry that had been posthumously awarded thirty-five years earlier to Trevelyan Richards, coxswain of the Penlee lifeboat. It had been donated to the safe keeping of the RNLI by his family. Despite massive publicity and a police investigation, the medal was never recovered. The case is now closed – unless any new information should come to light.

It was December 1981, and the *Union Star*, a 900-ton coaster, was making her maiden voyage. It was a relatively short trip between the port of Ijmuiden, Holland, to Arklow on Ireland's east coast, where she would deliver her cargo of fertiliser. Her captain was Henry Morton, and as well as his crew of four he had on board his wife (who one report says was pregnant) and two step-daughters, both in their teens.

The windy weather was worsening as he rounded the coast of Cornwall on the 19th, but Morton was an experienced sailor, and despite the *Union Star*'s engines failing he had men working on it and existing recordings of his communications with coastguards at around 6 pm indicate that he had no particular cause for concern. What none of the crew were aware of at the time was that seawater had somehow got into the *Union Star*'s fuel tanks, and no amount of tinkering with the engine was going to re-start her that evening. She would be floating helplessly, at the mercy of the ever-worsening storm.

Janet Madron was woken by her husband, Stephen, the Penlee lifeboat's mechanic, who wanted her to look at the ominously dramatic red morning sky. Later that day, Janet took one of their children to a friend's birthday party; when she returned, the weather had deteriorated and Stephen was on standby for the lifeboat. When the call came, Janet had a premonition that led her to say something she had never uttered before.

'I don't want you to go …'

'I've got to go. There's women and children out there.'

She knew he was right, of course, and all she could do was watch him leave their house for what would prove to be the last time.

With no progress being made on re-starting the *Union Star*'s engines and the wind increasing to storm-force, Morton still wasn't panicking but began to think of his family. He asked the coastguard about the possibility of helicopter extraction for his wife, Dawn, and the girls. Officers at the Falmouth station alerted RAF Culdrose but no rescue mission was considered necessary at that time, neither was there an emergency call-out for the lifeboat *Solomon Browne*. The coastguard put Morton in contact with a Penzance salvage tug but he was still hopeful of restarting the ship's engines, and when he was told that there would be a charge for the vessel to be called out whether or not her services were ultimately needed (which was standard practice) he declined that offer.

'All he is interested in is the money at the moment,' Morton told the coastguard, rather unfairly, but understandably. 'We are holding steady as we are. We don't seem to be drifting into land.'

Kevin Smith, 23 years old, was one of the Penlee lifeboat volunteers. He was supposed to have been still away at sea on 19 December because of his day job as a merchant seaman with the Cunard line, but his tour of duty had ended unexpectedly early. His sister recalled him muttering words to the effect of 'God, what a night!' as he left the house. His father listened into the radio chatter between lifeboat and the shore, something many family members of crewmen regularly did, and when it became clear that contact had been lost, he put it down to the atrocious weather. Kevin Smith's body would be one of the three never to be recovered.

Morton told the coastguard that his ship was not in difficulties 'touch wood', but at 6.30 pm he requested a weather update and was informed that the Land's End readings were Gale Force 8, gusting to 10 or 11 (11 being the penultimate category, a 'violent storm', and one step short of a hurricane). The skipper reported that his engines were still being worked on, and he would let them know once he was given a report from below on whether or not they could be fixed.

Janet Madron also often listened in to the communications between lifeboat and shore using a radio scanner. She heard Stephen inform the coastguard that they had managed to get four people off the *Union Star* so far. They were the last words she would hear spoken by her husband. From that point on, the only sound to be heard was the forlorn and unacknowledged repetitions of 'Falmouth coastguard to Penlee Lifeboat … Falmouth coastguard to Penlee Lifeboat …'

Despite his offer of help being dismissed by Morton, the Penzance tug put to sea. Perhaps the skipper sensed that he would be needed regardless of what the *Union Star*'s captain thought, and, anyway, it has been reported that Morton eventually heard from the ship's owners that they were prepared to recover any costs involved. But time was already running out.

Nigel Brockman, the *Solomon Browne*'s assistant mechanic, reported for duty when the shout went up that night, and so did his son Kevin. The latter was annoyed and disappointed to be turned away by coxswain Trevelyan Richards, partly because of his youth, but also because of the coxswain's rule of only allowing one member of any family in his crew on any one call-out. Richards' foresight and wisdom saved Kevin's life that night.

The first inkling that the situation might be taking a more ominous turn arose at around 7 pm. The *Union Star*'s engine problems naturally affected her power supply, which, in turn, meant that there was no radar. It was at this time that Morton's engineer got to the bottom of the problem – seawater in the fuel supply. The Falmouth coastguard sent an officer to the radar station at Gwennap Head to get a better fix on the *Union Star*'s position. The worrying news was relayed that the ship was two-and-a-half miles closer to land than Morton had assumed, and that she was drifting ever closer. Falmouth coastguard now requested that the navy rescue helicopter at Culdrose be scrambled.

Barrie Torrie was 33 and a fisherman. He and his wife had planned a night out on the 19th, and had arranged for someone to look after their two young children. When he got the call, their parting had none of the foreboding of the Madrons'. Barrie left the house with a breezy 'I'll see you later'.

The weather conditions, further to the east, where the Culdrose rescue helicopter was located, was not quite as extreme as it was where the drama was unfolding. That, together with the request for help not being an actual Mayday call, meant that the Sea King wasn't in the air as quickly as it would have been in a full-on emergency. Whether a full Mayday scramble would have made any difference is impossible to say.

Trevelyan Richards was a 56-year-old 'giant of a man with a big heart … a brilliant seaman' according to a fellow Mousehole resident. A fisherman, he had been coxswain of the Penlee lifeboat for eleven years. He was at home with his widowed mother when first warned that something might be in the offing. He had made his way to the lifeboat station, waiting with his selected crew to see whether they would be needed. The call came about twenty minutes after the helicopter had taken off.

By now, Morton on the *Union Star* had finally had one thing go right for him – one of his crew had managed to get a generator working, meaning that the ship's lights could be used to help the navy winchman when he made his descent to the deck. Unfortunately, getting the generator operational wasn't just the first thing that worked in favour of Morton and his crew that night; it was the only thing.

The gale was howling and the waves were mountainous beneath the Sea King as it vectored in towards the now illuminated *Union Star*. Such were the conditions that even when flying at an altitude of 400 feet, the helicopter was lashed by sea spray. The pilot, Lieutenant Commander Russell Smith (on detachment from the US Navy) manoeuvred his craft time and again to achieve a position from which he could begin lifting people off the deck, but the helicopter's line wasn't long enough to allow him to keep out of the way of the *Union Star*'s tall and violently swaying mast. Lieutenant Smith was obliged to inform Morton by radio link that it was simply unsafe for him to risk lowering a winchman.

By now, Trevelyan and the men of the *Solomon Browne* had made it to the coaster's location with his hand-picked crew of seven, as had the tug. Morton had lowered the *Union Star*'s anchor, but this presented a problem for the rescue vessels. The usual method of approach – to provide some respite from wind and wave as well as lessening the chances of being swept against the hull of the other vessel, was to come round to the relatively sheltered lee side. But at anchor, and with no engine power to adjust the ship's position, she was head-on to the waves: there was no lee side. The tug was unable to help, but Trevelyan Richards contacted Morton direct:

'Understand you had trouble with the chopper … Do you want for us to come alongside and take the women and children? Over.'

'Yes please. The helicopter is having a bit of difficulty getting to us, so if you could pop out I'll be very much obliged, over.'

When one final try by Lieutenant Smith in the Sea King failed, and with the *Union Star* now about 500 yards off the coast, the *Solomon Browne* became the only hope for those on board the ship, and she moved in. The gale was in full force, and Trevelyan battled through waves of twenty metres and more to get his lifeboat close to the ship. All the time, the *Union Star* was dragging on her anchor towards the shoreline, and disaster almost struck when the *Solomon Browne* was picked up and deposited on the deck of the ship. Incredibly, when she slipped backwards into the sea she was still intact and seaworthy. Thus, when he spotted a brief lull, Trevelyan was able to quickly move in.

Lieutenant Smith, from his aerial vantage point, saw flashes of orange life jackets as people scurried across the deck towards the waiting lifeboat, which took four people off before the two vessels were forced apart. Stephen Madron, the lifeboat's radio operator, initially reported that he had four men, then amended that to male and female. He also said that there were two people left on board, but this must also have been a misunderstanding in the heat of the moment, since if he had taken four into the *Solomon Browne* there must have been four still to be rescued (unless, of course, some had already been lost overboard).

Whatever the explanation, 'There's two left on board …' were the last words heard from Madron, or anyone on board the *Solomon Browne*. A loud, unidentifiable noise was heard over the radio, following which, much as everyone tried (including local fishing vessels) there was no further response.

And then the debris began to appear at the water's edge.

No one witnessed the fate that befell the *Solomon Browne*, and there is more than one theory as to what happened. One is that she hit a reef and sank or was overturned. Another was that there had been a catastrophic collision between ship and lifeboat. This was the conclusion of the Department of Transport enquiry, but it has been pointed out that the *Solomon Browne*'s engine compartment was discovered 300 yards from the *Union Star*, casting doubt on that scenario. And the 'noise' heard over the radio doesn't seem to have been the 'end' of the lifeboat and crew, because both the Sea King, returning to base to refuel, and the tug, caught glimpses of her – the latter over twenty minutes after the lifeboat's final transmission. Presumably, she must have sustained damage that put her radio out of action, either through collision or perhaps even capsizing and self-righting. The tug skipper reported her as being close to the shore. The *Union Star* was discovered on rocks close to the Tater Du lighthouse, about three miles south-west of Penlee Point, in the morning.

William 'Trevelyan' Richards was described in a BBC documentary as a 'hell of a character' who was without doubt 'the boss' on a shout. In addition to his posthumous gold medal, the crew of the *Solomon Browne* were awarded bronzes. Only eight of the sixteen bodies from both crews were ever found. Trevelyan was buried on Christmas Eve, some others on Boxing Day. Ever since that time, the famous Mousehole Christmas lights have been dimmed on 19 December from 8 till 9 pm.

Part VIII

Wartime

Chapter 34

Hartlepool's Hero

Bill Bennison

8 August 1917

Just before noon, while prowling the Bay of Biscay, Captain Saltzwedel of the German submarine *UC-71* spotted the British collier *Bolverton* about 130 miles off Ushant. He gave the 'dive' order and changed of course to intercept. Surfacing in the rear of the merchantman, *UC-71* opened fire.

On board, and waiting for the approach of *UC-71*, was Seaman Bill Bennison – but he wasn't a merchant seaman, and the *Bolverton* wasn't a true collier. She was HMS *Dunraven*, and she was a 'Q ship' – an armed vessel disguised as a merchantman, acting as submarine bait. Bill Bennison was a Royal Navy gunlayer, his job being to aim and elevate the particular gun he was assigned to.

The Q ship concept was a risky one for both sides. Sometimes, the element of surprise led to the sinking of the U-boat; other times, especially as the war progressed and submarine captains became familiar with the tactic, it backfired. This was to be one of those encounters.

The *Bolverton* went through the usual charade of making smoke as if she'd been badly damaged, and lowering a boat containing a 'panic party' to give the impression that the ship was being abandoned. Whether it was the initial long range or the *Dunraven* captain's desire to keep his powder dry until he was certain of scoring a direct hit on the submarine, the few accounts of the confrontation indicate that the navy ship had taken several hits before replying. Unfortunately, one of these landed close to where her depth charges were stored. There was no catastrophic explosion, but soon the *Dunraven*'s stern was on fire, and the 'fake' smoke was no longer needed. She continued to take direct hits, including a torpedo strike.

Even now, the warship strived to maintain its merchant appearance, waiting for the U-boat to close with them. But eventually a hit from *UC-71* exposed one of *Dunraven*'s 4-inch guns, and the submarine dived. The navy ship finally launched two torpedoes, but they both missed, and, happy that its target was sinking, *UC-71* stole away.

One crewman had been killed, and Bill Bennison was among the injured, being hospitalised with wounds to the scalp and right leg. HMS *Christopher*, a destroyer, came on scene and took off the Q ship's crew. Talking about it later, Bennison said, 'We thought, if we abandon ship we'll give the game away, so we stuck though the decks were getting red hot where we were laid and kneeling.' One of the *Dunraven*'s officers was awarded a VC, and for his part in staying at his post as the flames blazed around him, Bennison gained the Conspicuous Gallantry Medal – but it could easily have been more. There was one further VC to be allocated to the *Dunraven*'s crew, and the recipient was chosen by ballot. It went to one of Bennison's fellow gunlayers. (It was, in fact, a case of second time unlucky, because in June of the same year he had taken part in a similar action while on board the Q ship HMS *Pargust*. This action was successful and the submarine they encountered was destroyed, but yet again Bennison's name wasn't drawn out of the hat.)

Bill was then only 21 years old, and although he might have missed out on the highest award for military gallantry, he would one day to win the RNLI's own version of it.

26 January 1942

Another decade, another war. Bill Bennison was now too old to fight, but he was not past trying to save others. At around seven in the morning, there was an alert from the coastguard concerning a merchant ship firing distress rockets off Seaton Carew, just north of the estuary of the River Tees. Lifeboatmen always respond immediately to such a call, but in the case of Bill and some of his crew, it wasn't quite that simple. Bill lived on St Hilda Street in Hartlepool,[1] which, as the crow flies was a short distance to the

---

1. St Hilda Street no longer exists. It ran adjacent to Baptist Street.

lifeboat station – but the journey entailed a very short ferry journey to avoid what would be almost an hour's walk around the Victoria Dock and the Old Harbour. Ordinarily, this wouldn't be a problem, but the shout had come at a time when crowds of local men were on their way to work; the ferry was busy and crowded, and Bill and some of his men had to wait for it to disgorge its passengers and return before embarking.

They finally launched at 7.35. Being the middle of winter it was still dark, and the gale that had caused the ship they were heading for to run aground blew snow and sleet into their faces. Their target was a collier, the SS *Hawkwood*, carrying coal from Blyth to London. The position they had been given was to the south, close to the mouth of the River Tees. Bill's lifeboat, the *Princess Royal*, arrived in the vicinity and began to search for the exact location. As it began to get light, they sighted what was effectively two wrecks: the ship had broken in two, with the forward part (with the bridge) about 200 yards offshore and the stern in shallow water closer to the beach. Some crewmen were sighted in the stern, although unknown to the lifeboat crew there were also five men stranded out of sight on the forward section.

Bill's problem was that, because of the low tide, neither section of the wreck lay in water currently deep enough to take the *Princess Royal*. The only bonus was that despite the rough seas further out, the shallow water in which the two sections lay wasn't currently threatening the remaining structures or crew; therefore Bill returned to Hartlepool to wait for the tide to come in.

The lifeboat reappeared on the scene at around midday, but even with the higher tide she only had enough clearance to approach *Hawkwood*'s bow. Fortunately, a rocket crew were assembling and preparing an attempt to fire breeches buoy apparatus towards the stern section, which was nearer and on which the majority of the collier's crew awaited rescue.

Wary of the rougher, deeper waters, which were not only washing over and rocking the broken fragment of ship, but violently tossing the *Princess Royal* herself, Bill guided the lifeboat alongside the forward part of the collier just close enough, and held her for just long enough, for the five shivering and fatigued sailors to make the jump. This was accomplished without any injuries (although the overall ordeal itself left the poor stranded men in need of medical treatment) and the lifeboat finally put back in to Hartlepool so that they could be cared for in hospital. In the meantime, the Teesmouth lifeboat had been making her way to the scene, but by the time she arrived the *Princess Royal* had already left with the rescued men, so the Teesmouth boat returned to base.

After landing the exhausted men, Bill Bennison and his crew, with the wind lessening somewhat, set off again within the hour to add their assistance to the efforts of the rocket crew working to get a line to the twenty-three men on the *Hawkwood*'s stern. The *Princess Royal* arrived by the middle of the afternoon, but even with the easing of conditions the sea was still too rough and still too shallow for the lifeboat's draft. They tried pouring oil to calm the waves at least a little, but it was ineffective. The *Princess Royal* had its own rocket apparatus on board, but Bennison couldn't even get close enough to be able to use it. At one point the lifeboat crew were sent sprawling when the boat touched bottom, slightly injuring a couple of men. The men on the deck of the *Hawkwood* appeared to be safe for the time being and since there was little point in continuing for the present, Bennison returned once again to Hartlepool. It was late afternoon and already dark by the time they reached the lifeboat station, and the Hartlepool men had been at sea for seven hours all-told; still, though, they were prepared to go out again when the tide changed. Luckily, the rocket brigade had finally achieved success, and Bennison was informed that the remaining crewmen from the *Hawkwood* had been safely removed.

In addition to Bill's gold medal, Herbert Jefferson, the motor mechanic, gained a silver medal, while the six other crewmen got the bronze. The *Hawkwood*'s master wrote a letter of thanks, saying that he and his crew would 'always remember the fearless and persistent determination' of the crew of the *Princess Royal*. 'We all deeply appreciate that we owe our lives to these men … It was apparent that these men were wholly fearless and inspired by the spirit of self-sacrifice and determination not to be beaten by the tremendous odds against them.'

Bennison himself displayed a modesty typical of lifeboat crew: 'As far as I was concerned,' he told a local reporter, 'it was all in a day's work, and I have nothing but admiration for the splendid help given me by the crew.'

Mechanic Herbert Jefferson, one of whose sons was a prisoner of war at this period, is worth mentioning because he had previously taken part in the major operation to save the men on board the *Rohilla* (see Part 5, Chapter 21). And he was just as humble as Bennison: 'All I want to do is pay my tribute to the coxswain. But for his coolness and resource we would not have been able to accomplish what we did.'

Bill Bennison was Hartlepool born and bred, and enrolled in the Royal Naval Volunteer Reserve in January 1915 when he was 18. As well as his RNLI gold and Conspicuous Gallantry Medal, he had been awarded the *Medaille Militaire* (the third highest French military honour) for his part in the rescue of a French airman who had ditched in the sea in 1917.

In his service records, he is described as fair haired and blue eyed, with WHB tattooed on his left forearm. His height is given as 5 feet, 5 inches, but he was either still growing or the navy had a faulty measuring tape, because by 1925, if not earlier, his height is stated to be 5 feet 9 inches. It appears that he remained in the RNVR until at least 1929, training in Portsmouth but based in his home town of Hartlepool. He was promoted to leading seaman; in later years he was routinely referred to as 'Lieutenant Bennison', but I have been unable to find details of this promotion and it wasn't common for a rating to reach commissioned officer rank.

In 1930, presumably after leaving the navy, he joined the Hartlepool lifeboat crew as bowman, becoming second coxswain four years later, and coxswain five years after that. After the Second World War he was appointed dredger master for the Hartlepool Port and Harbour Commission. By the time of his *Hawkwood* exploits he was married with three children.

He retired from his post as coxswain in 1957. In that year, a local newspaper reporter went out with him on an exercise, and his observation of Bill was that he 'gives the impression of saying very little but thinking quite a lot'. William 'Bill' Bennison died in 1980, at the age of 84.

Chapter 35

The Fate of the *Stolwijk*

John Boyle

I n early December 1940, U-boat *U-140* (Captain Hans-Peter Hinsch) was lurking off the coast of Ireland when she intercepted a distress signal from a British merchant ship. The SS *Ashcrest* was part of the thirty-two-ship convoy SC-13 with a Royal Navy escort, having left Newfoundland bound for Liverpool.[1] In horrendously stormy conditions, the *Ashcrest* had sustained damage to her rudder and was gradually becoming separated from the rest of the convoy – the ideal scenario for a U-boat skipper. Hinsch plotted a course and moved in for the kill.

The navy escort consisted of a sloop, two corvettes and three destroyers, but *U-140* managed to evade them all. The first torpedo, fired at just before 8.30 pm on 8 December, missed its target; the next one slammed home right below the bridge, ripping a hole that split the *Ashcrest* in two. Within minutes, the two halves of the ship, along with every man on board, had been swallowed by the raging sea. Most of the thirty-eight crewmen had been Irish, dying virtually within sight of their homeland.

Part of the same convoy was SS *Stolwijk*, a Dutch merchant ship carrying a cargo of newspaper and steel bars, with a crew of twenty-eight. She also suffered rudder damage near the Irish coast. This was a couple of days before the loss of the *Ashcrest*, and although she wasn't hunted down by Captain Hinsch or any of his comrades, whether she was ultimately luckier is a moot point.

---

1. The 'SC' stood for 'slow convoy'. In theory this meant ships capable of no more than 12 knots, but in practice speeds were often appreciably slower than that.

The *Stolwijk* had been effectively consigned to a nomadic life for some months, being herself unable to return to Holland because of the German invasion, which had happened while she was away at sea. She had continued, however, to contribute to the war cause as part of the Dutch merchant fleet in exile ever since. The weather had been extremely stormy since her departure from northern Canada, and at one stage her captain, Albert Kooning, even changed course to try to avoid the worst of the elements (thus by sheer luck avoiding another U-boat wolfpack that was hunting for the convoy). But on 5 December this didn't prevent the *Stolwijk*'s rudder from falling victim to the pounding she was taking. An initial repair was made, but this also eventually failed, as did the last throw of the dice – a manually operated replacement rudder. Captain Kooning decided that there was nothing for it but to drop anchor off the coast of Donegal, but even anchor and chain were no match for the storm; his ship broke free and was soon being carried landwards. The skipper tried to reverse his way to safety on full power, but it was too late to halt his ship's inexorable progress towards disaster. Realising the gravity of his situation, Captain Kooning sent out a distress message by radio, and issued an order for the crew to don their life jackets.

In a race against time, Lieutenant Commander Brian Dean, commanding officer of HMS *Sabre*, one of the escorting navy ships, bravely took his own vessel towards the apparently doomed *Stolwijk* to try to save the crew. Exact details of what happened are sparse, but either the two ships collided or the *Sabre*, which is said to have sailed dangerously close to shore herself, struck submerged rocks. But in all events, the rescue bid had to be abandoned when Dean's own ship was damaged and some of his crew were injured (accounts vary between two and four casualties). Dean himself was the most seriously injured, sustaining a fractured skull. Another example of how the lack of solid information regarding this case has led to conflicting claims is that at least one version declares that Dean's injuries proved fatal. Fortunately, as we shall see below, the reports of his death were greatly exaggerated.

The *Stolwijk*'s first casualty occurred before she came to grief herself, when a big wave swept the radio operator into the sea, never to be seen again.

Finally, at 11.30 on a wild and black night, the *Stolwijk* crashed into rocks close to windswept and desolate Tory Island, nine miles north of the Irish mainland. The ship had been carrying two lifeboats, but the sea had already carried one away before she had foundered, and the other was now badly damaged. Nine of her crew took their chances and jumped overboard, swimming for the lifeboat that was still floating near the ship. It was a fateful decision. Not all made it to the boat, and while it is believed that some did, the lifeboat eventually capsized and all were lost. That left eighteen men on board the ship, waiting for help.

The nearest lifeboat station was on the island of Arranmore, approximately twenty-four miles down the west coast. This was the base for the motor lifeboat *KTJS*, which had previously seen service in Orkney and Shetland. Although the crew got the call soon after the *Stolwijk* had hit the rocks, coxswain John 'Jack' Boyle wasn't able to launch in those dark and stormy conditions. It was not until it began to get light at 6.30 the following morning that the *KTJS* finally ventured forth into the hurricane-strength winds and mountainous waves of the Atlantic. Spray and snow drastically reduced visibility, and it was around six hours before the lifeboat crew could pick out the masts of the *Stolwijk* in the distance. Jack Boyle and his men found that the cargo ship had hit a reef called locally Carraignacrubog ('The Rock of Crabs') situated between the islands of Inishbeg and Inishdooey off the north-west coast of Ireland, and her crew had crew congregated in the after part of the ship.

Boyle anchored the *KTJS* to windward of the *Stolwijk*, where he dropped anchor and slowly let out the cable, allowing the lifeboat to be carried towards the ship until they were near enough to fire a line to set up a breeches buoy extraction. The firing would still be at more or less maximum range because of the danger of the lifeboat being swept towards the *Stolwijk*'s hull. At times, waves lifted the lifeboat higher than the deck of the much larger ship, but the line was secured and the operations began. Each transfer took around five minutes, but after the fifth sailor had been brought off, the fraying breeches buoy line, rubbing against the damaged steel structure of the ship, snapped. The whole procedure of firing a new line and securing it had to be gone through again before the rescue could be resumed, only for the same thing to happen once more after a further ten men had been rescued. On the final occasion when the lifeboatmen tried to fire the line towards the *Stolwijk*, it was discovered that water had entered the mechanism. There were just four cartridges left, and the first three failed. On the last attempt the firing was successful, but even then the danger wasn't over because there were three men left on board the ship, and if the line failed now the survival of whoever was left on board would have been in jeopardy. It held. The whole procedure of removing the eighteen men to safety took four fraught, hand- and face-numbing hours.

Once all were aboard, including Captain Kooning, it was with great relief that Jack Boyle was able to turn away from the wreck and set a course for home. They were unable to work their way back into their base on Arranmore, and so had to set out once more and make for Burtonport, the nearest mainland port. Five hours had passed before the *KTJS* sailed into harbour, and by this time the lifeboat had been out for sixteen hours in the worst conditions imaginable. Jack and his crew were virtually in as bad a state as the eighteen men they had taken off the wreck, and had to be helped ashore themselves.

Of the ten sailors who lost their lives trying to get clear of the wreck, only three bodies were ever found. They were buried in the churchyard at Killult, Donegal, but exhumed and re-interred in Holland in 2000. In 2017, a monument was erected on Arranmore commemorating the rescue.

Jack Boyle was born in approximately 1892 and became coxswain in 1928. In 1946, Jack's son was granted a reward of £10 for saving a drowning boy from the sea off Arranmore. The district judge who presented him with the cheque remarked that Jack's son 'really was a chip off the old block ... the heroic son of a heroic father'. Jack died in 1949. As well as his RNLI gold medal for his part in the rescue, the *KTJS*'s motor mechanic, Teague Ward, received the silver medal; and Jack's brother Philip, who had been acting second coxswain, was one of six bronze medal recipients. Jack and his crew were also honoured by Queen Wilhelmina of the Netherlands.

Earlier that year, Lieutenant Commander Brian Dean had commanded HMS *Sabre* in the Dunkirk evacuation, during which she made ten return journeys and was damaged by enemy fire while ferrying nearly 6,000 soldiers back to Britain. (And several thousand more in operations after Dunkirk.) Dean was subsequently awarded the DSO. But the head injury he sustained as a result of trying to save the crew of the *Stolwijk* prevented him from returning to active duty. In later life, after the death of his wife, he decided to emigrate to New Zealand, where he had family. It seems that he was too modest to tell them about his other heroic exploit, and it was only when his obituary made no mention of it that others who knew what he had done informed the family of that night in December 1940.

Because the loss of the *Stolwijk* happened in wartime, there was no great desire to publicise it and details for this event are even more sketchy than for even some of the other First and Second World War stories in this book, perhaps because the convoy did suffer at least one loss to a U-boat. From what I can tell from my own research, the story received little if any mention in the newspapers at the time of the event; it was only when the gallantry medals were awarded that any coverage was given, and that brief. As a result, certain 'facts' copied and repeated by successive writers over the years are hard to verify. We have seen how Lieutenant Commander Dean has been described in at least one version of the story as having succumbed to his injuries. In its archives, one of the RNLI's own magazines erroneously claims that four crewmen were killed, when, in fact, they were injured but not fatally. Thankfully, the main substance of the story and the bravery of the crews of the Arranmore lifeboat and HMS *Sabre* are not in doubt in any of the retellings.

Chapter 36

The Year of Three Medals

Paddy Murphy

The Newcastle lifeboat station in County Down was opened in 1854, and located on the eastern side of Dundrum Bay, where eight years earlier the famous SS *Great Britain* had run aground. By the time of the Second World War the lifeboat's coxswain was Patrick Murphy, and his name was about to be added to the illustrious list of RNLI gallantry medals awarded to the men of that station.

19 January, 1941

The *Hoperidge*, a 5,000-ton cargo ship, ran ashore at the western end of Dundrum Bay in a gale. At just before seven in the morning, Paddy Murphy led the *L.P. and St Helen* motor lifeboat out into the easterly gale; it still wasn't fully light, and heavy snow hampered his crew's visibility as they probed the bay in search of the vessel. It may be that the *Hoperidge* was carrying some sensitive or secret wartime cargo, because Murphy was given the task by the ship's captain of passing on a message to the Admiralty. The ship had sustained casualties when coming up against the rocks, and required medical assistance.

This meant returning to shore and dropping off William Murphy, the lifeboat's second coxswain to get help. When an army doctor and his orderly arrived, the enormous waves made it impossible for the men to wade back out to the *L.P. and St Helen*. The only way the transfer could be achieved was for Paddy to edge the lifeboat up to a flat area of rock, using all his skill and experience at the controls to keep her prow steady against the ledge while the three men were helped into the boat.

The lifeboat left the scene for a time, but returned twice more early that afternoon: once to take the army doctor off, and again to take a second doctor to the ship.

For this exploit, Paddy Murphy received the RNLI's bronze medal.

28 January 1941

On 26 January, the MV *Sandhill* hit a mine off the coast of Lancashire, and although she remained afloat, the explosion had left her completely without power. At the mercy of wind and tide, she was carried slowly westwards till she managed to drop anchor just under two miles off the coast of Country Down on the morning of the 28th. The Newcastle lifeboat station was alerted, and after a difficult job of working out into open water, Paddy Murphy got the *L.P. and St Helen* to the ship, a much smaller vessel than the *Hoperidge* he had attended to a few days earlier. In view of the dangerous conditions and the fact that the *Sandhill* was safely anchored, no rescue attempt was made yet. Instead, Murphy returned to base on the understanding that he and his crew would come back and take the crew off.

A close eye was kept on the vessel and messages were passed from ship to shore. With the weather unchanged on the 29th, the plan was for the lifeboat to come to the *Sandhill*'s aid on the 30th. By then, though, the storm had increased in intensity; her anchors were struggling to hold her in place and she was moving inexorably towards the rocky coast. Paddy Murphy took the *L.P. and St Helen* out at 9.30 am; both boats were being tossed so violently that the lifeboat faced the inevitable risk in such circumstances of coming to grief against the hull of the *Sandhill*. Nevertheless, Murphy was able to hold his boat steady enough to save four crewmen, including the captain; but not only were there ten men still left on board, he was told that nine soldiers had tried to make it to shore in a ship's boat.[1] Thus, after landing the four crewman Murphy decided to go in search of the additional soldiers, since the deteriorating conditions

---

1. It is notable that the captain didn't insist upon being the last off according to custom, although perhaps there is some reason for this that wasn't reported.

meant that they were at much greater risk than those still on the *Sandhill*.

Unable to find any trace of the boat and her escapees by mid-afternoon, Murphy turned his attentions back to the ship, still dragging her anchors shorewards. Despite the *L.P. and St Helen* taking a battering against the sides of the ship, her crew managed to get off those left on board and fight through the towering waves back to Newcastle by 6 pm. By the time the storm began to abate the following day, the *Sandhill* had survived the night without being driven onto the rocks. Consequently, the lifeboat's final act in this mission was to take the crew back out to their ship, which was towed to safety by a local tug.[2]

So it was that Paddy Murphy was awarded a clasp to his bronze medal.

21 January 1942

Life on board the SS *Browning* was rarely dull – although, given a choice, her crew would probably have much preferred it to have been so.

On the afternoon of 5 September 1939, near the start of the war and when perhaps a vestige of naval chivalry still existed, the lookouts on board the *Browning*, then about 300 miles off Cape Finisterre en route to Brazil, spotted a surfaced U-boat heading rapidly towards them. A series of small explosions erupted in the water around them when the deck gun of the submarine, *U-48*, opened up, prompting the cargo ship's captain to order the lowering of the boats so that his crew could escape before the *Browning* was torpedoed.

But no torpedo was fired. The U-boat continued to close the distance, instead making for the fleeing lifeboats. Their crews were sitting ducks and must have feared the worst – but instead, the *U-48* captain hailed them. What transpired was that Captain Herbert Schultze had earlier intercepted another British cargo ship, the *Royal Sceptre* and had opened fire in order to make her stop, killing

---

2. I have been unable to discover any mention of the fate of the nine soldiers.

and wounding several of those on board. Her crew had also taken to the lifeboats, but a radio operator had been left at his post. Even though the man was sending distress signals that would have alerted any nearby Royal Navy warships, Schultze took the time to get him off and make sure all her crew were clear before sinking the *Royal Sceptre*. He had then spotted the distant *Browning* and had made for her, but not with the intention of consigning her to the same fate. He now ordered her crew to re-embark, and told them where they would find the drifting lifeboats of the other British ship and rescue the crew – which they duly did. (Herbert Schultze became a U-boat 'ace', sinking twenty-six ships during his wartime career. On his first patrol he sank a ship called the *Firby* in a similar fashion, and sent a cheeky radio message across the airwaves (knowing that it would be intercepted by the British) to 'Mr Churchill', telling him what he'd done and where the crew could be picked up. He was awarded the Iron Cross 2nd Class, Iron Cross 1st Class, the Knight's Cross, and the Knight's Cross with oak leaves. His nickname among his men was 'Daddy' Schultz because of the paternal care he took of them. He survived the war, dying in 1987 at the age of 77.

In October 1942 the *Browning* loaded cargo at Barrow-in-Furness, then embarked on what Captain Thomas Sweeney warned his crew would be a 'very hazardous journey', but they weren't told of the destination. He wanted no panic, but made the ominous statement that if there was, he had a revolver in his cabin and would not hesitate to use it. The reason for this cloak-and-dagger stuff was the nature of the ship's cargo: a large amount of TNT and artillery shells for use by the military, together with petrol and highly inflammable pitch for the repair of runways.

The *Browning* proceeded into the Mediterranean in a large convoy. By the afternoon of 12 November she was part of a detachment from the main convoy of around twelve ships following a navy minesweeper towards the port of Oran, but before they could get very far, a tremendous explosion shook the whole ship. She had been torpedoed – though luckily the explosives, which would surely have blown the ship out of the water, remained intact. The crew were given the order to abandon ship. They manned the lifeboats and rowed for all they were worth to get clear of what was, in effect, a very large floating bomb.

As they opened up the distance, the sound of a succession of small explosions form within the *Browning* echoed across the water, followed by one huge blast that destroyed the ship, spreading the combustible cargo across the water until the sea itself seemed to be on fire. The crew were safe, though, and rescued by a navy corvette.

Seven months before her dramatic end, the *Browning* had had another close call – this time at the hands of nature rather than the enemy. It was a stormy day on 21 January – so bad, in fact, that several ships, part of a convoy being escorted by the corvette HMS *Montbrettia*, had been blown ashore off County Down. At around five in the morning, Paddy Murphy and his men received a call from the coastguard telling them that four ships were in trouble along the coast near Ballyquintin Point, several miles north-east of their station. The Cloughey lifeboat a little further to the north was the closest, but she was busy attending to some of the other stranded vessels. The *L.P. and St Helen* launched at about 5.30, sailing into sleet and snow and struggling against high seas for five hours. It was fully light by then, and although a dismal day there was no missing the appalling sight of no fewer than seven ships on the rocks. Murphy made for the one furthest out – the SS *Browning* – whose stern had caught on a reef.

During the night a number of the merchant ship's crew had been pulled ashore by breeches buoy, but thirty-nine remained on board. Murphy made three attempts to get close to the *Browning*, but the waves and heaving seas, which at times were breaking over the steamer's bridge, were lifting and dropping the *L.P. and St Helen* dramatically, and only the lifeboat's anchor cables prevented her from being swept against the ship's sides or even being tossed onto her deck. But at least Murphy was now close enough to be able to communicate with the ship, and her captain informed the coxswain that on the lee side, despite the rocks, there was enough relatively calm water for him to get the lifeboat into a good position. To get there, though, Paddy Murphy would have to carefully guide his lifeboat between the *Browning*'s bow and more rocks; he waited for a fleeting lull in the swirling seas, then charged for the gap. There was just a few feet of clearance on either side, but he made it; his reward was a spot that was almost like the calm eye of the storm, sheltered by the larger vessel's bulk. Now the removal of the remaining crew was relatively straightforward – other than the fact that there were far more sailors than the *L.P. and St Helen* was designed to carry. Knowing that he daren't risk trying to do this all over again – which in any case would take many hours, during which time the ship might be lost – he decided that the overloading the lifeboat was the lesser of two evils, and he crammed them all in.

The *L.P. and St Helen* was sitting so low that water was washing across her decks; there were miles to travel before reaching safety. Even before that, there was the small matter of extricating himself from his current position, which was so tight that the lifeboat couldn't be turned round to make her go back the way she came. Ahead was the reef on which the stern of the *Browning* was trapped, with only shallow water over it – but this was the only way out. In what one newspaper described as 'an act of almost reckless daring', Murphy waited for a swell to pass over the reef, then gunned the *L.P and St Helen* right over it. The *Browning*'s mate later wryly remarked that if he'd known what Murphy had intended to do he would never have left his ship – but the gamble paid off. The coxswain still had ten miles to go – Newcastle was out of the question so he was continuing north, picking his way through rocks and reefs as he did so, and the stranded sailors were finally landed at the first available haven – Portavogie, a little fishing village.

Some of the *Browning*'s men were in a bad way and taken to hospital, and even the exhausted lifeboat men had been working for nine hours. All of the seven stranded ships were eventually refloated.

Paddy Murphy received his gold medal as a result of this to add to his other awards, thus becoming the only man to receive three RNLI medals within twelve months. William Murphy, the second coxswain got a silver, as did Robert Agnew the mechanic. Four other crewmen were awarded the bronze medal. Paddy was given the BEM soon afterwards. He died in 1969, aged 81.

Chapter 37

Tondin's Jock

John Buchan McLean

21 March 1954

It was a windy morning along the north-east coast of Scotland, and with conditions worsening, two Lerwick seine-net fishing vessels, the *Northern Light* and the *John West*, decided to put into Peterhead Bay, around twenty-five miles north of Aberdeen. Before too long, though, the *John West* ran aground, and the water was too shallow for her companion vessel to approach and throw a line to get her off.

While they were trying to work out what to do, two men came down from the quayside, climbed into a fishing yawl called the *Lizzie*, and set off across the harbour. In their little boat they were able to get close enough to the *John West* to grab a line thrown down to them, and they then proceeded to take it out to the *Northern Light*, which took over the tow into deeper waters.

The crews of both vessels were naturally grateful, but at the time they weren't to know that they could hardly have been in better hands – their heroes were John Buchan McLean and his brother Peter. Not only were they both lifeboatmen, but 'Tondin's Jock', as John was known to his friends, was the recently retired, gold medal-winning coxswain of the Peterhead lifeboat.

23 January 1942

Gale-force winds and driving snow were causing chaos in the north sea; off the coast of Aberdeenshire that morning, the Whitby steamer *Runswick*, carrying a cargo of coal, and another Whitby ship, the

Saltwick, collided. Both were damaged, particularly the *Runswick*. A distress call was made to the coastguard and relayed to the Peterhead lifeboat station. The crew of the *Julia Park Barry* was assembled, and Jock McLean led his men out in search of the ships at just before 8 am. It was ten degrees below freezing when they departed that morning, and the angry sea was washing away large sections of breakwater.

Finding that the *Runswick*, in the western part of the bay, was not in a sinking condition, McLean instructed her to follow him into Peterhead Bay, with the *Saltwick* coming after her, joined by the SS *Fidra*, another ship seeking shelter. Even after anchoring in the relative protection of the bay, though, the conditions were testing and the ships far from safe. In the early hours of the 24th, a Saturday, the *Runswick*'s anchor cable parted and she sent out a distress signal, which was picked up by the harbour master and passed on to the lifeboat station. Once again, the *Julia Park Barry* went into action, motoring the short distance from their base in the inner harbour out into the bay. It was too dark to see much, but when the *Runswick* switched on her searchlight and began to probe, Jock McLean and his men could see that the merchantman had grounded below Smith Embankment at the northern end of the harbour.

Jock drew the lifeboat close to the *Runswick* as she rose and fell dramatically in the rolling seas, and a rope tossed up was grabbed by a crewman on deck so that the *Julia Park Barry* could be secured alongside the ship. But the strain on the line meant that it kept breaking. After the fourth such failure, the *Runswick*'s men dropped four of their own ropes, and once these were tied in place on the lifeboat they withstood the forces on them while the ship's crew began descending by the way of a ladder, with Jock keeping the *Julia Park Barry* in position by judicious application of the motor's power.

When the forty-fourth and last man had scrambled down the side of the ship and was helped into the crowded lifeboat, the ropes were let go and Jock steered them back into the harbour. It was just before four in the morning when they disembarked and everyone was able to get into the warmth and try to get some sleep.

When daylight, such as it was, arrived on the Saturday, the *Saltwick* and *Fidra* remained safely at anchor in the bay. The wind, however, was blowing even harder, and Jock and a couple of his men took it in turns to keep watch on the ships throughout that day and the following night. Their concerns were justified on the Sunday morning, when, with the storm reaching its peak and gusting to over 100mph, the *Saltwick* finally succumbed and was driven ashore, her anchors failing to hold her. A coastguard rocket crew failed in their attempt to fire a line to the ship, but later some sailors from the Royal Navy managed to get to her in a boat; it was only big enough to take four of the crew off, so, being so close in to shore, six others decided to try to make it to land in the *Saltwick*'s own boat. The decision was to have fatal consequences.

Despite the short distance, the turbulent sea wasn't about to let them land easily and they battled for an hour, tossed around like matchwood. And although the boat did make it to the beach, the men were so exhausted and the surf so powerful that they were repeatedly swept off their feet, the waves washing over them. More navy men came to their aid, but it was too late for two of the *Saltwick*'s crew, who had drowned by the time they were dragged ashore. Even some of the survivors were said to have been delirious by this stage.

Before the day was out, the inevitable happened – the *Fidra* suffered the same fate as the other two ships, and sounded her siren. The *Julia Park Barry* was ready to go, but wasn't initially needed as shore-based rescuers had gone to her aid. But by midnight on the Sunday, word was passed to Jock McLean that the team that had gone to help the *Fidra*'s crew had reached the limits of their physical endurance, having struggled to help the stranded men for sixteen hours without a break. He trudged along the seafront through the wind and snow to ascertain the ship's position, and by the time he had returned, the *Fidra*'s master had let those on shore know that time was running out – his vessel was breaking up and his crew of twenty-five were in mortal danger. Jock and his men boarded the *Julia Park Barry* and set out in the early hours of Monday morning. It didn't take long to get to her, and in the beam of a coastal defence searchlight he could see that she was stern-on to the shore. He positioned the lifeboat in a similar attitude alongside her, and although at one point the *Julia Park Barry* was almost swamped by a great wave that came crashing down over both ship and lifeboat, he was able to keep coming close enough for a small number of men to leap aboard each time. It was a slow, physically and mentally draining process that lasted almost an hour, and all the time Jock McLean was having to use all his skill get the get the balance just right – close enough and long enough to take men off, while avoiding a damaging collision with the ship's hull. They all reached dry land at 3.15 am, but the lifeboat crew's labours still weren't over.

There were still sailors left on board the *Saltwick*, and there were growing concerns over the condition they must be in by now. Jock McLean and his men put out yet again at first light, but as they attempted to manoeuvre into position alongside the ship, which was now lying on its side, disaster almost struck the lifeboat itself. A succession of big waves tossed them onto submerged rocks and engulfed the *Julia Park Barry*, washing crewmen off their feet and almost over the side. They held on, and the boat was badly bashed but luckily still seaworthy. Jock reversed her out of danger and finally into the lee of the *Saltwick*, affording him some protection from the elements. A relatively smooth transfer of stranded sailors was able to take place. Of the forty men still left on board, the *Julia Park Barry* took off thirty-six, leaving her captain and three of his officers. By late morning they were all landed safely.

It was now Monday morning, 26 January, and Jock and his men had been in action or on standby since eight o'clock on Friday the 23rd. It was calculated that they had had no sleep or rest for the last twenty-seven hours, and although they had been able to snatch sleep at times during the whole period, they had spent just under ten hours at sea in all, in the worst possible stormy, freezing, snowy winter conditions.

Jock McLean's gold medal was Scotland's first in just over 100 years. Motor mechanic David Wiseman got a silver, and six crewmen were issued with the bronze award.

Two of the three ships involved in the events of 23–26 January 1942 became casualties of war the following year. In March 1943 the SS *Fidra*, carrying a cargo of iron ore and part of a convoy, was sunk by

U-130 off the coast of Portugal. Seventeen of her twenty crew were killed, including her master, Master Hugh McLarty. (I have been unable to ascertain whether he was on board her when she grounded in Peterhead Bay.) Then, in October of the same year, a convoy that included the SS *Saltwick*, carrying Red Cross parcels to Gibraltar, was attacked and sunk by the Germans. Thankfully, most of her crew were saved. (Possibly all – there is a report that one man was killed, but other accounts suggest that everyone escaped.)

John Buchan 'Tondin's Jock' McLean was born in 1893. He worked on an Aberdeen trawler before becoming coxswain of the Peterhead lifeboat in 1937. He retired in January 1954, but as we saw at the start of the chapter, his life-saving exploits weren't quite over. And three years before he went to the aid of the Lerwick fishing boats in his little *Lizzie*, at the age of 58, he dived into the harbour fully clothed to rescue an eight-year-old girl. For this act he was presented with a Royal Humane Society award. When he died in 1956, he was still living in his house on Lodge Walk, close to the seafront and a stone's throw from the lifeboat station.

Part IX

Miscellany

Chapter 38

Royal Shipmate

Robert Howells

In 2001, an Empire Gallantry Medal (the precursor to the George Cross) was put up for auction, with an estimated value of around £2,000. It was one of a handful won by RNLI coxswains over the years. The man to whom it had been presented nearly eighty years earlier was Robert Howells, coxswain of the Fishguard lifeboat. It went for double the estimated price.

During a storm on 3 December 1920, the *Hermina*, a three-year-old Dutch schooner with three masts and a small engine, had put out from Fishguard in ballast but soon found herself forced to return by stormy weather. Her master, one Notgodacht, brought her to anchor close to the harbour breakwater. But the anchors couldn't hold her, and she was gradually dragged eastwards across the bay in sea 'mountains high' towards the Needle Rock, a prominent, arched feature at the foot of the cliffs.

Back across the bay in the direction from which the schooner was being carried, lay the Fishguard lifeboat station, and when the distress flares were seen in the early evening, coxswain Robert Howells and his crew launched the *Charterhouse* lifeboat and were soon motoring towards the *Hermina*. By the time they had arrived, the schooner was already touching bottom on submerged rocks around the landmark.

The ferocity of the wind and the towering waves made it difficult for Howells to get into a position from which he could take the ten-man crew off, but the 66-year-old was as experienced a seaman as they come, and after several attempts managed to bring the lifeboat alongside. The *Charterhouse* was in a precarious position, as wave after wave lifted her above the schooner's deck level only for her to plummet back down again. One by one, however, seven men were evacuated. But not all of those on board wished to be rescued. Her master, Captain Notgodacht, along with his first and second mates, was determined to stay with their vessel, and despite Howells' warning that the *Hermina* was in imminent danger of breaking up, they couldn't be persuaded to change their minds.

Neither were Howells' own problems over. After he pulled away from the schooner, the lifeboat's engine spluttered and died, and nothing could be done to restart it. The *Charterhouse* was, when new, Wales' first motorised lifeboat, but at a time when lifeboats still also carried sails and oars and in many ways still had the appearance of sailing boats. The *Charterhouse* had two masts, and the only way to get back to shore was by a combination of oar and sail. The howling wind tore at the lifeboat's sails as they tried to work their way back, eventually ripping away the mizzen sail. The mainsail held, but brave crewman Thomas Holmes risked his life to shimmy along the curved forward part of the lifeboat to raise the jib sail. After a gruelling three hours, by which time the lifeboat had taken in a lot of water, Howells, his crew and the rescued men were back on dry land.

Not long after this, the coastguard reported again seeing distress flares being fired from the direction of the *Hermina*. Howells' work was at an end because the *Charterhouse*'s engine couldn't be repaired in time to send her out again; the coastguard rocket crew were deployed, but couldn't do anything till first light, leaving the three sailors to spend a harrowing night in the open.

But in the morning, rather than firing a rocket with a line attached – presumably because the schooner was so close in to shore at the foot of a steep cliff, meaning that the rocket couldn't be fired at such an acute, downward angle – a more dramatic attempt took place.

One of the men involved, William Morgan, volunteered to be lowered 160 feet to the men below while being blown around by the strongly gusting wind that whipped along the sheer cliff-face, in imminent danger of being slammed against it, or of the rope becoming frayed by the sharp edges of the rocks.

He made it safely, but unfortunately it was already too late for one of the three men who had wanted to stay with their vessel, which, since Howells' visit, had been thrown against the rocks and almost broken in half. The impact had brought the *Hermina*'s mainmast crashing down, knocking the second mate overboard. He was killed either by the impact or drowning. The captain and first mate were also sent tumbling into the sea, but managed to scramble up onto the rocks. After several punishing hours, the intrepid Morgan and the two survivors were hauled to safety

The combined operations to save the crew of the *Hermina* quite rightly resulted in the issuing of numerous awards for bravery. Howells travelled to London to receive his gold medal with not only his crew, but the *Charterhouse* herself, which was transported by train and put on show outside the Houses of Parliament. The lifeboat still exists, and is now at the centre of a restoration project. Three of Howells' colleagues received silver medals, and the rest of the thirteen men were awarded bronzes. (Glimpses of the wreckage of the *Hermina* can still be seen at low tide in the vicinity of the Needle Rock.)

As well as the Empire Gallantry Medal mentioned at the start of the chapter, Howells was also recognised by the Dutch, being presented with a gold watch by the queen, as was Morgan for his dramatic cliff rescue.

When Howells was presented with his gold RNLI medal by King George V, it was, in fact, a meeting of old shipmates – because they are believed to have served together when they then young Prince of Wales had been a naval cadet. However, despite mixing with royalty as a youth, there is reason to believe that as a young man Robert Howells had a problem with either authority, drink or both, because it must be said that his disciplinary record was patchy to say the least …

He went to sea as a boy. In 1868 at the age of 15 he is listed in Royal Navy records as having been born in Manorbier; he was 5 feet 4½ inches, with black hair, blue eyes and a dark complexion. He enlisted as a Boy, First Class; sadly, he didn't stay 'first class' for long, and the comments section of his subsequent naval history ranges between Very Good, Good, Fair and Indifferent – he experienced as many peaks and troughs as he would later on the seas during his lifeboat exploits.

Howells served in a variety of ships, but the first blip on his record came in 1873, when he would have been 20, when he was locked up for a few days for 'insubordination'. Something serious must have happened the next year, because for some reason he served a month's imprisonment in Hull. Howells found himself locked up in the ship's cells for a week on six separate occasions over the next sixteen years during a lengthy navy career.

His last recorded indiscretion was in 1890, and by 1910 he had presumably left all that behind him because it was when he became coxswain of the Fishguard lifeboat, a position he held for eleven years.

Robert Howells died at the age of 72, in March 1925. He had lived just long enough to meet his old naval colleague George V again at an event to mark RNLI's centenary in 1924 (see Appendix I). At that time, he was one of just eight living recipients of the gold medal.

Chapter 39

A Seaman Through and Through

Patsy Sliney

(*Title from a poem published in the Irish Examiner after his gold medal-winning exploit.*)

By Tuesday 11 February 1936, the weather off the south coast of Ireland had been steadily intensifying from gale force to hurricane strength. Robert Mahony, the honorary secretary of the lifeboat station in the little harbour of Ballycotton, Cork, struggled to prevent himself being blown over as he watched stones weighing a ton being dislodged from the quay and 'flung around like sugar lumps'. Directly to the east of the short promontory on which Ballycotton stood, there were two islands; upon the furthest one, Daunt Rock, was a lighthouse around 50 feet tall but getting on for 200 feet above sea level. Sea spray was being blown over the top of this building. Anchored nearby was the Daunt Rock lightship the *Comet*, 98 feet long and with a crew of eight on board; the violent seas were placing an intolerable strain on her mooring cables …

Meanwhile, the coxswain of the Ballycotton lifeboat had been busy trying to save his own vessel from being destroyed by the elements. His small motorboat had been torn from her moorings, and he and some friends spent the whole night fighting to reach and secure her, which they thankfully managed to achieve. Patrick 'Patsy' Sliney was around 51 years old, and was probably born in Midleton, about twelve miles north of Ballycotton, in 1885. He seems to have lost his father at an early age, since his mother Margaret is the only adult shown in the household in the census returns taken when Patsy was a child. He was by now an experienced lifeboatman, having been Ballycotton's coxswain for fourteen years, and its second coxswain for eleven years before that. As is so often the case in lifeboat communities, the lifeboat crew was something of a family affair: brother Thomas was the mechanic of Ballycotton's *Mary Stanford*, and son William, 22, was a crewman. When Patsy himself had been appointed coxswain, he had succeeded both the father and uncle of his wife, Catherine, in that role.

At just after eight o'clock on the morning of 11 February, Patsy Sliney was visited by the lifeboat station secretary Robert Mahony, relaying news of a phone call he had received. He was lucky to receive the call at all since the storm had knocked out most phone lines, but local calls were still getting through. It was worrying news: the lightship anchored off Daunt Rock was adrift and being carried landward, and had no power. Mahony knew what it was like out there as well as Sliney did, and although he didn't say so he was of the opinion that the *Mary Stanford* wouldn't even be able to get out of the harbour, let alone effect a rescue alongside the much larger lightship.

Patsy had other ideas. His men were already assembled, which he was glad about; he didn't like the idea of having to fire the maroons to alert them because he knew it would worry the whole village.

When Mahony arrived, he could hardly believe his eyes. He later told the RNLI magazine, *The Lifeboat*:

> To my amazement, the life-boat was already at the harbour mouth, dashing out between the piers … As I watched the lifeboat I thought every minute that she must turn back. At one moment a sea crashed on her; at the next she was standing on her heel. But she went on. People watching her left the quay to go to the church to pray. I watched her till she was a mile off, at the lighthouse … The life-boat seemed to hesitate. She turned round. We thought she was coming back. Then to our horror the coxswain took her through the sound between the two islands. That way, as we knew, though it was much more dangerous than the open sea, he would save half a mile.

Patsy had discussed the plan with John Walsh, his second coxswain, before committing to the drastic course of action. The *Mary Stanford* was being lashed by waves, and Sliney had everyone squeeze into the cabin for their safety. It was so bad that he even carried out a head-count to make sure no one had been washed over the side. At one point a gigantic wave lifted them high above normal sea-level, and their stomachs lurched as it dropped them with such a crash that Patsy's brother Thomas had to check that the engines hadn't been damaged. Luckily, the boat had survived intact. 'After that, she'll go through anything,' was Thomas Sliney's droll observation. The boat and its engines had certainly got them through the treacherous sound in one piece, but there were more trials to come.

The *Mary Stanford* was being tossed and buffeted, and Patsy had to employ the drogue, a sea-anchor that slows the progress of a boat being propelled forward at a dangerous rate. It helped, but when the cockpit door was opened so that the drogue could be deployed, the men inside were sent tumbling by a tremendous wave that engulfed the boat. No one was hurt and Patsy pressed on, but the combination of gloom, waves, rain and spray reduce visibility considerably, and finding the drifting *Comet* lightship was going to be another matter.

After patrolling for an hour or two, he took the *Mary Stanford* into the relative calm of Cork Harbour and called in at Cobh (formerly Queenstown, and still referred to it as such by some at the time) to see if there was any word on the *Comet*'s location. This move paid off, because, although the phone lines were still down, word had reached Cobh that the lightship had managed to anchor close to Daunt Rock.

Sliney gathered his men together again and headed back into the storm. Two ships were on the scene when the Ballycotton lifeboat arrived at the *Comet*'s position in the early afternoon. One of them, the steam packet *Innisfallen*, departed to resumed her own voyage once the *Mary Stanford* arrived. The other vessel was the naval destroyer HMS *Tenedos*, and she remained on station to offer what help she could. But it transpired that the lightship crew didn't want any help – or at least, they didn't want to be taken off their ship just yet. It was a selfless stance rather than a stubborn one, arising out of the fear that any vessels caught in the storm in that vicinity might well assume that the lightship was in her normal position, and soon find themselves in danger.

But there was no telling how long the *Comet*'s anchors would hold, so Patsy agreed to stand by – which he could only do by the continuous applying and easing of power together with deft steering and in order to keep roughly on station, since the lifeboat's own anchors would have been of no use. This went on until the middle of the afternoon, when HMS *Tenedos* attempted to take advantage of a slight lull in the storm. By paying out her anchor cable she closed the distance between herself and the lightship, then let go a buoy with a towing cable attached. The navy crew couldn't get the buoy close enough to the lightship, and, although Patsy was able to intervene and toss it aboard, the cable gave way under the strain and snapped before any real progress had been made; a second attempt ended the same way. By now, Patsy's men were weary, wet and hungry, and since darkness was setting in and nothing more could be done – and with the *Tendedos* staying to keep an eye on things, the coxswain took the *Mary Stanford* back to Cobh to re-equip, and for the crew to rest and gather their strength for the morning (although the crew did take their rest in shifts so that three men would always be aboard the lifeboat in case there was any sudden change in the *Comet*'s situation).

The *Mary Stanford* set off again at first light on Wednesday 12 February, and because she was back on scene and the weather had improved somewhat, HMS *Tenedos* finally took her leave.[3] With the wind dropping, the crew of the *Comet* were still hopeful of staying with their vessel. The *Mary Stanford* maintained a watch all day and all night, shrouded in a fog that had descended on the coast. On the Thursday, Patsy had to return to Cobh once more to refuel both boat and men. A delay in getting petrol to Cobh by lorry meant that, in those short winter days, the light was already fading by the time the lifeboat was able to set out again.

By now, the *Comet* had new company, because the lightship tender the SS *Isolda* had arrived from her base at Rosslare with the aim of towing the lightship to safety. When the lifeboat reached the

<hr>

3. In 1942, the *Tenedos* was destroyed by Japanese bombers while undergoing repairs at Columbo, Ceylon (Sri Lanka), with the loss of thirty-three men.

light-vessel again, around dusk, Sliney and his men found that the *Isolda* was already in position. Her captain told the coxswain that he intended to stand by all night and in the morning would try to take the *Comet* in tow. But the lull in the storm had only been temporary, and as evening wore on the weather deteriorated again. The *Comet* was showing two red lights, a signal to passing ships that she was out of position, but a big wave put one of them out of action. She was being driven towards Daunt Rock, and her crew donned their life jackets and began to congregate in the stern, fearing the worst.

The sea was now too heavy for the *Isolda* to offer assistance, so Patsy manoeuvred the *Mary Stanford* closer.[4] Lifeboat station secretary Robert Mahony described the plight of the *Comet*:

> The seas were going right over her. She was plunging tremendously ... rolling from 30 to 40 degrees, burying her starboard bow in the water and throwing her stern all over the place. She was fitted with rolling chocks, which projected over two feet from her sides, and as she rolled these threshed the water.

Patsy's only realistic option was to dash towards her leeward side and hope for a quick extraction before he was driven away. He got close enough to shout his plan to the bedraggled *Comet* crewmen, because it was vital that they knew what to expect and how they should act: he would have to come for them as fast as he could, kill his speed just long enough for the men to make the leap into the lifeboat, then reverse away from the ship equally rapidly to get out of the range of the great chocks flailing wildly as the ship plunged and rolled. On the first run, only one of the lightship crew had time to make the jump before the *Mary Stanford* had to hastily back off. Patsy came powering up again, and this time no one was able to jump. He managed to pick up five men on his next run, but on the fourth go the *Comet* was thrown against the Mary Stanford, destroying some of her rails and

---

4. Four years later, the *Isolda*, considered a neutral vessel, was bombed and sunk, killing six and wounding seven of her crew. Her then captain, Albert Bestic, had survived the sinking of the *Lusitania*.

damaging the fender and deck. A lifeboatman aiming the spotlight just avoided being crushed. Once more, Patsy took his battle-scarred boat in, and, once again, neither of the two remaining crewmen could be extracted – in fact, they appeared to be paralysed with fear.

Time was running out and on the sixth run there could be no hesitation. Lifeboatmen were posted forward, and the instant the *Mary Stanford* was within reach the hesitant lightship men were roughly grabbed and yanked aboard. There was no careful or gentle way to do it, and both were injured. Despite having been saved, one of the pair had some sort of panic attack and had to be restrained in order to prevent him from harming himself or anyone else. After a sixty-three-hour operation, forty-nine of them at sea in a diabolical winter tempest, the Ballycotton lifeboatmen and their eight exhausted charges reached land at eleven o'clock that night when the *Mary Stanford* put into Cobh. Patsy and his men were suffering from exposure and salt-water burns, and the coxswain himself had developed an infection in his arm, presumably from a wound incurred during all the tossing and bumping he had endured. This was Thursday, and it was said that none of the lifeboat crew had managed more than three hours' sleep since that Tuesday morning when they had first fought their way out of Ballycotton harbour.

The Sliney family amassed three medals for their part in this rescue. As well as Patsy's gold, his son William was issued with a bronze medal, while brother Thomas, the lifeboat mechanic, received a silver. Three other crewmen were awarded bronze medals, and second coxswain John Walsh a silver.

Patsy had already won four medals during the First World War when he had served in the Royal Navy Reserve. We know from this records that he was just over 5 feet 8 inches tall, with a fresh complexion and blue eyes. William's son Colm Sliney, Patsy's grandson, continued the family tradition, as did his own son Will – still a Ballycotton lifeboatmen at the time of writing. Patsy's medal collection came to public attention in 2018 when the family decided to donate them to Cork Public Museum. His granddaughter Agnes Dunlea told the *Irish Examiner* that Patsy was a very patient man who, despite his very poor hearing in later years, entertained visitors from all over the world who were anxious to hear about his exploits at sea. We never knew too much about it, but we were aware of the Daunt Rock rescue, and we'd sometimes see the medals taken out of a box when people called to see him.

Patrick 'Patsy' Sliney retired as coxswain in 1950 at the age of 65, and died in 1972 aged 87.

Chapter 40

Maid of the Isles

Grace Darling

Before losing sight of the wreck, they saw it strike the rock a second time, and then divide into two pieces ... Here they remained for some time, when their situation was descried by the keeper of the outer lighthouse, whose only companion was his daughter, a girl of about 19 years of age...

G race Darling wasn't actually awarded the RNLI gold medal, so technically speaking does not belong in this book. But the part she played in the following story quickly became part of lifeboat (using that term in its loosest sense) legend, deservedly so, and almost demands to be in any book of this kind. Rescues at sea, especially in the oar-pulling days before motor lifeboats, required not only great physical strength but a knowledge of the sea and its ways, which is why most lifeboat crew were not only men but fishermen for at least the first century of the RNLI's life. It was, therefore, only natural that a daring rescue featuring a young woman who led a largely sedentary landlubber's life should create a sense of both fascination and admiration, a sensation even, among the general public. There are several instances in this book of people who seemingly deserved a gold medal but who were rewarded with something less; readers can judge for themselves whether this is one of those cases.

The Longstone lighthouse had been built at least partly thanks William Darling's recommendation. His case for it was prompted by the number of times he had been called upon to try to save victims of vessels wrecked while trying to negotiate the shallow and rocky waters between the inner Farne Island and the coast. Longstone Rock was much further out – around six miles from the coast – than the Brownsman lighthouse. This had been his original posting, and the place where his daughter Grace had joined him when just weeks old. To their credit the authorities heeded his advice, and the beacon of the 26-metre-tall Longstone lighthouse began shining out across the waters off the Northumberland coast in 1826.[1] The Darlings were a large family, but by the time the events related in this story took place the only residents at the lighthouse were William Darling, his wife Thomasin, and Grace, their daughter.

At just before 5 am on 7 September 1838, Grace caught sight of some sort of calamity unfolding through the window of her bedroom. It seemed that a ship had come to grief on the rock known as the Big Harcar; but it was still dark, and she was unable to get a clear view of the full situation. She alerted her father, and all they could do was keep a frustrated vigil till daylight revealed the extent of the disaster. It was only then, aiming her telescope through the billowing spray and froth about half- to three-quarters of a mile out to sea, that she got a good view of the steamer that had come to grief during the night – and her lens picked out a number of tiny figures stranded on Big Harcar itself. The poor creatures must have been on the barren crag throughout the stormy night, and somehow they had to be saved.

> The Dundee and Hull Steam Packet Company have the pleasure to announce that their splendid New Steam Ship FORFARSHIRE (450 tons burthen and 200 horse power) James Kidd, Commander, is appointed to sail … [departing on] Saturdays at 5 o'clock … Wednesdays at 3 o'clock … The Cabins and Sleeping Apartments have been fitted up with every possible attendance; and in this respect they will not be found inferior to any Steamer in Hull. Provisions, Wines, Spirits &c provided by the Steward … and a female Attendant is engaged expressly for the ladies.

---

1. It still does to this day, albeit now unmanned.

Thus was the maiden voyage of the *Forfarshire* announced to the world through the press in April 1836. In May 1838, John Humble had replaced Kidd as captain of the ship, having previously commanded at least two other similar vessels.[2] Humble, a North Shields man, was still the *Forfarshire*'s master on 5 September of that year when she left Hull at around 6 pm for one of her regular runs to Dundee. As well as a mixed cargo, she carried around forty passengers. The specific number could never be established, since the names of those buying tickets were entered into a book that was subsequently lost with the ship. In total, though, there were said to be approximately sixty-three people on board, including the crew. One of them was Humble's own wife.

Despite the proud fanfare that accompanied her foray into this coastal trade, things hadn't always gone smoothly for the *Forfarshire*. A year previously almost to the day (before Humble had joined her) she had run aground on Holme Sand (probably Foul Holme Sand near the mouth of the Humber). She was floated off again the next day and although it appeared that no harm had been done, there were concerns about whether her boilers might have been damaged. An inspection was carried out by an engineer and they were given the all-clear, but – regardless of whether it had anything to do with the grounding – rumours about *Forfarshire* boiler troubles were circulating in Dundee right up until this September sailing.

Sure enough, there were problems with one of the ship's three boilers almost as soon as the ship was under way. It was shut off, and the steamer sailed slowly on through the night. During the following day, Thursday the 6th, the weather worsened, and a thick mist descended on the coastal waters.

The *Forfarshire* had got as far as Berwick, just about sixty-five miles from her destination, when the third boiler was restarted. After that minor success, however, things started to go downhill fast.

Once restarted, the troublesome boiler soon began leaking scalding hot water at an alarming rate, flooding the engine room and soaking the coal needed to keep the furnaces going. By 8 pm

---

2. John Humble had previously commanded the *Eclipse* and the *Neptune*.

all boilers were inoperable, and the ship's engineer told Humble that there was no possibility of restarting the engines. At this time steamships still had masts and carried sails, and the captain ordered these to be set. But it wasn't quite as simple as that. The *Forfarshire* was a paddle steamer, and the bulky paddles and housings on either side acted as an impediment to traditional sailing progress. A letter in the press from a Lloyd's agent described a paddle steamer with her engines disabled as 'the most helpless craft that can float upon the ocean'. The ship had been steaming into strong winds, and was now unable to make headway. The *Forfarshire* was forced southwards, back in the direction from which she had come. This was still more an inconvenience than a disaster – until, at four o'clock on Friday the 7th, a lookout spotted breakers ahead, the sign, dreaded by sailors, of white water passing over submerged rocks.

Humble tried to take the steamer between what he realised must be the islands and the coast, but by now the *Forfarshire* was being tossed around in the darkness and not responding adequately to the helm. Before long, those passengers who were awake realised the dangerous position they were now in and began to rush up on deck. A Perthshire farmer called Ritchie, dressed only in his shoes and trousers, emerged and encountered a young man called Bell, who cried 'It's all over with us!' He shook hands with Ritchie, adding, 'Farewell!' A calmer voice below was that of the Reverend Robb of Dunkeld, who tried to sooth the frayed nerves of a woman called Sarah Dawson, a Dundee woman living in Hull, who had two children with her.

The last person to see John Humble alive was John Tulloch, the ship's carpenter. He encountered his captain hurrying towards the stern, he assumed to rouse any passengers who might still be sleeping in their cabins.

'Oh,' cried Humble, 'this is a dreadful affair!'

Seconds later, the *Forfarshire* hit the rocks.

In the ensuing chaos, eight crewmen scrambled into one of the ship's boats and managed to get clear. One or two passengers were able to join them before the boat departed. Ritchie, saw the boat pulling away, and with a running jump managed to land on board; he spent much of the journey bailing water with his shoe, until a passing sloop came upon them and took them to safety.

Those left on board the *Forfarshire* were running around in terror, trying to find other boats or at least a place of safety on the ship. Sarah Dawson remained in the cabin with her children, but she asked the Reverend Robb to go up on deck and see what was happening. This he did, but now fate played its final cruel trick.

The steamer was lifted off the rocks by a tremendous wave, then came crashing back down with such force that she was broken in two amidships. (John Kidd, the ship's fireman – not to be confused with her former master of the same name – said she snapped 'like a carrot'.) Survivors described the 'agonising shrieks' of those on board rising above the sound of the wind and the waves that swept over the ship in those last minutes. The fore half of the vessel was left snared on the rock, but the sternmost part, where most of the passengers were located, instantly slipped backwards into the inky cold sea and disappeared from view. Among them were Ritchie's uncle. In his haste to get away, the farmer hadn't even had time to wake him. Sarah Dawson, along with her boy and girl, were in the forward cabin and for the time being at least, unharmed – but the Reverend Robb didn't survive the breaking up of the *Forfarshire*.

Up on deck, Tulloch had had the presence of mind to grab hold of the windlass, and urged four others with him to do the same; thanks to their secure grip, they were not lost overboard when the destruction of the ship occurred. Before the stern went down he witnessed on that part of the ship the distressing sight of an elderly woman emerging from below, soon followed by a younger woman. They embraced each other, the younger one, probably a relative, crying 'Oh, my dear …' It was the last he saw either of them.

Even those down in the forward cabin were by no means completely protected from the elements. Sarah Dawson and her children were lashed by the freezing seawater that swept in through the doorway every time a wave cascaded over the wreck. The children soon began to suffer badly from the cold and wet, and several times Sarah went up to beg Tulloch and the others to do something for them; but they were obviously even more exposed to the fury of the wind and waves, and it was all they could do to continue to keep their hold on the windlass. Tulloch yelled to her over the cacophony around them to remain in the cabin, where it was safer despite the water rushing in. Sarah herself was thrown backwards down the stairs into the cabin by another wave, and stayed there.

> And here it is our gratifying duty to record an effort made for the rescue of the unfortunate sufferers by two individuals whose heroism ... never was exceeded in any similar case, and it of so extraordinary a character that, had we not heard its truth attested to by those who were benefited by it, we could not have been induced to give it our belief, ranking, as it does, amongst the noblest instances of purely disinterested and philanthropic exertions in behalf of suffering individuals that ever reflected honour upon humanity.
>
> (*Morning Chronicle*, 20 September 1838)

The story as it is often told is that Grace Darling wanted them to put out in their coble for Big Harcar, but her father, William, was strongly against the idea given the severity of storm. After much urging on Grace's part, he caved in and with a heavy heart, and with the assistance of Thomasin, Grace's mother, they pushed the boat off from their island. There is a little more to it than that, as we shall see in due course, but launch the boat they did.

With Grace at one oar and William the other, they pulled with all their might as the waves tossed the little boat around and the spray drenched them. Rather than take the shortest, straightest course, they had to pick out a more circuitous route, taking into account rocks, tide and currents. But the Darlings' optimism and confidence were rewarded when they safely achieved their goal. William leapt out of the boat onto the rock, leaving Grace at the oars to keep it steady and prevent any collisions – no mean feat in itself.

Here, amid what was left of the *Forfarshire*, they had come upon nine pitiful, prostrated, shivering souls, including Tulloch and the four men who had been holding on to the windlass, together with a bereaved and distraught Sarah Dawson, whose two children had died from exposure in the night.

The Darlings knew these waters; even before setting out, they were aware that the tide would be against them for the return journey, and that the only way they could make it back was if some of the survivors had enough strength left to help man the oars. Fortunately, a couple of them did. The rescue entailed two trips, because William decided that nine people was four too many for his little boat. William first took Sarah Dawson and four men off, leaving Grace behind ministering to the rest. Then he and the two least affected of those he'd picked up came back for Grace and the remaining four men. They all found themselves welcomed into the sturdy shelter of the Longstone lighthouse at around 9 am. One of those rescued later told a reporter, with tears in his eyes, of their relief and amazement upon seeing the boat come into view, and even more so when they saw that one of the two rowers was a young woman.

It was the plight of Sarah Dawson that affected Grace the most. She was to write later that Sarah's sufferings 'seemed to me to be unequalled, having struggled nearly two hours to save her dear children, until they both died in her hands'.

When the wreck of the *Forfarshire* had been first sighted on the Friday morning by Grace Darling and others on shore, the waves were crashing over the Seahouses harbour walls, carrying away stores piled on the quayside and washing right up to the houses. It was considered impossible to put a boat out in search of survivors. However, Mr Smeddle, the steward of Bamburgh Castle, offered a reward to any Seahouses (at that time still known as 'North Sunderland') fisherman who would go out to the rock, and after some time a boat did put out containing seven men, one of whom was William Darling (known by his middle name of Brooks), Grace's brother. They were worried that the Seahouses lifeboat was too light and of too shallow draught to cope with the conditions, so they took out one of their own fishing smacks.

After a tremendous struggle they reached the Great Harcar rock, but unknown to them they had arrived an hour after the visit by the Darlings, and to their dismay they were met only with the tragic sight of the bodies of the Reverend Robb and Sarah Dawson's two children: Matilda, aged 5, and James, 7. Assuming that everyone else had perished, they moved the corpses away from the clutches of the waves to the highest part of the rock, for later collection, and departed with heavy hearts. Their cox decided it would be too risky to try to put back to Seahouses and so they made the still difficult trip to the lighthouse, where they now discovered that there were survivors after all. It was still an unpleasant time for the boatmen, since the Darlings hadn't been prepared for such a sudden influx of people and had neither the food, beds, nor spare, dry clothing to be able to offer much in the way of comfort. The Seahouses boatmen had to remain two days and nights in this trying state, housed in some old workmen's huts, or 'barracks', left over from the days when the lighthouse had first been built.

For days afterwards there was confusion regarding how many people had originally been on board the *Forfarshire*, and thus how many lives had been lost. The only thing for sure was that eighteen had been saved: nine in the ship's own lifeboat, and nine by the Darlings. The best estimate of the number involved is around sixty-three passengers and crew, and that between forty-three and forty-five people lost their lives. Among these were at least three more children in addition to Sarah Dawson's son and daughter.

The sea never relinquished its hold on most of those who drowned. The body of Mrs Patrick, wife of one Captain Patrick of Hull, was picked up by a steamer towards the end of September, several miles south of 'Shields' (presumably North). William Darling himself found 'a little tin box, inside which was a purse, and a receipt bearing the owner's name'. It was that of the wife of the *Forfarshire*'s master, John Humble. One report said that Humble and his wife died in each other's arms, which may or may not a mawkish embellishment of a kind common in journalism of the day. The absence of a passenger list and the fact that losses of vessels during storms wasn't uncommon meant that when bodies were later found, it wasn't always possible to match them with certainty to the *Forfarshire*. At least two such subsequent gruesome discoveries were listed as 'supposed' to have been passengers on board that unlucky ship.

The stern of the ship washed up at Cambois near Blyth, many miles to the south of where it first slid into the sea. By that time, only two survivors were still left in Bamburgh. John Tulloch, the *Forfarshire*'s carpenter, was, amazingly, considering what he'd been through 'working at the wreck' – probably keeping an eye on any salvageable cargo. Poor Sarah Dawson had been taken in by the local minister, said, quite understandably, to be in a 'very depressed state of mind'.

One rumour circulating among the towns and villages on that part of the coast that eventually made it into the press was that the crew of the *Forfarshire* were 'exceedingly vain' regarding her sailing (i.e. steaming) prowess, and that she often took delight in outdoing other more powerful vessels. 'These objectionable practices compelled them to keep up immense fires, and by such a proceeding the boilers have been worn out by abuse, rather than use', reported the *Berwick Advertiser*. This was never confirmed, but what is certainly true is that the *Forfarshire*'s boilers needed attention just before her final sailing and were scheduled to undergo further work, possibly a major overhaul, after the ship's arrival in Dundee. Clearly, there were serious concerns over their condition, and it became a major topic of discussion, though without any clear-cut conclusions being reached.

The very earliest reports of what happened to the *Forfarshire* naturally focused on the awful human tragedy; but within days, the part played by Grace was starting to capture the imagination of press and public. The emphasis in the reporting of events quickly morphed from 'Darling and his daughter' to 'Grace Darling and her father' as her feat and its journalistic potential sank in, and Grace's status rapidly burgeoned into that of a national heroine. It was the nineteenth-century version of a story going 'viral'.

By early October 1838 a subscription was opened to get an engraving of the pair made; melodramatic paintings of the rescue began to appear, along with portraits of Grace herself (she sat for at least seven artists and one sculptor) and her father, not to mention poems and songs. As well as the silver medallion from the Royal National Institution for the Preservation of Lives from Shipwrecks that she and William her were awarded, they also received gold ones from the Royal Humane Society, along with numerous other such tangible accolades.

There is no doubt as to Grace's courage and her deserved place in the annals of rescues at sea, but in the rush to lionise, almost beatify her, there is a risk that the truth may have become slightly distorted – although I would suggest only in some of the details, rather than the overall part she played. For example, probably the most often repeated version of the way the drama unfolded is that it was Grace who first spotted the wreck and who persuaded a reluctant father to go out to it. However, a very detailed and apparently well-informed account doing the rounds in the press just ten days after the drama reports that the roles were reversed: although Grace wasn't a reluctant volunteer, in this version it was William who sighted the ship, came up with the plan and suggested it to his daughter, who 'cheerfully complied'.

In fact, it *is* possible to ascertain the general facts of the situation with some confidence – since a report written by William Darling himself for his employers, Trinity Lighthouse, was reproduced in a little-known late-Victorian publication, *Grace Darling: Her True Story, From Unpublished Papers in Possession of her Family*. No author's name appears in the book, but Jessica Mitford in her biography of Grace Darling tells us that it was a combined effort between one of Grace's sisters, called Thomasin after their mother, and author Daniel Atkinson.

In it, William clearly states that it was indeed Grace who first spotted the wreck. As for the debate as to whether it would be possible to get a lightweight coble out to 'Harkers Rock' as his letter terms it, and who argued in favour and who (if any) against the rescue mission, well, perhaps neither version is right. William says that once it was light enough to see and survivors could be made out, '*we* agreed that if we could get to them some of them would be able to assist us back, without which we could not return' (author's italics).

The way in which a heroic rescue effort by numerous brave and selfless people mutated into 'the Grace Darling' rescue apparently didn't go down well with everyone on the Northumberland coast. In the book mentioned above, there is talk of grumbles among the boatmen over the way their part had been so overshadowed, and queries regarding how difficult and dangerous it had actually been for Grace and William to row out to the wreck. At least one boatman declared that by the time they went, it had been an 'easy' thing to accomplish. To be fair to the boatmen, none of those who went out to the rock thinking there were still lives to be saved – including Grace's own brother – received medals for bravery, although they were rewarded financially.

The idea, though, that Grace and William's efforts were accomplished with ease doesn't hold water, if readers will pardon the pun. The very fact that the Seahouses men daren't risk their own lifeboat (within an hour of the Darlings doing so), but had to put out in a fishing smack much larger and sturdier than the Darlings' coble, *and* then couldn't make it back to their home port, gives the lie to that idea.

Grace Darling told a correspondent that she was born and raised 'on the islands' but although she was certainly raised there, the Atkinson book quotes her father as saying that she was born in Bamburgh, in a house not far from the parish church.[3]

She was taught to read and write by her parents. From various descriptions we know that she was of slender build, and not quite 5 feet 3 inches in height. She sewed, and undertook housekeeping duties, but perhaps surprisingly for a lighthouse keeper's daughter, claimed to have 'no time so spare'. She enjoyed reading, but her father insisted that the literature be mostly of a Christian nature, along with some historical and biographical non-fiction; William wouldn't allow novels and plays in the home, and Grace says he referred to playing cards as 'the Devil's books'. If this makes him sound almost puritanical, someone who knew him is quoted in the Atkinson book as refuting this, stressing that he was 'far from morose

---

3. There is a house bearing a plaque declaring it to be where she was born, but the Atkinson book, written with the input of Grace's sister it must be remembered, says that the present building is 'upon the site of' the house she was born in, thus implying that it was demolished and replaced. This is something of a mystery, one I have discussed with John Harper of the excellent Grace Darling website, who remains confident that it *is* the actual building Grace was born in.

and Pharisaical', that he loved singing and playing the violin, and was a keen naturalist.

The memoir says that Grace had offers of marriage, but remained single for the rest of her life – which, sadly, was a very short one.

In the spring of 1842, just four years after the *Forfarshire* tragedy and when she was still only 26, Grace first 'manifested symptoms of delicacy', which was one of several euphemisms for consumption, or what we now call tuberculosis. It was a depressingly common, then incurable, and much-dreaded disease (Grace's contemporaries Emily and Anne Brontë would succumb just a few years later). It is perhaps somewhat surprising that someone who led such an isolated existence should catch an infectious disease of that kind, and it's possibly no coincidence that it seems to have first been noticed during a trip to the mainland. It was an illness that could linger for years, but soon after Grace's symptoms first manifested, her health went downhill rapidly.

She developed the tell-tale persistent cough, tried a 'change of air' as was often prescribed in such cases then, but it failed to halt her decline. The Duke of Northumberland, who had taken her under his wing and considered himself her patron, invited her to stay at Alnwick where his own physician could treat her, and she was also tended to by his wife, the duchess. But when it became apparent that nothing could be done and that the end was in sight, she was moved back closer to home, to her sister Thomasin's house in Bamburgh. According to biographer Constance Smedley, she spent her last days lying in the same box-bed in which she had been born. Within a week, in the poignant words of Thomasin, Grace 'went like snow', dying in William's arms at 8.15 pm on 20 October 1842.

Appendix I

A Special Gathering

On Monday 30 June 1924, centenary celebrations for the RNLI were held in London and went on for several days. Dignitaries from around the world – as far afield as Japan – attended, and the lifeboats of five different nations converged on the capital and sailed up the Thames. Present during the course of this period were the king and Prince of Wales, as well as cabinet minister Winston Churchill, who gave a rousing speech in praise of the Institution.

The real stars, though, were the seven out of the remaining eight living recipients of the gold medal for gallantry:

Thomas McCombie of Kingstown, Ireland, who had won his award back in 1895. He had been the master of the SS *Tearaght*, which had saved the crew of the Finnish barque the *Palme* after the Kingstown lifeboat's own attempt ended with it capsizing and the loss of all fifteen of her crewmen. (His story is not one of those included in this book.)

Major Herbert Burton of the Royal Engineers, who had held the rank of captain at the time of the epic *Rohilla* rescue in 1914.

Robert 'Scraper' Smith, coxswain of the Tynemouth lifeboat, the other surviving member of the three who were awarded golds for their part in that operation. (Sadly, Langlands, the third man, had died the previous year.) By now, Smith himself was in his early 70s and almost blind. He thought he would be able to recognise George V from his naval uniform but His Majesty wore civilian clothes, and although he talked with Smith for some time the old lifeboatman assumed it was just another one of the numerous dignitaries. When he asked one of his colleagues when they were going to be presented to the king, he was told 'Scraper, you've just been talking to him!' Smith later admitted to being rather deflated by the thought that his big moment had come and gone without him realising it. On reflection, though, he was very impressed by His Majesty's 'homely' manner and the friendly way in which he shook hands with them all. Smith's daughter even said that the king (possibly recognising that Smith could see very little) leapt over a table in his eagerness to shake her father's hand. When Smith returned to his home village of Cullercoats, hundreds of villagers were waiting at the railway station to greet him. He was cheered all way to his house, where the crowd congregated outside singing 'For He's a Jolly Good Fellow'. Perhaps feeling almost like royalty himself, he felt obliged to wave to them from an upstairs window, tears filling his age-dimmed eyes.

Henry Blogg of Cromer, who had so far won one gold for the *Fernebo* rescue in 1917 but would go on to accrue two more.

William Fleming of the Gorleston lifeboat, which had rescued the crew of the *Hopelyn* in 1922.

John Swan, coxswain of the Lowestoft lifeboat, which had taken part in the same mission.

Robert Howells of Fishguard, who led the rescue of the crew of the *Hermina* in 1920. As we have seen, His Majesty recognised Howells as a former shipmate from their cadet days.

John O'Shea, the lifesaving Catholic priest, was the eighth gold medal winner still alive at that time, but, unfortunately, he was unwell and unable to make the journey from Ireland.

Rockets and Mortars

The stories in this book often feature references to 'rocket crews', the employing of 'Manby's apparatus' and so on, and it's worth a brief look at what this was all about.

Even though many vessels came to grief virtually within hailing distance of land, very often factors like rocks, currents, powerful waves and the like made it all but impossible for rescuers to get out to the wreck. A number of people had been working independently on a method by which a rope might be fired to a ship in order to convey survivors to land or be used by rescuers in boats to haul themselves out to the wreck.

The innovations of two men, in particular, emerged from the pack in the early nineteenth century, eventually going head-to-head as the main and best means of effecting a physical communication with a wreck or stranded vessel. As we have seen described in several of the stories, these were:

- *The Manby mortar*, a cannon-like device designed to fire ropes attached to an iron shot;
- *Dennett's rocket*, which was more like an industrial-sized firework system.

George Manby (who as we saw in Part I, Chapter 1, was also an early advocate of a national lifeboat service) was a Norfolk man, a writer and a thinker who had served in the Cambridgeshire militia. He was galvanised into action after seeing the massive loss of life from a shipwreck just fifty to sixty yards offshore. He later got hold of an ordinary military mortar, and after some tinkering and experimentation had soon made the necessary adjustments to allow it to accurately and safely fire a line two hundred yards and more. Within a year (February 1808) it had been employed successfully in a real-life rescue.

John Dennett was from Newport on the Isle of Wight. He was fifteen years younger than Manby, and use of Manby's Mortar was already well established by the time he came up with his own take on the concept. While the mortar fired a round shot or one with barbs depending on the circumstances, Dennett's rockets were encased in iron, on the end of an 8 foot wooden pole. The apparatus first went into action in the early 1830s, and again soon proved its worth in the real world of life-saving. (Henry Trengrouse of Cornwall had invented a rocket before Dennett, but had tried in vain to get it adopted nationally.) With both systems being employed in different locations around the country (mainly by the coastguard) there came a time when it was decided there was a need to assess which method was the most effective, and thus worth investing in.

The Royal National Institution for the Preservation of Life at Cowes on the Isle of Wight asked the island's coastguard station to undertake a trial of the two pieces of equipment. In May 1827, both sets of systems were set up in Freshwater Bay, and Dennett was on hand to instruct in the use of his newer invention; naval and army officers were also present. The target was two flagstaffs two hundred yards off shore and eight yards apart. The naval men present, especially those employed by the coastguard, were already very familiar with the Manby mortar; it had saved many lives, and some later admitted they expected it to triumph – but the rocket won hands down. Lest it be thought that the witnesses were favouring the local man, the Inspecting Commander of the coastguard convincingly listed its advantages:

- Ships didn't always run aground in convenient places, and one of the drawbacks of the mortar was its weight and the difficulties in getting into the best place for firing. (And anyway – perhaps surprisingly – the rocket had a greater range of fire than the mortar.[1])

- Dennett's rocket, the inspector realised, could be carried for miles along a rocky coastline by just two men, if need be, and reach places where the mortar (which took ten men to transport it) just couldn't go.
- It also took less time to set up and get into action.
- Furthermore, the rocket was basically a giant firework and looked like one in action, so when it was fired, its fiery trail helped to temporarily illuminate the wreck, thus helping pinpoint its location to other rescuers on shore. (The flame also acted like a modern tracer round, helping those firing the equipment to adjust their aim where necessary.)
- Finally, in stormy weather it was understandably common for a shot from either piece of equipment to go astray – however, a line shot from Dennett's rocket could be hauled back in a re-used, but not one from Manby's mortar.

The military officers present were unanimous in concurring with the above assessment and in recommending its deployment around the coasts of Britain and Ireland, although use of the mortar did continue for some time.

Later, a lighter version of the rocket device came into use that was small and portable enough to be carried on, and fired from, the lifeboat itself.

---

1. Even in military use, the squat, short-barrelled mortar was considered a short-range weapon.

Bibliography

Atkinson, Daniel, *Grace Darling: Her True Story*. Hamilton, Adams & Co, London 1880 (Internet Archive).

Brittain, Colin, *Into the Maelstrom: The Wreck of HMHS* Rohilla. History Press, Stroud 2014.

Cox, Barry (ed.), *Lifeboat Gallantry: RNLI Medals & How They Were Won*. Spink, London 1998.

Farrington, K. and Constable, N., *Mayday! Mayday! The History of Sea Rescue Around Britain's Coastal Waters*. Collins, London 2011.

Gleeson, Janet, *The Lifeboat Baronet: Launching the RNLI*. History Press, Stroud 2014.

Hennesey, Sue, *Hidden Depths: Women of the RNLI*. History Press, Stroud 2010.

Hippisley Coxe, Antony D., *Smuggling in the West Country 1700–1850*. Tabb House, Padstow 1984.

Kelly, Robert, *For Those in Peril*. Shearwater Press, Douglas, Isle of Man 1979.

Leach, Nicholas, *Lifeboats of the Humber: Two Centuries of Gallantry*. Amberley, Stroud 2013.

Mitford, Jessica, *Grace Had an English Heart*. Viking Penguin, London 1998.

O'Byrne, William R., *A Naval Biographical Dictionary*. John Murray, London 1849 (Google Books).

Parliament (UK), *Report from Select Committee on Shipwrecks of Timber Ships*. August 1839 (Google Books).

Smedley, Constance, *Grace Darling and her Times*. Hurst & Hackett, London 1932 (Internet archive).

Treanor, Rev. Thomas Stanley, *Heroes of the Goodwin Sands*. Religious Tract Society, London 1904 (Project Gutenburg).

Wake-Walker, Edward, *Lifeboat Heroes*. Haynes, Yeovil 2009.

Wood, Stephen, *Those Terrible Grey Horses: An Illustrated History of the Royal Scots Dragoon Guards*. Osprey, Oxford 2015.

Other Media

For Those In Peril – The Story of Henry Blogg, Anglia Television documentary 1962, East *Anglian Film Archive* (http://www.eafa.org.uk/catalogue/204878)

The Story of the Stolwijk (John Boyle), YouTube (https://www.youtube.
com/watch?v=lY5HS0YRL_4&feature=youtu.be&fbclid=IwAR0V05_
LBXM5RSRgZ7XLRoYI0h2OeFAUs92W38_QTEH8wHy6iH0FJF
NdxpE)

'Rohilla' *Wrecked off Whitby*, British Film Institute (https://player.bfi.org.uk/
free/film/watch-rohilla-wrecked-off-whitby-1914-online)

Principal Websites

BBC People's War (re SS *Browning*)

British Newspaper Archive (www.britishnewspaperarchive.co.uk)

Benyon, P., Index of 19th Century Naval Vessels (http://www.pbenyon.plus.com/
18-1900/Index.html)

Cromer Website (https://enjoycromermore.co.uk/news/end-of-an-era-as-eighth-
generation-rnli-coxswain-at-norfolk-lifeboat-station-retires-after-36-
years-1-5586797)

Executed Today (re Francis Spaight) (http://www.executedtoday.com/
2017/12/19/1835-patrick-obrien-francis-spaight-apprentice-boy)

Grace Darling (www.gracedarling.co.uk)

The Life Saving Awards Research Society (www.lsars.org.uk/site/medal-rolls.
php)

Lloyd's List (http://www.maritimearchives.co.uk/lloyds-list.html)

National Archives (www.nationalarchives.gov.uk/)

Old Bailey Online (www.oldbaileyonline.org)

Oxford Dictionary of National Biography (www.oxforddnb.com)

RNLI Lifeboat magazine archive (https://lifeboatmagazinearchive.rnli.org)

RNLI main and various regional sites (https://rnli.org)

Times Digital Archive (https://gale.com)

Uboat.net (www.uboat.net/)

Victoria Cross Online (vconline.org.uk) (http://www.bbc.co.uk/history/ww2
peopleswar/stories/76/a4040876.shtml)

Wreck Site (www.wrecksite.eu)

Index